Ian Nicolson

BOAT DATA BOOK

Nautical

First published by
NAUTICAL PUBLISHING COMPANY LIMITED
Nautical House, Lymington, Hampshire, England

in association with
George G. Harrap & Co. Ltd
London

ISBN 0 245 50993 3

Printed in England by
BAS Printers Limited, Over Wallop, Hampshire
Bound by Kemp Hall Bindery, Oxford

To Jeremy and Clare Lines

My thanks are due to the people, often unknown, who devised many of the formulae in this book but particularly to McKechnie Metals Ltd of Walsall for permitting me to use many of their tables. Also to my partner Alfred Mylne for suggestions, and our draughtsman Graeme Mackie for help in preparing material and ideas for inclusion. Special thanks are due to Mrs. M. V. Hannigan for typing pages of facts and figures at terrific speed.

Thanks are also due to many other people and companies in the ship- and boat-building industries for their help and permission to use data and graphs etc. The list includes The British Standards Institute, Calor Gas, Camping Gaz, Caterpillar, M. S. Gibb, Ian Proctor Metal Masts, Lewmar, Marlow Ropes, Norseman Ropes, Ormiston, Simpson Lawrence, South-Western Marine Factors. Sparlight. Apologies are offered for inadvertently omitting any companies whose data has been used.

CONTENTS

Note: A full index of contents is given at the head of each section

INTRODUCTION

This book is for owners, chandlers, builders, repairers, designers, draughtsmen, students. In fact for anyone concerned with the technical side of boats and small ships.

One of its most valuable uses is saving time and trouble when specifying anything for a boat. By simply quoting a page anyone can order equipment without having to look up the correct size and write out lengthy details.

An owner can phone a marina or chandler and simply say: 'Put a new anchor on my boat. Size as specified in *Boat Data Book*.' Designers can reduce long lists of rigging to: 'As detailed in *Boat Data Book*, page 99, column for yachts between 9 m and 11 m.'

Anyone buying a boat can check the standard of equipment by referring to the lists in this book. There is a widespread practice of fitting boats with totally inadequate anchors, chain, winches and so on. When buying a new or second-hand boat it is most unlikely that more than half the essential safety gear will be on board. Reference to pages 16 to 23 will show what is needed.

When buying a boat it is important to check dimensions of berths, galley top heights and so on. There is a tendency also to save on building costs by fitting furniture which is under-size and as a result inconvenient, besides being uncomfortable to use.

Dimensions are given in metres (or millimetres) as well as feet and inches. Speed is in knots because this is still the universal unit at sea, but there are conversion tables from knots to kilometres per hour and miles per hour.

ERRORS AND OMISSIONS

Great care has been taken to ensure that the data in this book is accurate. However the information has to pass through so many processes, typesetting, printing, correcting, and so on, resulting in alterations which may inadvertently introduce errors. As a result no guarantee is given or implied that the information in this book is accurate; no responsibility can be accepted for the use, or consequences of the use, of this data. In some instances deliberate approximations have been used, where acceptable, to round up or down figures to the nearest whole number or simple fraction.

SECTION 1 — Boat equipment

Anchor sizes relative to boat length and type

1 Recommended sizes of 'patent' anchors such as Danforth, Meon, C.Q.R., Plough etc. For Fisherman types increase the weight by 20%.

2 Lloyd's tested anchors are recommended.

3 For inshore racing a light kedging anchor is likely to prove inadequate if the yacht has to anchor in severe weather in an unprotected anchorage.

4 Long-range cruising assumes that the yacht may have to ride out a hurricane. In these conditions a modest increase in weight and size of anchor over the average will sometimes save the ship.

BOAT LENGTH OVERALL	METRES 6 / 20 FEET	METRES 8 / 26 FEET	METRES 10 / 33 FEET	METRES 12 / 39 FEET	METRES 14 / 46 FEET	METRES 16 / 52 FEET	METRES 18 / 59 FEET	METRES 20 / 66 FEET	METRES 22 / 72 FEET
FOR INSHORE RACING	KILOS 5 / 10 LBS	KILOS 7 / 15 LBS	KILOS 9 / 20 LBS	KILOS 14 / 30 LBS	KILOS 18 / 40 LBS	KILOS 29 / 65 LBS	KILOS 36 / 80 LBS	KILOS 23 / 50 LBS & KILOS 41 / 90 LBS	KILOS 29 / 65 LBS & KILOS 68 / 150 LBS
FOR COASTAL CRUISING	KILOS 5 / 10 LBS & KILOS 14 / 30 LBS	KILOS 7 / 15 LBS & KILOS 18 / 40 LBS	KILOS 10 / 22 LBS & KILOS 23 / 50 LBS	KILOS 16 / 35 LBS & KILOS 27 / 60 LBS	KILOS 20 / 45 LBS & KILOS 34 / 75 LBS	KILOS 25 / 56 LBS & KILOS 43 / 95 LBS	TWO AT KILOS 32 / 70 LBS & ONE AT KILOS 57 / 125 LBS	TWO AT KILOS 39 / 85 LBS & ONE AT KILOS 79 / 175 LBS	TWO AT KILOS 54 / 120 LBS & ONE AT KILOS 113 / 250 LBS
FOR LONG RANGE CRUISING	KILOS 9 / 20 LBS & KILOS 14 / 30 LBS	KILOS 11 / 25 LBS & KILOS 20 / 45 LBS	KILOS 16 / 35 LBS & KILOS 32 / 70 LBS	KILOS 23 / 50 LBS & TWO AT KILOS 41 / 90 LBS	KILOS 27 / 60 LBS & KILOS 36 / 80 LBS & TWO AT KILOS 59 / 130 LBS	KILOS 32 / 70 LBS & KILOS 45 / 100 LBS & TWO AT KILOS 77 / 170 LBS	KILOS 36 / 80 LBS & TWO AT KILOS 54 / 120 LBS & TWO AT KILOS 100 / 220 LBS	KILOS 41 / 90 LBS & TWO AT KILOS 64 / 140 LBS & TWO AT KILOS 127 / 280 LBS	KILOS 45 / 100 LBS & TWO AT KILOS 73 / 160 LBS & TWO AT KILOS 159 / 350 LBS

Fisherman anchors—proportions

A folding Fisherman anchor has the virtue of being effective in all types of holding ground. Where the sea-bed is covered with layers of kelp it is one of the few types of anchor that may penetrate the weed and obtain a firm grip on the bottom.

This graph shows the proportions which have in practice been found to give an effective anchor. It is important that the palms are sharp and there must be good fillets where the shank meets the arms to ensure adequate strength.

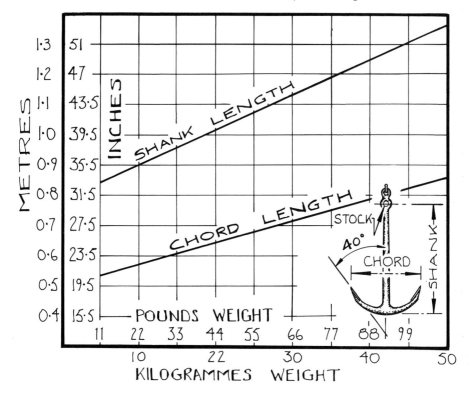

Danforth type anchors—proportions

There are several variations on the basic Danforth type of anchor. These figures are based on the standard type which has been developed and tested extensively. Wide variations from these proportions may be treated with caution.
A side elevation is shown at the bottom of the facing page.

WEIGHT OF ANCHOR	DIMENSIONS												SHACKLE	
	INS A	MM	INS B	MM	INS C	MM	INS D	MM	INS E	MM	INS F	MM	INS.	MM
LBS 17 / 7.7 KILOS	$4\frac{1}{4}$	108	$10\frac{3}{8}$	264	$9\frac{5}{16}$	237	24	610	$14\frac{5}{8}$	372	$1\frac{1}{8}$	48	$\frac{3}{8}$	9.53
LBS 30 / 13.6 KILOS	$5\frac{3}{4}$	146	$13\frac{3}{4}$	349	$12\frac{1}{8}$	308	32	813	$19\frac{5}{8}$	499	$2\frac{1}{4}$	57	$\frac{1}{2}$	12.7
LBS 43 / 19.5 KILOS	$6\frac{3}{8}$	162	$15\frac{9}{16}$	395	$13\frac{7}{16}$	341	36	914	$21\frac{15}{16}$	558	$2\frac{9}{16}$	64	$\frac{1}{2}$	12.7
LBS 55 / 25 KILOS	$7\frac{1}{8}$	181	$17\frac{5}{16}$	440	$14\frac{7}{8}$	378	40	1016	$24\frac{3}{4}$	619	$2\frac{5}{16}$	58	$\frac{1}{2}$	12.7
LBS 75 / 34 KILOS	8	203	$19\frac{3}{4}$	502	$16\frac{13}{16}$	427	$45\frac{5}{8}$	1159	$24\frac{7}{8}$	708	$2\frac{15}{32}$	62	$\frac{1}{2}$	12.7
LBS 100 / 45 KILOS	$8\frac{3}{8}$	213	$20\frac{9}{16}$	521	$17\frac{1}{2}$	445	$47\frac{1}{2}$	1207	$28\frac{15}{16}$	736	$1\frac{19}{32}$	41	$\frac{5}{8}$	15.9
LBS 150 / 68 KILOS	9	229	$21\frac{1}{4}$	540	$18\frac{7}{8}$	479	49	1245	$29\frac{3}{8}$	759	$1\frac{29}{32}$	49	$\frac{3}{4}$	19
LBS 200 / 90 KILOS	$9\frac{3}{4}$	248	$22\frac{3}{4}$	578	$20\frac{9}{16}$	522	$52\frac{1}{4}$	1334	$32\frac{1}{16}$	813	$2\frac{5}{32}$	54	$\frac{7}{8}$	22.2

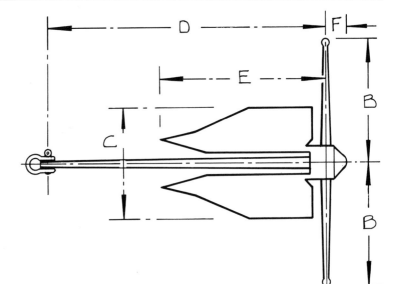

Anchor ropes and mooring warps—sizes

Anchor ropes—polyamide (nylon) or polyester (terylene/dacron). Warps should be of the same material or polypropylene (courlene etc).
All ropes and chains are detailed by *diameter*.
Protect against chafing at the bow fairlead.
Never use a floating rope (such as polypropylene) on an anchor.

YACHT'S LENGTH OVERALL	UP TO 5.5 METRES 18 FEET	5.5 TO 7.3M 18 TO 24FT	7.3 TO 9M 24 TO 30FT	9 TO 11M 30 TO 36FT	11 TO 13.5M 36 TO 44FT	13.5 TO 16.5M 44 TO 54FT
THAMES TONNAGE	DAYBOATS AND DINGHIES	2 - 4 TONS	4 - 8 TONS	8 - 12 TONS	12 - 18 TONS	18 - 30 TONS
ANCHOR ROPE WITH SHORT LENGTH OF CHAIN	30M. OF 10 MM PLAITED PLUS 5M. OF 5MM CHAIN — OR — 100FT OF 3/8 INCH DIAM PLAITED PLUS 18FT OF 3/16 INCH CHAIN	42M. OF 13 MM PLAITED PLUS 5M. OF 6.5MM CHAIN — OR — 140 FT OF 1/2 INCH DIAM PLAITED PLUS 18FT OF 1/4 INCH CHAIN	55M. OF 13 MM 3-STRAND PLUS 5M. OF 8MM CHAIN — OR — 180FT OF 1/2 INCH DIAM 3-STRAND PLUS 18FT OF 5/16 INCH CHAIN	70M. OF 16MM 3-STRAND PLUS 7M. OF 10MM CHAIN — OR — 240FT. OF 5/8 INCH DIAM 3-STRAND PLUS 24FT OF 3/8 INCH CHAIN	90M. OF 16 MM 3-STRAND PLUS 7M. OF 11MM CHAIN — OR — 300FT. OF 5/8 INCH DIAM 3-STRAND PLUS 24FT OF 7/16 INCH CHAIN	120M. OF 19 MM 3-STRAND PLUS 7M. OF 13 MM CHAIN — OR — 400FT. OF 3/4 INCH DIAM 3-STRAND PLUS 24FT OF 1/2 INCH CHAIN
MOORING WARPS 3-STRAND OR PLAITED	2, 3 OR 4 REQUIRED EACH 9M. OF 10 MM — OR — 30FT. OF 3/8 INCH DIAM.	3 OR 4 REQUIRED EACH 14 M. OF 11MM — OR — 45FT OF 7/16 INCH DIAM.	4 REQUIRED EACH 18M. OF 13mm — OR — 60FT OF 1/2 INCH DIAM.	4 REQUIRED EACH 23M. OF 13mm — OR — 75FT OF 1/2 INCH DIAM.	4 OR 5 REQUIRED EACH 27M. OF 16mm — OR — 90FT OF 5/8 INCH DIAM.	5 OR 6 REQUIRED EACH 30M OF 19mm — OR — 100FT OF 3/4 INCH DIAM.

Danforth anchor—side elevation

Tools for small craft

The selection of hand tools carried on board is at least partly a matter of personal preference and experience. The available space for stowage and working will also affect the size of the list.

Racing boats are usually skinned out and carry only the minimum equipment to deal with emergencies. At the other end of the scale boats which have to be entirely self reliant will carry all the tools listed here up to List E, even when the craft's overall length is 12 metres, 40 ft overall.

These lists are based on the need to deal with emergencies afloat, including damage control and repair. They are also worked out on the principle that some maintenance will be done afloat, and on larger craft alterations will be carried out on board without extensive shore facilities. The dividing line between these requirements will be a matter of owners' preference.

Only the best tools are adequate for work afloat and even the best lack proper corrosion resistance. It seldom pays to buy second best even on the principle that annual replacement of tools is part of the ship's maintenance schedule. When tools are wanted afloat they are needed badly and breakages are intolerable.

Chisels, screwdrivers, saws etc. should have hard plastic handles. Full corrosion protection should be carried out including the use of oil impregnated tool-kit lining papers, the use of Lanolin etc.

List A is for boats up to 6 metres 20 ft overall.
List B is for boats up to 9 metres 30 ft overall.
List C is for boats up to 12 metres 40 ft overall.
List D is for boats up to 15 metres 50 ft overall.
List E is for boats up to 18 metres 60 ft overall.

List A. Knife, with marline spike or multi-purpose blades.
Medium-large screwdriver (size 330 mm or 13 in overall
length).
Mini-mole grip.
Oil can.

If the vessel has an engine—set of engine tools.

List B. All List A plus:
Wire cutters for largest size of rigging. (Only required if the
vessel is a sailing yacht.)
Junior hacksaw and 4 spare blades.
Surform.
Hand-drill.
Set of about 8 twist drills (from 2 mm to 6 mm; $\frac{1}{16}$ in to $\frac{1}{4}$ in).
Counter-sink for steel (12 mm, $\frac{1}{2}$ in size), with shank to fit hand
drill. This tool can be used for wood or soft metals in
emergencies.
Pair of pliers, single-joint side-cutting type (180 mm or 7 in
length).
Small screwdriver set (handle and various accessories).
Metre rule. (Folding wood type which shows millimetres and
inches.)
Adjustable spanner to open up to 40 mm or $1\frac{1}{2}$ in.

List C. All lists A and B plus:
Portable or table vice.
Engineers ball pein hammer (0·75 kg, $1\frac{1}{2}$ lb size).
Ratchet brace with assorted drill bits (8 mm to 30 mm; $\frac{3}{8}$ in to
$1\frac{1}{4}$ in).
Two screwdriver bits (6 mm and 9 mm; $\frac{1}{4}$ in and $\frac{3}{8}$ in).
Centre punch.
Chisel (12 mm; $\frac{1}{2}$ in).
Mole grip.
Full size hacksaw, of the type which will take any size of blade.
Packet of assorted fine, medium and coarse hacksaw blades.
Special wood cutting hacksaw blade.

Tools for small craft—continued

List D.   All Lists A, B and C plus:

Hand-saw (500 mm or 20 in).
Full set of counter-sinks for ratchet brace.
Swedish file (medium cut on one side, smooth on the other).
Rat-tail file.
Round (cylindrical) surform.
Large screwdriver.
Square (250 mm or 10 in).
Pinch bar or wrecking bar.
Plane (50 mm or 2 in cutter width).
Electric drill to work off ship's power or the cordless type pre-
    charged ashore. To take up to 8 mm, $\frac{3}{8}$ in drills.
Set of twist drills from 6 mm to 9 mm, $\frac{1}{4}$ in to $\frac{3}{8}$ in.
Carborundum stone—double sided, coarse and fine.
Chisels, 6 mm, $\frac{1}{4}$ in and 18 mm, $\frac{3}{4}$ in.
Mole grip with bench cramp on handle.
2 small cramps.
Expanding bit (size 12 mm to 35 mm, $\frac{1}{2}$ in to $1\frac{1}{2}$ in).
Adjustable spanner to fit largest nut on board.
Cold chisel (8 mm, $\frac{3}{8}$ in).
Stubby screwdriver.
Wood scraper(s).
Full packet of fine hacksaw blades.
Full packet of medium hacksaw blades.
Full packet of coarse hacksaw blades.

List E.   All Lists A, B, C and D plus:

Pad saw.
Tenon saw.
Adjustable spokeshave.
Mallet.
'Soft' hammer with a selection of faces or tips.
Large hammer, e.g. 2 kilos, 5 lb.
Small hammer, e.g. 0·2 kg, $\frac{1}{2}$ lb.
Full set of files.
Set of bradawls.
Set of gouges up to 20 mm, $\frac{3}{4}$ in.
Set of cold chisels from 6 mm to 25 mm, $\frac{1}{4}$ in to 1 in.
Set of socket spanners and/or ring spanners, and/or open ended
      spanners.
Set of Allen keys.
Spanner to fit keel bolt nuts where applicable.
Chain type pipe wrench.
Nail punch 1$\frac{1}{2}$ mm, $\frac{1}{16}$ in.
Inside/outside calipers.
2 large clamps (jaw opening at least 250 mm, 10 in).
Mechanic's vice with swivel base—90 mm, 3$\frac{1}{2}$ in jaw width.
Woodworker's vice.
Soldering iron (electric to work off ship's supply, or traditional
      type heated by an external source).
Blow-lamp (to use the same fuel as other items on board, e.g.
      calor or paraffin).
Adaptor to turn electric drill into a reciprocating saw.
Bench pedestal to turn electric drill into grinder etc.
Set of tools for electric drill including wire brushes, grinding
      points, buffs etc.
Adjustable cutters or set of hole cutters.
Magnet.
Breast drill with chuck opening to 15 mm, $\frac{5}{8}$ in.
Metal drills up to 15 mm, $\frac{5}{8}$ in.
Set of wood drills up to 15 mm, $\frac{5}{8}$ in, which have shanks to fit 8
      mm, $\frac{3}{8}$ in electric drill.
Paint brushes. Two each size: 12 mm, 25 mm, 35 mm and 50
      mm; $\frac{1}{2}$in, 1 in, 1$\frac{1}{2}$ in and 2 in.
Bevel gauge.
Spirit level—at least 300 mm, 12 in and plumb gauge.
Tap wrench and set of taps, 4 mm to 16 mm; $\frac{3}{16}$ in to $\frac{5}{8}$ in.
Stocks and dies, 4 mm to 16 mm; $\frac{3}{16}$ in to $\frac{5}{8}$ in.

Safety equipment—craft under 5·5 m (18 ft) L.O.A.

Item No.	Safety Item	Number Required	Status	Type & Size
1.	Lifejacket	1 for each person.	Essential. To be worn when conditions are dangerous.	To BSI Specification Childrens size where appropriate, SBBNF approved buoyancy aid may be used in sheltered waters.
2.	Lifebuoy	1	Recommended. 2 are recommended where possible especially on motor cruisers. A rescue quoit of DOTI approved pattern may be substituted.	Horse-shoe type. Orange or Yellow.
3.	Anchor with warp and/or Chain.	1	Recommended. 2 recommended for sea-angling and 2 suggested for extended cruising.	See Tables on pages 8 et seq.
4.	Bilge Pump.	1	Recommended	Non-choke diaphragm 45 litres (10 galls) per minute.
5.	Bucket or Bailer.	1	Essential	Even with a self-bailer a hand bailer or bucket is required.
6.	Paddle or Oar with Rowlock	1	Recommended by DOTI but 2 suggested certainly if oars are carried and even if paddles are carried.	To suit size and freeboard of craft.
7.	Distress Signals	2 at least	Essential. It is suggested that for serious cruising the requirements for 13·7 m (45 ft) craft be followed.	5-star Red hand-held flares for night use. Orange smoke flares for day use.
8.	Compass	1	Recommended. For serious cruising a second or hand-bearing compass is suggested.	Marine type with a card at least 75 mm (3 in) across.
9.	First Aid Kit.	1	Recommended	See next column

Equipment	Stowage	Overhaul or Test Frequency
Whistle recommended. Water-proof light self-activated by seawater recommended	Away from engine, exhaust pipe etc. Preferably not in extreme bow.	Annually
30 m (100 ft) of buoyant line of at least 115 kilos (250 pounds) breaking strain — e.g. 4 mm ($\frac{5}{32}$ in) diam. Ulstron-tied to one lifebuoy. Self-igniting light if sailing at night.	On deck close to Helmsman.	Annually
Chocks and Lashings on deck where appropriate.	End of warp secured inboard. Anchor(s) on foredeck or ready for instant use	Annually
Strum Box to prevent pipe choking.	Bolted down near helmsman is normally best. However a portable pump which can draw water from the sea can sometimes be used for fire-fighting.	Each voyage.
Lanyard		Annually
Lanyards on rowlocks. Leather on oars.	Locate oars and paddles where they cannot be trodden upon etc. or accidentally broken.	Annually
Waterproof container. A polythene bag alone is not enough as it is too vulnerable.	Away from engine heat, and not in a locker with sharp or heavy items. Near helmsman.	See the 'Shelf-Life' stamped on the flares. It is usually about 3 years.
Gimbals on a sailing craft. Correction card. Light and dimmer switch.	Near helmsman and away from steel fittings, instruments which generate a magnetic field etc.	Whenever opportunity offers. Certainly every 2 months.
Instruction book and contents as recommended by current medical authorities.	In a waterproof container.	Half yearly.

10.	Torch	1	Recommended. 2 suggested for serious cruising	Waterproof type at least large enough to take 2 U-2 batteries
11.	Radar Reflector	1	Essential in shipping lanes at night or thick weather	At least 300 mm (12 ins) cube.
12.	Radio Receiver	1	Recommended for weather forecasts.	For extended cruising a DF type is an asset in many areas.
13.	Engine Tool Kit.	1	Essential whenever there is an engine on board	To suit engine, and to include essential spares such as pump rotors etc.
14.	Firefighting equipment.	2	Extinguishers essential. 1 may be carried but if there is no galley or engine an extinguisher may be omitted.	1·5 kilo (3 lbs) Dry powder. Carbon dioxide or foam extinguishers of equal capacity may be fitted. BCF & BTM should not be fitted for use in confined spaces as they give off toxic fumes.
15.	Auxiliary firefighting equipment.	1	Should only be carried IN ADDITION to the above equipment.	Bucket with lanyard.
		1		Blanket or rug.
		1		Asbestos blanket.

All the above items are on the British DOTI List. Experience suggests the items below are almost

16.	Charts	As required to cover cruising area.	Essential in strange waters, in thick weather in home waters.	Large scale Admiralty.
17.	Depth gauge: Either echo- sounder or lead and line.	1	Frequently most valuable often essential.	Yacht size echo-sounder. 1·5 kilos (3 lbs) lead and 25 m (12 fathoms) of 5 mm ($\frac{3}{16}$ in) plaited terylene rope.
18.	Signalling cloth	1	Suggested since it shows up at a con- siderable distance. May also be used as weather protection, as a storm sail etc.	Day-Glo Orange waterproof cloth 2 m x 2 m (6 ft x 6 ft)

Spare batteries and bulbs.	One near helmsman. Well clear of drips, bilge water etc.	Each voyage.
At least two securing points (top and bottom) if portable; 3 securing bolts or screws at least if permanently fixed.	'Flat' side up at least 3 m (10 ft) above sea level. Rigidly secured at masthead or other high point if possible.	Annually.
Spare batteries.	Away from drips, bilge water and rigidly secured.	Each voyage.
Tools with moving parts such as pliers need coating with grease or similar treatment to prevent rusting and seizure.	In a waterproof container.	Monthly.
Operating instructions posted up by extinguishers. Also a notice warning crew of dangerous fumes if BCF or BTM types are carried.	In a securing bracket on bulkhead or similar location away from drips etc. Also not close to probable source of fire such as galley or engine.	Half yearly.
This is often carried for bailing in any case		Annually
Soaked in seawater		
Specially made for firefighting.		
Always as important.		
A flat working surface, parallel rulers or equivalent, pencil and rubber etc.	Away from drips etc. Stowed flat not rolled.	Annually.
Spare batteries.	Within sight of helmsman.	Each voyage.
Eyeholes at 500 mm (18 in) intervals all round with lanyards.		Annually.

Safety equipment—continued

19.	Storm canvas		Essential for sailing craft making passages more than 5 miles from base	To suit vessel. Consult designer or builder for recommended size.
20.	Warm and Waterproof clothing.	1 set for each person on board.	Essential.	Good quality well fitting oilskins and seaboots.

For craft between 5·5 m (18 ft) and 13·7 m (45 ft) L.O.A.

Item No.	Safety Item	Number Required	Status	Type & Size
21.	Safety Harness	One for each person on board. For power craft only those on deck are likely to need harnesses so 2 may do.	Essential. To be worn in rough weather or medium weather at night.	To BSI Specification. Childrens size where appropriate.
22.	Lifebuoys	2 or more	Recommended	Horseshoe type. Orange or Yellow.
23.	Inflatable liferaft or Rigid dinghy or Inflatable dinghy	1	Recommended.	Of DOTI type or equivalent. With permanent not inflated buoyancy, and oars and row-locks secured. May be collapsible type. With at least 2 separate inflatable compart-ments, one to be kept permanently inflated.
24.	Bilge pump	1, 2 or 3	Recommended.	
25.	Flares	6	This is an absolute minimum number.	Two to be the rocket parachute type. The rest to be '5-Star' Reds.

		Half yearly.
Safety harness integral is a great advantage.		Monthly.

Equipment	Stowage	Overhaul or Test Frequency
A long safety line is needed for general use with short line or extra clip at half line length for use when the vessel is doing more than 8 knots since it can be dangerous to fall overboard at this speed.	Generally near the companionway.	Monthly
One should have a 30 m (100 ft) buoyant line with a breaking strain of 1150 kilos (2500 pounds) e.g. 10 mm ($\frac{3}{8}$ in) diam. Ulstron (polypropylene multifilament). A self-igniting light and smoke signal should be attached to one.	Near helmsman.	Annually
Bailer, painter, oars and rowlocks or paddles. Duplications of many of the parent yachts safety equipment such as flares etc. are found in inflatable liferaft packs and are recommended for inflatable dinghies or rigid dinghies. Also recommended; CO_2 inflation and an overall canopy.	On deck or in a locker opening directly onto the deck.	Annually
Strum box needed to prevent pipe becoming choked.	One near the helmsman. If 2 are fitted one should be below deck.	Each voyage
A tube fixed on deck is needed for some types of rocket. In a waterproof container. A polythene bag alone is not rugged enough.	Away from engine heat and not in a locker with sharp or heavy objects.	See the 'Shelf-life' stamped on the flares. It is usually 3 years after date of manufacture.

26.	Daylight Distress Smoke Signals.	2	This is an absolute minimum number.	The smallest size acceptable is 180 mm (7 in) × 90 mm (3½ in) diam.
27.	Towrope	1	Recommended.	Normally a pair of mooring warps or the anchor warp will do.
28.	Lifelines	1 or 2 3	Recommended. Far better when children are on board.	All round vessel so far as possible. 5 mm $\frac{3}{16}$ in wire minimum diameter.
29.	Recognition. NAME and/or NUMBER	1 each side 1 on deck	Recommended. Optional.	Figures and letters at least 220 mm (9 in) high and 300 mm (12 in) much to be preferred.
30.	Firefighting Equipment.	1	Recommended for vessel under 9 m (30 ft) if it has only an engine but no cooking facilities or vice versa.	1·5 kilos (3 pounds) capacity dry powder. See notes on item 14.
		2	Recommended for vessel under 9 m (30 ft) if it has both engine and cooking facilities.	As above.
		3	Recommended for vessels of between 9 m and 13·7 m (30 ft & 45 ft)	Two, each 1·5 kilos (3 pounds) capacity dry powder or equivalent and one or more of 2·5 kilos (5 pounds) capacity dry powder or equivalent.
		2	Recommended for all craft over 9 m (30 ft).	Buckets
		1	Recommended for all craft over 9 m (30 ft).	Bag of sand
31.	Anchors	2	SEE ITEM 3 FOR TYPE, SIZE ETC.	
32.	Compass	2	Recommended. One arranged for taking bearings.	Marine type with a card of at least 100 mm (4 in) across.
33.	First Aid Box.	1	Recommended.	SEE ITEM 9 FOR SIZE,
34.	Charts.		SEE ITEM 16 FOR NUMBERS ETC.	
35.	Torch		SEE ITEM 10 FOR NUMBERS ETC.	
36.	Radar Reflector.		SEE ITEM 11 FOR TYPE ETC.	

(45 ft) L.O.A.—continued

	Near helmsman.	See the 'Shelf-life' stamped on the signals. It is usually 3 years after the date of manufacture.
A smooth fairlead at the bow, and well bolted. Strongly based mooring post or cleat. Also chafing gear to wrap round the warp.		Annually
Threaded through stanchions at 1·8 metres (6 ft) intervals.	Permanently rigged and kept taut.	Annually
	Name and/or number on dodgers or on topsides, and/or numbers on sail.	Annually
See notes on item 14.	See notes on item 14.	Half yearly.
	When 2 or more extinguishers are carried they should be located at different points throughout the vessel.	
Gimballed on a sailing craft. Correction card. Light and dimmer switch.	Near helmsman and away from all steel etc. as well as away from instruments and electric wiring which generates a magnetic field.	Whenever opportunity permits. Certainly every two months.
37.	Radio Receiver.	SEE ITEM 12 FOR TYPE ETC.
38.	Engine tool kit.	SEE ITEM 13 FOR TYPE ETC.

ALSO RECOMMENDED FOR THIS SIZE OF VESSEL ITEMS 17, 18, 19 and 20.

Sheet winches—power ratio

There is a good deal of controversy about the correct size of sheet winch to fit on a boat. This is because crew strengths vary, different yachts are used for different purposes and some are much harder driven than others. Dominating all is the high cost of powerful winches which is the reason why so many standard boats are marketed with winches of inadequate power.

The graph shows upper and lower limits for winches to suit the sail area of the largest genoa to be set, which should be taken as the basis. If the crew is weak, if the boat is to be raced hard in all weathers, go for the larger size of winch. If in doubt use the right hand side of the graph curve. For multihulls increase the power ratio by 20%.

$$\text{Power ratio} = \text{gear ratio} \times \frac{\text{radius of handle}}{\text{radius of drum} + \text{rope}}$$

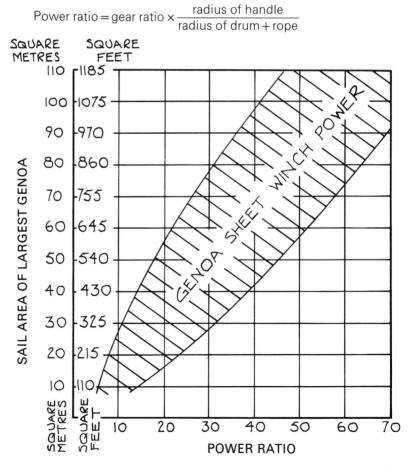

Lights and shapes needed on small craft

It is not enough to know what lights and shapes are needed; their exact spacing must be known when designing and building small craft. These lists should be treated with some reserve because alterations and additions are pending during the period that this book is going to press.

Small craft are frequently found with lights and gear for hoisting shapes which do not stand up to severe conditions at sea. For instance a light which is not rigidly secured will oscillate in quite a moderate sea and in time the electric cable insulation becomes cracked and faulty. No light (or other fitting) should be held by less than three fastenings.

1　　　　**Lights for power-driven vessels.**

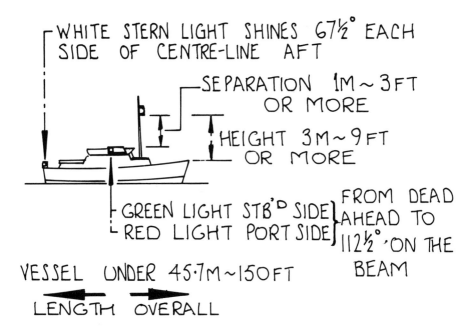

WHITE STERN LIGHT SHINES 67½° EACH SIDE OF CENTRE-LINE AFT

SEPARATION 1M ~ 3FT OR MORE

HEIGHT 3M ~ 9FT OR MORE

GREEN LIGHT STB'D SIDE
RED LIGHT PORT SIDE
FROM DEAD AHEAD TO 112½° ON THE BEAM

VESSEL UNDER 45·7M ~ 150FT
LENGTH OVERALL

2   **A vessel at anchor** hoists a spherical black shape forward where it can be clearly seen all round.

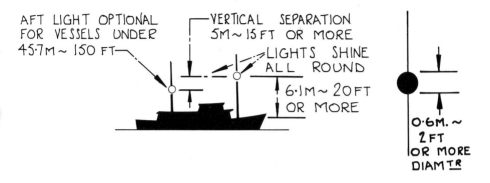

AFT LIGHT OPTIONAL FOR VESSELS UNDER 45·7M ~ 150 FT

VERTICAL SEPARATION 5M ~ 15 FT OR MORE

LIGHTS SHINE ALL ROUND

6·1M ~ 20 FT OR MORE

0·6M. ~ 2 FT OR MORE DIAM⊤ᴿ

3   **A vessel not under command** hoists two black spherical shapes. This signal is for ships unable to keep clear of others, for example the steering gear may have broken down. Though it is not a distress signal, ships flying this signal should be kept under observation since they may need help later.

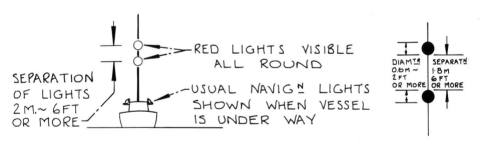

RED LIGHTS VISIBLE ALL ROUND

SEPARATION OF LIGHTS 2 M. ~ 6 FT OR MORE

USUAL NAVIGᴺ LIGHTS SHOWN WHEN VESSEL IS UNDER WAY

DIAM⊤ᴿ 0.6M ~ 2 FT OR MORE

SEPARAᵀᴺ 1·8 M 6 FT OR MORE

4   **A vessel aground** hoists three black spherical shapes. This signal is not required for vessels power-driven under 19·8 metres (65 ft) or sailing vessels under 12·1 metres (40 ft).

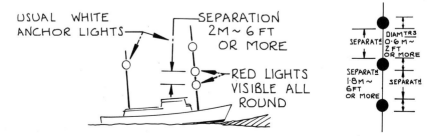

USUAL WHITE ANCHOR LIGHTS

SEPARATION 2M ~ 6 FT OR MORE

RED LIGHTS VISIBLE ALL ROUND

SEPARATᴺ 1·8M ~ 6FT OR MORE

DIAMTRS 0·6 M ~ 2 FT OR MORE

SEPARATᴺ

5   **Pilot vessels** show the usual nagivation lights when under
way, or anchor lights when at anchor.

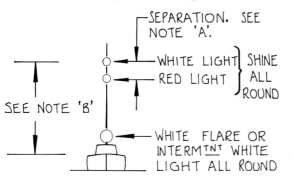

SEPARATION. SEE NOTE 'A'.

WHITE LIGHT
RED LIGHT } SHINE ALL ROUND

SEE NOTE 'B'

WHITE FLARE OR INTERM<u>INT</u> WHITE LIGHT ALL ROUND

Note: A The light separation is 2·43 metres (8 ft) or more. But
it is 1·22 metres (4 ft) or more if the vessel is under 19·8 metres
(65 ft) long.
Note: B Height of top light is 6·1 metres (20 ft) or more. But it
is 2·7 metres (9 ft) or more if the vessel is under 19·8 metres
(65 ft) long.

6   **A vessel trawling** with gear extended 150 metres (500 ft)
hoists a single triangle with the point upwards on the side of the
ship that is in the direction of the gear.

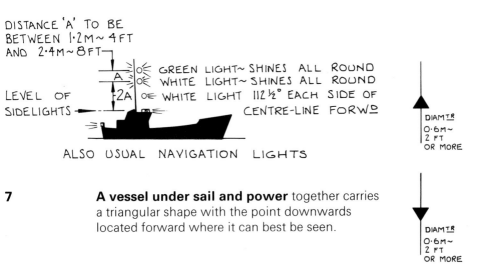

DISTANCE 'A' TO BE BETWEEN 1·2M ~ 4FT AND 2·4M ~ 8FT

GREEN LIGHT ~ SHINES ALL ROUND
WHITE LIGHT ~ SHINES ALL ROUND
WHITE LIGHT 112½° EACH SIDE OF CENTRE-LINE FORW<u>D</u>

LEVEL OF SIDELIGHTS

ALSO USUAL NAVIGATION LIGHTS

DIAM<u>TR</u> 0·6M ~ 2 FT OR MORE

7   **A vessel under sail and power** together carries
a triangular shape with the point downwards
located forward where it can best be seen.

DIAM<u>TR</u> 0·6M ~ 2 FT OR MORE

Lights and shapes—continued

8   **Sailing vessels** under 12 metres (39·4 ft) may show a single light at the masthead which is divided into three sectors as shown. Alternatively they may show red and green lights forward and a white light aft as illustrated in the plan view. If this is the case the red and green lights may be separated or combined into one housing.

When under sail and power together they must show lights as for a small craft under power (lower drawing).

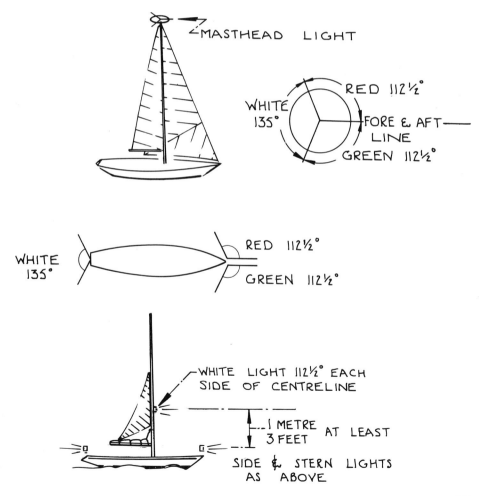

9   **A fishing vessel with lines, trawl or nets** (but not a fishing vessel trolling (for which see Section 6) carries twin diamonds with the points together.

A fishing vessel under 19·8 metres (65 ft) hoists a basket forward where it can best be seen (right hand sketch, below)

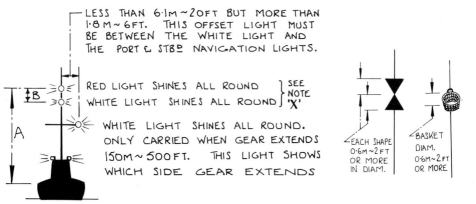

LESS THAN 6·1m ~20FT BUT MORE THAN 1·8 M ~ 6FT. THIS OFFSET LIGHT MUST BE BETWEEN THE WHITE LIGHT AND THE PORT & STB⁰ NAVIGATION LIGHTS.

RED LIGHT SHINES ALL ROUND ⎫ SEE
WHITE LIGHT SHINES ALL ROUND ⎬ NOTE 'X'

WHITE LIGHT SHINES ALL ROUND. ONLY CARRIED WHEN GEAR EXTENDS 150m ~ 500FT. THIS LIGHT SHOWS WHICH SIDE GEAR EXTENDS

EACH SHAPE 0·6m~2FT OR MORE IN DIAM.

BASKET DIAM. 0·6m~2FT OR MORE

ALSO USUAL NAVIGATION LIGHTS

NOTE 'X' SPACING OF THESE LIGHTS AS ON TRAWLER UNLESS LENGTH IS UNDER 12M~40FT WHEN DIMENSION 'A' MAY BE 2·7m ~ 9FT OR MORE AND DIMENSION 'B' MAY BE 1m ~ 3FT OR MORE

10   **A vessel unable to give way** because it is engaged in work which makes it impossible for her to keep clear of others, eg cable laying, refuelling at sea etc, carries two red balls separated by a white diamond.

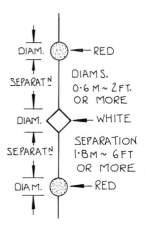

SEPARATION OF LIGHTS 2m.~ 6FT. OR MORE

RED LIGHT ⎫
WHITE LIGHT ⎬ LIGHTS SHINE ALL ROUND
RED LIGHT ⎭

USUAL NAVIGATⁿ LIGHTS SHOWN WHEN UNDER WAY OR ANCHOR LIGHTS WHEN AT ANCHOR

DIAM.
SEPARATⁿ
DIAM.
SEPARATⁿ
DIAM.

RED
DIAMS. 0·6 M ~ 2FT. OR MORE
WHITE
SEPARATION 1·8m ~ 6FT OR MORE
RED

11 **Vessels towed and towing.** A tug with a tow having a length from the stern of the tug to the stern of the aftermost vessel in the towline in excess of 180 metres (600 ft) carries a diamond shape located forward where best seen and this is repeated on the towed vessel.

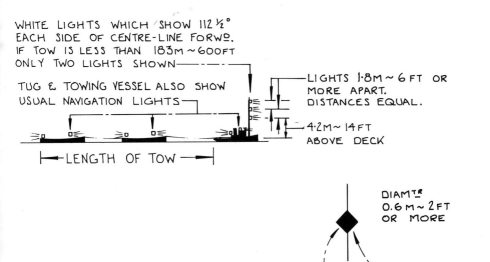

WHITE LIGHTS WHICH SHOW 112½° EACH SIDE OF CENTRE-LINE FORWD. IF TOW IS LESS THAN 183m ~ 600FT ONLY TWO LIGHTS SHOWN

TUG & TOWING VESSEL ALSO SHOW USUAL NAVIGATION LIGHTS

LIGHTS 1·8M ~ 6 FT OR MORE APART. DISTANCES EQUAL.

4·2M ~ 14FT ABOVE DECK

←LENGTH OF TOW→

DIAMTR 0.6 M ~ 2FT OR MORE

180M ~ 600 FT. OR MORE

SECTION 2 — **Materials**

Brass rod (metric measure)—weight in kg/m and lb/ft

DIAMETER OR WIDTH ACROSS FLATS MILLIMETRES	DECIMAL EQUIVALENT INCHES	WEIGHT KG./M.	WEIGHT LB./FT.	WEIGHT KG./M.	WEIGHT LB./FT.	WEIGHT KG./M.	WEIGHT LB./FT.
1	.0394	.0067	.0045	.0073	.0049	.0085	.0057
2	.0787	.0266	.0179	.0293	.0197	.0339	.0228
3	.1181	.0598	.0402	.0659	.0443	.0762	.0512
4	.1575	.1064	.0715	.1173	.0788	.1354	.0910
5	.1969	.1664	.1118	.1833	.1232	.2118	.1423
6	.2362	.2395	.1609	.2642	.1775	.3049	.2049
7	.2756	.3261	.2191	.3595	.2416	.4152	.2790
8	.3150	.4258	.2861	.4695	.3155	.5422	.3643
9	.3543	.5389	.3621	.5942	.3993	.6862	.4611
10	.3937	.6654	.4471	.7337	.4930	.8471	.5692
11	.4331	.8050	.5409	.8877	.5965	1.0249	.6887
12	.4724	.9581	.6438	1.0563	.7098	1.2199	.8197
13	.5118	1.1243	.7555	1.2398	.8331	1.4316	.9620
14	.5512	1.3040	.8762	1.4378	.9661	1.6602	1.1156
15	.5906	1.4970	1.0059	1.6507	1.1092	1.9059	1.2807
16	.6299	1.7031	1.1444	1.8780	1.2619	2.1686	1.4572
17	.6693	1.9228	1.2920	2.1201	1.4266	2.4481	1.6450
18	.7087	2.1555	1.4484	2.3748	1.5971	2.7445	1.8442
19	.7480	2.4018	1.6139	2.6483	1.7795	3.0580	2.0548
20	.7874	2.6612	1.7882	2.9343	1.9717	3.3883	2.2768
21	.8268	2.9340	1.9715	3.2352	2.1739	3.7357	2.5102
22	.8661	3.2200	2.1637	3.5507	2.3859	4.0998	2.7549
23	.9055	3.5194	2.3649	3.8808	2.6077	4.4811	3.0111
24	.9449	3.8321	2.5750	4.2254	2.8393	4.8792	3.2786
25	.9843	4.1582	2.7941	4.5850	3.0809	5.2943	3.5575
26	1.0236	4.4975	3.0221	4.9591	3.3323	5.7263	3.8478
27	1.0630	4.8500	3.2590	5.3480	3.5936	6.1753	4.1495
28	1.1024	5.2160	3.5049	5.7514	3.8647	6.6411	4.4625
29	1.1417	5.5952	3.7597	6.1696	4.1457	7.1240	4.7870
30	1.1811	5.9878	4.0235	6.6023	4.4364	7.6239	5.1229
31	1.2205	6.3935	4.2961	7.0498	4.7371	8.1405	5.4700
32	1.2598	6.8127	4.5778	7.5120	5.0477	8.6741	5.8286
33	1.2992	7.2452	4.8684	7.9890	5.3682	9.2248	6.1986
34	1.3386	7.6909	5.1679	8.4805	5.6985	9.7922	6.5799
35	1.3780	8.1500	5.4764	8.9866	6.0386	10.3768	6.9727
36	1.4173	8.6223	5.7938	9.5075	6.3886	10.9783	7.3769
37	1.4567	9.1079	6.1201	10.0430	6.7484	11.5966	7.7924
38	1.4961	9.6069	6.4554	10.5932	7.1181	12.2318	8.2192
39	1.5354	10.1192	6.7996	11.1579	7.4976	12.8841	8.6575
40	1.5748	10.6448	7.1528	11.7366	7.8871	13.5533	9.1072
41	1.6142	11.1837	7.5149	12.3318	8.2864	14.2395	9.5683
42	1.6535	11.7359	7.8860	12.9406	8.6955	14.9426	10.0407
43	1.6929	12.3015	8.2660	13.5643	9.1146	15.6627	10.5246
44	1.7323	12.8802	8.6549	14.2025	9.5434	16.3997	11.0198
45	1.7717	13.4724	9.0528	14.8554	9.9821	17.1536	11.5264
46	1.8110	14.0778	9.4596	15.5230	10.4307	17.9243	12.0443
47	1.8504	14.6964	9.8753	16.2053	10.8892	18.7122	12.5737
48	1.8898	15.3285	10.3000	16.9021	11.3574	19.5169	13.1144
49	1.9291	15.9739	10.7337	17.6137	11.8356	20.3385	13.6665
50	1.9685	16.6326	11.1763	18.3400	12.3236	21.1772	14.2301

DIAMETER OR WIDTH ACROSS FLATS MILLIMETRES	DECIMAL EQUIVALENT INCHES						
		WEIGHT KG./M.	WEIGHT LB./FT.	WEIGHT KG./M.	WEIGHT LB./FT.	WEIGHT KG./M.	WEIGHT LB./FT.
51	2.0079	17.3045	11.6278	19.0810	12.8215	22.0862	14.8409
52	2.0472	17.9897	12.0882	19.8367	13.3293	22.9052	15.3912
53	2.0866	18.6882	12.5576	20.6068	13.8468	23.7947	15.9889
54	2.1260	19.4002	13.0360	21.3917	14.3742	24.7010	16.5979
55	2.1654	20.1254	13.5233	22.1914	14.9116	25.6243	17.2183
56	2.2047	20.8638	14.0195	23.0056	15.4587	26.5647	17.8502
57	2.2441	21.6157	14.5247	23.8346	16.0157	27.5219	18.4934
58	2.2835	22.3807	15.0388	24.6782	16.5826	28.4959	19.1479
59	2.3228	23.1591	15.5618	25.5366	17.1594	29.4870	19.8139
60	2.3622	23.9508	16.0938	26.4096	17.7460	30.4952	20.4913
61	2.4016	24.7558	16.6347	27.2973	18.3425	31.5201	21.1800
62	2.4409	25.5741	17.1846	28.1996	18.9488	32.5620	21.8801
63	2.4803	26.4057	17.7434	29.1166	19.5650	33.6210	22.5917
64	2.5197	27.2507	18.3112	30.0482	20.1910	34.6966	23.3145
65	2.5591	28.1088	18.8878	30.9944	20.8268	35.7893	24.0487
66	2.5984	28.9805	19.4735	31.9555	21.4726	36.8992	24.7945
67	2.6378	29.8652	20.0680	32.9312	22.1282	38.0256	25.5514
68	2.6772	30.7635	20.6716	33.9216	22.7937	39.1693	26.3199
69	2.7165	31.6748	21.2840	34.9266	23.4690	40.3296	27.0996
70	2.7559	32.5996	21.9054	35.9464	24.1543	41.5072	27.8909
71	2.7953	33.5376	22.5357	36.9806	24.8492	42.7015	28.6934
72	2.8347	34.4892	23.1751	38.0299	25.5543	43.9131	29.5075
73	2.8740	35.4537	23.8232	39.0934	26.2689	45.1411	30.3327
74	2.9134	36.4317	24.4804	40.1719	26.9936	46.3864	31.1695
75	2.9528	37.4230	25.1465	41.2650	27.7281	47.6484	32.0175
76	2.9921	38.4277	25.8216	42.3726	28.4724	48.9277	32.8771
77	3.0315	39.4455	26.5055	43.4949	29.2265	50.2236	33.7479
78	3.0709	40.4768	27.1985	44.6322	29.9907	51.5367	34.6302
79	3.1102	41.5212	27.9003	45.7837	30.7645	52.8665	35.5238
80	3.1496	42.5792	28.6112	46.9503	31.5484	54.2136	36.4290
81	3.1890	43.6502	29.3309	48.1315	32.3421	55.5771	37.3452
82	3.2284	44.7347	30.0596	49.3271	33.1455	56.9580	38.2731
83	3.2677	45.8324	30.7942	50.5376	33.9589	58.3556	39.2122
84	3.3071	46.9435	31.5438	51.7629	34.7822	59.7704	40.1629
85	3.3465	48.0678	32.2993	53.0024	35.6151	61.2019	41.1248
86	3.3858	49.2055	33.0638	54.2569	36.4581	62.6504	42.0981
87	3.4252	50.3565	33.8372	55.5261	37.3109	64.1158	43.0828
88	3.4646	51.5207	34.6195	56.8100	38.1736	65.5984	44.0790
89	3.5039	52.6984	35.4108	58.1083	39.0460	67.0976	45.0864
90	3.5433	53.8892	36.2110	59.4214	39.9284	68.6141	46.1054
91	3.5827	55.0935	37.0202	60.7492	40.8206	70.1472	47.1356
92	3.6221	56.3110	37.8383	62.0919	41.7228	71.6975	48.1773
93	3.6614	57.5417	38.6653	63.4488	42.6366	73.2645	49.2303
94	3.7008	58.7858	39.5013	64.8208	43.5565	74.8486	50.2947
95	3.7402	60.0432	40.3462	66.2072	44.4881	76.4494	51.3704
96	3.7795	61.3140	41.2001	67.6085	45.4297	78.0675	52.4577
97	3.8189	62.5980	42.0629	69.0242	46.3810	79.7022	53.5561
98	3.8583	63.8954	42.9347	70.4550	47.3424	81.3541	54.6661
99	3.8976	65.2059	43.8153	71.9000	48.3134	83.0228	55.7874
100	3.9370	66.5300	44.7050	73.3599	49.2944	84.7086	56.9202

Brass rod (metric measure)—weights—continued

DIAMETER OR WIDTH ACROSS FLATS MILLIMETRES	DECIMAL EQUIVALENT INCHES	WEIGHT KG./M.	WEIGHT LB./FT.	WEIGHT KG./M.	WEIGHT LB./FT.	WEIGHT KG./M.	WEIGHT LB./FT.
101	3.9764	67.8671	45.6035	74.8343	50.2851	86.4111	58.0642
102	4.0158	69.2178	46.5111	76.3237	51.2859	88.1309	59.2198
103	4.0551	70.5816	47.4275	77.8275	52.2964	89.8673	60.3866
104	4.0945	71.9588	48.3529	79.3461	53.3168	91.6209	61.5649
105	4.1339	73.3492	49.2872	80.8792	54.3470	93.3911	62.7544
106	4.1732	74.7530	50.2305	82.4272	55.3872	95.1787	63.9556
107	4.2126	76.1701	51.1827	83.9897	56.4371	96.9827	65.1678
108	4.2520	77.6006	52.1439	85.5672	57.4971	98.8040	66.3916
109	4.2913	79.0443	53.1140	87.1590	58.5667	100.6422	67.6268
110	4.3307	80.5012	54.0930	88.7658	59.6464	102.4972	68.8733
111	4.3701	81.9715	55.0810	90.3969	60.7357	104.3693	70.1312
112	4.4095	83.4551	56.0779	92.0228	61.8350	106.2584	71.4006
113	4.4488	84.9521	57.0838	93.6733	62.9440	108.1642	72.6812
114	4.4882	86.4623	58.0986	95.3387	64.0631	110.0871	73.9733
115	4.5276	87.9858	59.1223	97.0186	65.1919	112.0269	75.2768
116	4.5669	89.5227	60.1550	98.7132	66.3306	113.9838	76.5917
117	4.6063	91.0728	61.1966	100.4224	67.4791	115.9574	77.9179
118	4.6457	92.6363	62.2472	102.1465	68.6376	117.9480	79.2555
119	4.6850	94.2130	63.3067	103.8851	69.8059	119.9556	80.6045
120	4.7244	95.8032	64.3752	105.6385	70.9841	121.9802	81.9649
121	4.7638	97.4064	65.4525	107.4062	72.1719	124.0217	83.3367
122	4.8032	99.0232	66.5389	109.1891	73.3699	126.0802	84.7199
123	4.8425	100.6531	67.6341	110.9862	74.5775	128.1553	86.1143
124	4.8819	102.2965	68.7384	112.7983	75.7951	130.2479	87.5204
125	4.9213	103.9530	69.8515	114.6249	77.0225	132.3569	88.9376
126	4.9606	105.6229	70.9736	116.4662	78.2598	134.4831	90.3663
127	5.0000	107.3061	72.1046	118.3222	79.5069	136.6263	91.8064
128	5.0394	109.0028	73.2447	120.1931	80.7641	138.7866	93.2580
129	5.0787	110.7124	74.3935	122.0784	82.0309	140.9635	94.7208
130	5.1181	112.4356	75.5514	123.9785	83.3077	143.1574	96.1950
131	5.1575	114.1720	76.7182	125.8931	84.5942	145.3685	97.6806
132	5.1969	115.9219	77.8940	127.8224	85.8906	147.5961	99.1776
133	5.2362	117.6848	79.0786	129.7666	87.1970	149.8409	100.6860
134	5.2756	119.4612	80.2723	131.7252	88.5131	152.1027	102.2058
135	5.3150	121.2508	81.4748	133.6985	89.8391	154.3811	103.7368
136	5.3543	123.0539	82.6864	135.6866	91.1750	156.6770	105.2795
137	5.3937	124.8701	83.9068	137.6893	92.5207	158.9893	106.8333
138	5.4331	126.6997	85.1362	139.7067	93.8763	161.3189	108.3987
139	5.4724	128.5425	86.3745	141.7388	95.2418	163.6652	109.9753
140	5.5118	130.3988	87.6218	143.7856	96.6171	166.0288	111.5635
141	5.5512	132.2682	88.8780	145.8470	98.0023	168.4089	113.1628
142	5.5906	134.1511	90.1432	147.9231	99.3973	170.8062	114.7737
143	5.6299	136.0471	91.4172	150.0138	100.8022	173.2204	116.3959
144	5.6693	137.9566	92.7003	152.1192	102.2169	175.6517	118.0296
145	5.7087	139.8792	93.9922	154.2393	103.6415	178.0997	119.6746
146	5.7480	141.8153	95.2932	156.3743	105.0761	180.5646	121.3309
147	5.7874	143.7646	96.6030	158.5237	106.5204	183.0465	122.9986
148	5.8268	145.7272	97.9218	160.6877	107.9745	185.5454	124.6777
149	5.8661	147.7031	99.2495	162.8664	109.4385	188.0613	126.3683
150	5.9055	149.6924	100.5862	165.0600	110.9125	190.5945	128.0705

Brass rod—standard hexagons for bolts, screws and nuts

B.S.1083 WHITWORTH AND FINE Inches	NOMINAL SIZES		WIDTH ACROSS FLATS Inches
	UNIFIED		
	B.S.1768 NORMAL SERIES Inches	B.S.1769 HEAVY SERIES Inches	
	$\frac{1}{4}$		.4375
$\frac{1}{4}$			.445
	$\frac{5}{16}$		.500
$\frac{5}{16}$			.525
	$\frac{3}{8}$		.5625
$\frac{3}{8}$			.600
	$\frac{7}{16}$ Bolts & Screws		.625
	$\frac{7}{16}$ Nuts		.6875
$\frac{7}{16}$			.710
	$\frac{1}{2}$		.750
	$\frac{9}{16}$ Bolts & Screws†		.8125
$\frac{1}{2}$			.820
	$\frac{9}{16}$ Nuts†	$\frac{1}{2}$	.875
$\frac{9}{16}$			.920
	$\frac{5}{8}$		.9375
$\frac{5}{8}$			1.010
		$\frac{5}{8}$	1.0625
	$\frac{3}{4}$		1.125
$\frac{3}{4}$			1.200
		$\frac{3}{4}$	1.250
$\frac{7}{8}$			1.300
	$\frac{7}{8}$		1.3125
		$\frac{7}{8}$	1.4375
1			1.480
	1		1.500
		1	1.625
$1\frac{1}{8}$			1.670
	$1\frac{1}{8}$		1.6875
		$1\frac{1}{8}$	1.8125
$1\frac{1}{4}$			1.860
	$1\frac{1}{4}$		1.875
		$1\frac{1}{4}$	2.000
$1\frac{3}{8}$*			2.050
	$1\frac{3}{8}$†		2.0625
		$1\frac{3}{8}$†	2.1875
$1\frac{1}{2}$			2.220
	$1\frac{1}{2}$		2.250
		$1\frac{1}{2}$	2.375
$1\frac{3}{4}$			2.580
	$1\frac{3}{4}$		2.625
		$1\frac{3}{4}$	2.750
2			2.760
	2		3.000
		2	3.125

Not standard with B.S.W. thread.   † To be dispensed with wherever possible.

Note: To avoid confusion with standards now obsolete, purchasers of hexagon rods are advised to specify the decimal sizes across flats.

Brass rod (Imperial measure)—weight in lb/ft

DIAMETER OR WIDTH ACROSS FLATS INCHES	DECIMAL EQUIVALENT	MILLIMETRE EQUIVALENT	WEIGHT (lb.) PER FOOT (round)	(hex)	(square)
$\frac{1}{16}$	.0625	1.588	.0113	.0124	.0144
$\frac{5}{64}$	.0781	1.984	.0176	.0194	.0224
$\frac{3}{32}$	.0938	2.381	.0254	.0280	.0323
$\frac{7}{64}$	.1094	2.778	.0345	.0380	.0439
$\frac{1}{8}$	.1250	3.175	.0450	.0497	.0574
$\frac{9}{64}$	.1406	3.572	.0570	.0629	.0726
$\frac{5}{32}$	.1563	3.969	.0704	.0776	.0896
$\frac{11}{64}$	.1719	4.366	.0852	.0939	.1085
$\frac{3}{16}$	.1875	4.763	.1014	.1118	.1291
$\frac{13}{64}$	.2031	5.159	.1190	.1312	.1515
$\frac{7}{32}$	.2188	5.556	.1380	.1522	.1757
$\frac{15}{64}$	.2344	5.953	.1584	.1747	.2017
$\frac{1}{4}$	.2500	6.350	.1803	.1988	.2295
$\frac{17}{64}$	.2656	6.747	.2035	.2244	.2591
$\frac{9}{32}$	.2813	7.144	.2281	.2515	.2905
$\frac{19}{64}$	.2969	7.541	.2542	.2803	.3236
$\frac{5}{16}$	.3125	7.938	.2817	.3106	.3586
$\frac{21}{64}$	.3281	8.334	.3105	.3424	.3954
$\frac{11}{32}$	.3438	8.731	.3408	.3757	.4339
$\frac{23}{64}$	.3594	9.128	.3725	.4107	.4742
$\frac{3}{8}$	.3750	9.525	.4055	.4472	.5164
$\frac{25}{64}$	.3906	9.922	.4401	.4852	.5603
$\frac{13}{32}$	.4063	10.319	.4760	.5248	.6060
$\frac{27}{64}$	.4219	10.716	.5133	.5660	.6535
$\frac{7}{16}$	.4375	11.113	.5520	.6087	.7029
$\frac{29}{64}$	.4531	11.509	.5921	.6529	.7539
$\frac{15}{32}$	.4688	11.906	.6337	.6987	.8068
$\frac{31}{64}$	.4844	12.303	.6766	.7461	.8615
$\frac{1}{2}$	.5000	12.700	.7210	.7950	.9180
$\frac{33}{64}$	.5156	13.097	.7668	.8455	.9763
$\frac{17}{32}$	.5313	13.494	.8140	.8975	1.0363
$\frac{35}{64}$	.5469	13.891	.8625	.9510	1.0982
$\frac{9}{16}$	.5625	14.288	.9125	1.0062	1.1619
$\frac{37}{64}$	.5781	14.684	.9639	1.0629	1.2273
$\frac{19}{32}$	.5938	15.081	1.0167	1.1211	1.2945
$\frac{39}{64}$	.6094	15.478	1.0709	1.1809	1.3636
$\frac{5}{8}$	.6250	15.875	1.1265	1.2422	1.4344
$\frac{41}{64}$	.6406	16.272	1.1836	1.3051	1.5070
$\frac{21}{32}$	.6563	16.669	1.2420	1.3695	1.5814
$\frac{43}{64}$	.6719	17.066	1.3019	1.4355	1.6576
$\frac{11}{16}$	.6875	17.463	1.3632	1.5031	1.7356
$\frac{45}{64}$	.7031	17.859	1.4258	1.5721	1.8154
$\frac{23}{32}$	.7188	18.256	1.4899	1.6428	1.8970
$\frac{47}{64}$	.7344	18.653	1.5554	1.7150	1.9803
$\frac{3}{4}$	.7500	19.050	1.6223	1.7888	2.0655
$\frac{49}{64}$	.7656	19.447	1.6905	1.8641	2.1525
$\frac{25}{32}$	.7813	19.844	1.7602	1.9409	2.2412
$\frac{51}{64}$	.7969	20.241	1.8314	2.0193	2.3318
$\frac{13}{16}$	.8125	20.638	1.9039	2.0993	2.4241
$\frac{53}{64}$	.8281	21.034	1.9778	2.1808	2.5182
$\frac{27}{32}$	.8438	21.431	2.0531	2.2639	2.6141
$\frac{55}{64}$	.8594	21.828	2.1299	2.3485	2.7119
$\frac{7}{8}$	.8750	22.225	2.2080	2.4347	2.8114
$\frac{57}{64}$	.8906	22.622	2.2876	2.5224	2.9127
$\frac{29}{32}$	.9063	23.019	2.3686	2.6117	3.0158
$\frac{59}{64}$	.9219	23.416	2.4510	2.7025	3.1206
$\frac{15}{16}$	.9375	23.813	2.5348	2.7949	3.2274
$\frac{61}{64}$	.9531	24.209	2.6200	2.8889	3.3358
$\frac{31}{32}$	.9688	24.606	2.7066	2.9844	3.4461
$\frac{63}{64}$	.9844	25.003	2.7946	3.0814	3.5581
1	1.0000	25.400	2.8840	3.1800	3.6720

DIAMETER OR WIDTH ACROSS FLATS INCHES	DECIMAL EQUIVALENT	MILLIMETRE EQUIVALENT	WEIGHT (lb.) PER FOOT (round)	WEIGHT (lb.) PER FOOT (hexagon)	WEIGHT (lb.) PER FOOT (square)
$1\frac{1}{64}$	1.0156	25.797	2.9748	3.2801	3.7876
$1\frac{1}{32}$	1.0313	26.194	3.0671	3.3819	3.9051
$1\frac{3}{64}$	1.0469	26.591	3.1607	3.4851	4.0243
$1\frac{1}{16}$	1.0625	26.988	3.2558	3.5899	4.1454
$1\frac{5}{64}$	1.0781	27.384	3.3522	3.6963	4.2681
$1\frac{3}{32}$	1.0938	27.781	3.4501	3.8042	4.3928
$1\frac{7}{64}$	1.1094	28.178	3.5494	3.9137	4.5192
$1\frac{1}{8}$	1.1250	28.575	3.6500	4.0247	4.6474
$1\frac{9}{64}$	1.1406	28.972	3.7522	4.1373	4.7774
$1\frac{5}{32}$	1.1562	29.369	3.8556	4.2514	4.9091
$1\frac{11}{64}$	1.1719	29.766	3.9606	4.3671	5.0427
$1\frac{3}{16}$	1.1875	30.163	4.0669	4.4843	5.1781
$1\frac{13}{64}$	1.2031	30.559	4.1746	4.6031	5.3153
$1\frac{7}{32}$	1.2188	30.956	4.2837	4.7234	5.4542
$1\frac{15}{64}$	1.2344	31.353	4.3943	4.8453	5.5950
$1\frac{1}{4}$	1.2500	31.750	4.5063	4.9688	5.7375
$1\frac{17}{64}$	1.2656	32.147	4.6196	5.0938	5.8818
$1\frac{9}{32}$	1.2813	32.544	4.7344	5.2203	6.0280
$1\frac{19}{64}$	1.2969	32.941	4.8505	5.3484	6.1759
$1\frac{5}{16}$	1.3125	33.338	4.9681	5.4781	6.3256
$1\frac{21}{64}$	1.3281	33.734	5.0871	5.6093	6.4771
$1\frac{11}{32}$	1.3438	34.131	5.2075	5.7420	6.6304
$1\frac{23}{64}$	1.3594	34.528	5.3293	5.8763	6.7855
$1\frac{3}{8}$	1.3750	34.925	5.4525	6.0122	6.9424
$1\frac{25}{64}$	1.3906	35.322	5.5772	6.1496	7.1011
$1\frac{13}{32}$	1.4063	35.719	5.7032	6.2886	7.2615
$1\frac{27}{64}$	1.4219	36.116	5.8307	6.4291	7.4238
$1\frac{7}{16}$	1.4375	36.513	5.9595	6.5712	7.5879
$1\frac{29}{64}$	1.4531	36.909	6.0898	6.7148	7.7537
$1\frac{15}{32}$	1.4688	37.306	6.2215	6.8600	7.9213
$1\frac{31}{64}$	1.4844	37.703	6.3545	7.0067	8.0908
$1\frac{1}{2}$	1.5000	38.100	6.4890	7.1550	8.2620
$1\frac{33}{64}$	1.5156	38.497	6.6249	7.3048	8.4350
$1\frac{17}{32}$	1.5313	38.894	6.7622	7.4562	8.6098
$1\frac{35}{64}$	1.5469	39.291	6.9009	7.6092	8.7864
$1\frac{9}{16}$	1.5625	39.688	7.0410	7.7637	8.9649
$1\frac{37}{64}$	1.5781	40.084	7.1825	7.9197	9.1450
$1\frac{19}{32}$	1.5938	40.481	7.3255	8.0773	9.3270
$1\frac{39}{64}$	1.6094	40.878	7.4698	8.2365	9.5108
$1\frac{5}{8}$	1.6250	41.275	7.6155	8.3972	9.6964
$1\frac{41}{64}$	1.6406	41.672	7.7627	8.5594	9.8837
$1\frac{21}{32}$	1.6563	42.069	7.9113	8.7232	10.0729
$1\frac{43}{64}$	1.6719	42.466	8.0613	8.8886	10.2639
$1\frac{11}{16}$	1.6875	42.863	8.2127	9.0556	10.4566
$1\frac{45}{64}$	1.7031	43.259	8.3654	9.2240	10.6511
$1\frac{23}{32}$	1.7188	43.656	8.5196	9.3940	10.8475
$1\frac{47}{64}$	1.7344	44.053	8.6752	9.5656	11.0456
$1\frac{3}{4}$	1.7500	44.450	8.8323	9.7388	11.2455
$1\frac{49}{64}$	1.7656	44.847	8.9907	9.9134	11.4472
$1\frac{25}{32}$	1.7813	45.244	9.1505	10.0897	11.6507
$1\frac{51}{64}$	1.7969	45.641	9.3117	10.2675	11.8560
$1\frac{13}{16}$	1.8125	46.038	9.4744	10.4468	12.0631
$1\frac{53}{64}$	1.8281	46.434	9.6384	10.6277	12.2720
$1\frac{27}{32}$	1.8438	46.831	9.8039	10.8101	12.4826
$1\frac{55}{64}$	1.8594	47.228	9.9708	10.9942	12.6951
$1\frac{7}{8}$	1.8750	47.625	10.1390	11.1797	12.9094
$1\frac{57}{64}$	1.8906	48.022	10.3087	11.3668	13.1254
$1\frac{29}{32}$	1.9063	48.419	10.4799	11.5555	13.3433
$1\frac{59}{64}$	1.9219	48.816	10.6523	11.7456	13.5629
$1\frac{15}{16}$	1.9375	49.213	10.8263	11.9374	13.7844
$1\frac{61}{64}$	1.9531	49.609	11.0016	12.1307	14.0076
$1\frac{31}{32}$	1.9688	50.006	11.1783	12.3256	14.2326
$1\frac{63}{64}$	1.9844	50.403	11.3564	12.5220	14.4594
2	2.0000	50.800	11.5360	12.7200	14.6880

37

Brass rod (Imperial measure)—weight in lb/ft—continued

DIAMETER OR WIDTH ACROSS FLATS INCHES	DECIMAL EQUIVALENT	MILLIMETRE EQUIVALENT	WEIGHT (lb) PER FOOT		
			d ◯	d ⬡	d ▢
2 1/32	2.0313	51.594	11.8993	13.1206	15.1506
2 1/16	2.0625	52.388	12.2683	13.5274	15.6204
2 3/32	2.0938	53.181	12.6429	13.9405	16.0973
2 1/8	2.1250	53.975	13.0230	14.3597	16.5814
2 5/32	2.1562	54.769	13.4089	14.7851	17.0726
2 3/16	2.1875	55.563	13.8004	15.2168	17.5711
2 7/32	2.2188	56.356	14.1975	15.6547	18.0767
2 1/4	2.2500	57.150	14.6003	16.0988	18.5895
2 9/32	2.2813	57.944	15.0086	16.5490	19.1095
2 5/16	2.3125	58.738	15.4227	17.0056	19.6366
2 11/32	2.3438	59.531	15.8423	17.4682	20.1709
2 3/8	2.3750	60.325	16.2675	17.9372	20.7124
2 13/32	2.4063	61.119	16.6985	18.4123	21.2610
2 7/16	2.4375	61.913	17.1350	18.8937	21.8169
2 15/32	2.4688	62.706	17.5772	19.3812	22.3798
2 1/2	2.5000	63.500	18.0250	19.8750	22.9500
2 17/32	2.5313	64.294	18.4785	20.3750	23.5273
2 9/16	2.5625	65.088	18.9375	20.8812	24.1119
2 19/32	2.5938	65.881	19.4022	21.3936	24.7035
2 5/8	2.6250	66.675	19.8725	21.9122	25.3024
2 21/32	2.6563	67.469	20.3485	22.4370	25.9084
2 11/16	2.6875	68.263	20.8302	22.9681	26.5216
2 23/32	2.7188	69.056	21.3174	23.5053	27.1420
2 3/4	2.7500	69.850	21.8103	24.0488	27.7695
2 25/32	2.7813	70.644	22.3087	24.5984	28.4042
2 13/16	2.8125	71.438	22.8129	25.1543	29.0461
2 27/32	2.8438	72.231	23.3226	25.7164	29.6951
2 7/8	2.8750	73.025	23.8380	26.2847	30.3514
2 29/32	2.9063	73.819	24.3591	26.8592	31.0148
2 15/16	2.9375	74.613	24.8858	27.4399	31.6854
2 31/32	2.9688	75.406	25.4181	28.0269	32.3631
3	3.0000	76.200	25.9560	28.6200	33.0480

DIAMETER OR WIDTH ACROSS FLATS INCHES	DECIMAL EQUIVALENT	MILLIMETRE EQUIVALENT	WEIGHT (lb.) PER FOOT		
$3\frac{1}{16}$	3.0625	77.788	27.0488	29.8249	34.4394
$3\frac{1}{8}$	3.1250	79.375	28.1640	31.0547	35.8594
$3\frac{3}{16}$	3.1875	80.963	29.3019	32.3093	37.3081
$3\frac{1}{4}$	3.2500	82.550	30.4623	33.5888	38.7855
$3\frac{5}{16}$	3.3125	84.138	31.6452	34.8931	40.2916
$3\frac{3}{8}$	3.3750	85.725	32.8505	36.2222	41.8264
$3\frac{7}{16}$	3.4375	87.313	34.0785	37.5762	43.3899
$3\frac{1}{2}$	3.5000	88.900	35.2900	38.9550	44.9820
$3\frac{9}{16}$	3.5625	90.488	36.6020	40.3587	46.6029
$3\frac{5}{8}$	3.6250	92.075	37.8975	41.7872	48.2524
$3\frac{11}{16}$	3.6875	93.663	39.2157	43.2406	49.9306
$3\frac{3}{4}$	3.7500	95.250	40.5563	44.7188	51.6375
$3\frac{13}{16}$	3.8125	96.838	41.9194	46.2218	53.3731
$3\frac{7}{8}$	3.8750	98.425	43.3050	47.7497	55.1374
$3\frac{15}{16}$	3.9375	100.013	44.7133	49.3024	56.9304
4	4.0000	101.600	46.1440	50.8800	58.7520
$4\frac{1}{8}$	4.1250	104.775	49.0730	54.1097	62.4814
$4\frac{1}{4}$	4.2500	107.950	52.0923	57.4388	66.3255
$4\frac{3}{8}$	4.3750	111.125	55.2015	60.8672	70.2844
$4\frac{1}{2}$	4.5000	114.300	58.4010	64.3950	74.3580
$4\frac{5}{8}$	4.6250	117.475	61.6905	68.0222	78.5464
$4\frac{3}{4}$	4.7500	120.650	65.0703	71.7488	82.8495
$4\frac{7}{8}$	4.8750	123.825	68.5400	75.5747	87.2674
5	5.0000	127.000	72.1000	79.5000	91.8000
$5\frac{1}{8}$	5.1250	130.175	75.7500	83.5247	96.4474
$5\frac{1}{4}$	5.2500	133.350	79.4903	87.6488	101.2095
$5\frac{3}{8}$	5.3750	136.525	83.3205	91.8722	106.0864
$5\frac{1}{2}$	5.5000	139.700	87.2410	96.1950	111.0780
$5\frac{5}{8}$	5.6250	142.875	91.2515	100.6172	116.1844
$5\frac{3}{4}$	5.7500	146.050	95.3522	105.1388	121.4055
$5\frac{7}{8}$	5.8750	149.225	99.5430	109.7597	126.7414
6	6.0000	152.400	103.8240	114.4800	132.1920

Brass rod (decimals of an inch)—weight in lb/ft

Inches	Wt. (lb.) per foot	Add this for each .001 increase in d	Wt. (lb.) per foot	Add this for each .001 increase in d	Wt. (lb.) per foot	Add this for each .001 increase in d	Inches	Wt. (lb.) per foot	Add this for each .001 increase in d	Wt. (lb.) per foot	Add this for each .001 increase in d	Wt. (lb.) per foot	Add this for each .001 increase in d
.06	.0104	.00037	.0114	.00041	.0132	.00048	.54	.8410	.00314	.9273	.00347	1.0708	.00400
.07	.0141	.00044	.0156	.00048	.0180	.00055	.55	.8724	.00320	.9620	.00353	1.1108	.00408
.08	.0185	.00049	.0204	.00054	.0235	.00062	.56	.9044	.00326	.9973	.00359	1.1515	.00415
.09	.0234	.00054	.0258	.00060	.0297	.00070	.57	.9370	.00332	1.0332	.00366	1.1930	.00422
.10	.0288	.00061	.0318	.00067	.0367	.00077	.58	.9702	.00337	1.0698	.00372	1.2353	.00430
.11	.0349	.00066	.0385	.00073	.0444	.00084	.59	1.0039	.00343	1.1070	.00378	1.2782	.00437
.12	.0415	.00072	.0458	.00080	.0529	.00092	.60	1.0382	.00349	1.1448	.00385	1.3219	.00444
.13	.0487	.00078	.0537	.00086	.0621	.00099	.61	1.0731	.00355	1.1833	.00391	1.3664	.00452
.14	.0565	.00084	.0623	.00092	.0720	.00107	.62	1.1086	.00361	1.2224	.00398	1.4115	.00459
.15	.0649	.00089	.0716	.00099	.0826	.00114	.63	1.1447	.00366	1.2622	.00404	1.4574	.00466
.16	.0738	.00095	.0814	.00105	.0940	.00121	.64	1.1813	.00372	1.3025	.00410	1.5041	.00474
.17	.0833	.00101	.0919	.00111	.1061	.00129	.65	1.2185	.00378	1.3436	.00417	1.5514	.00481
.18	.0934	.00107	.1030	.00118	.1190	.00136	.66	1.2563	.00383	1.3852	.00423	1.5995	.00488
.19	.1041	.00113	.1148	.00124	.1326	.00143	.67	1.2946	.00390	1.4275	.00429	1.6484	.00496
.20	.1154	.00118	.1272	.00130	.1469	.00151	.68	1.3336	.00395	1.4705	.00436	1.6979	.00503
.21	.1272	.00124	.1402	.00137	.1619	.00158	.69	1.3731	.00401	1.5140	.00442	1.7482	.00510
.22	.1396	.00130	.1539	.00143	.1777	.00165	.70	1.4132	.00406	1.5582	.00448	1.7993	.00518
.23	.1526	.00135	.1682	.00149	.1942	.00173	.71	1.4538	.00412	1.6031	.00455	1.8511	.00525
.24	.1661	.00142	.1832	.00156	.2115	.00180	.72	1.4951	.00418	1.6485	.00461	1.9036	.00532
.25	.1803	.00147	.1988	.00162	.2295	.00187	.73	1.5369	.00424	1.6946	.00468	1.9568	.00540
.26	.1950	.00152	.2150	.00168	.2482	.00195	.74	1.5793	.00430	1.7414	.00474	2.0108	.00547
.27	.2102	.00159	.2318	.00175	.2677	.00202	.75	1.6223	.00435	1.7888	.00480	2.0655	.00554
.28	.2261	.00164	.2493	.00181	.2879	.00209	.76	1.6658	.00441	1.8368	.00487	2.1209	.00562
.29	.2425	.00171	.2674	.00188	.3088	.00217	.77	1.7099	.00447	1.8854	.00493	2.1771	.00569
.30	.2596	.00176	.2862	.00194	.3305	.00224	.78	1.7546	.00453	1.9347	.00499	2.2340	.00577
.31	.2772	.00181	.3056	.00200	.3529	.00231	.79	1.7999	.00459	1.9847	.00506	2.2917	.00584
.32	.2953	.00188	.3256	.00207	.3760	.00239	.80	1.8458	.00464	2.0352	.00512	2.3501	.00591
.33	.3141	.00193	.3463	.00213	.3999	.00246	.81	1.8922	.00470	2.0864	.00518	2.4092	.00599
.34	.3334	.00199	.3676	.00219	.4245	.00253	.82	1.9392	.00476	2.1383	.00525	2.4691	.00606
.35	.3533	.00205	.3896	.00226	.4498	.00261	.83	1.9868	.00482	2.1907	.00531	2.5296	.00613
.36	.3738	.00210	.4121	.00232	.4759	.00268	.84	2.0350	.00487	2.2438	.00537	2.5910	.00621
.37	.3948	.00216	.4353	.00239	.5027	.00275	.85	2.0837	.00493	2.2976	.00544	2.6530	.00628
.38	.4164	.00223	.4592	.00245	.5302	.00283	.86	2.1330	.00499	2.3520	.00550	2.7158	.00635
.39	.4387	.00227	.4837	.00251	.5585	.00290	.87	2.1829	.00505	2.4070	.00557	2.7793	.00643
.40	.4614	.00234	.5088	.00258	.5875	.00297	.88	2.2334	.00510	2.4626	.00563	2.8436	.00650
.41	.4848	.00239	.5346	.00264	.6173	.00305	.89	2.2844	.00516	2.5189	.00569	2.9086	.00657
.42	.5087	.00246	.5610	.00270	.6477	.00312	.90	2.3360	.00522	2.5758	.00576	2.9743	.00665
.43	.5333	.00250	.5880	.00277	.6790	.00319	.91	2.3882	.00528	2.6334	.00582	3.0408	.00672
.44	.5583	.00257	.6157	.00283	.7109	.00327	.92	2.4410	.00534	2.6916	.00588	3.1080	.00679
.45	.5840	.00263	.6440	.00289	.7436	.00334	.93	2.4944	.00539	2.7504	.00595	3.1759	.00687
.46	.6103	.00268	.6729	.00296	.7770	.00341	.94	2.5483	.00545	2.8099	.00601	3.2446	.00694
.47	.6371	.00274	.7025	.00302	.8111	.00349	.95	2.6028	.00551	2.8700	.00607	3.3140	.00701
.48	.6645	.00279	.7329	.00308	.8460	.00356	.96	2.6579	.00557	2.9307	.00614	3.3841	.00709
.49	.6924	.00286	.7635	.00315	.8816	.00364	.97	2.7136	.00562	2.9921	.00620	3.4550	.00716
.50	.7210	.00291	.7950	.00321	.9180	.00371	.98	2.7698	.00568	3.0541	.00626	3.5266	.00723
.51	.7501	.00297	.8271	.00328	.9551	.00378	.99	2.8266	.00574	3.1168	.00633	3.5989	.00731
.52	.7798	.00303	.8599	.00334	.9929	.00386	1.00	2.8840	.00580	3.1800	.00639	3.6720	.00738
.53	.8101	.00309	.8933	.00340	1.0315	.00393							

Aluminium rod (Imperial measure)—weight in lb/ft

Diameter or width across flats (Inches)	Decimal equivalent	Millimetre equivalent	Weight (lb.) per foot		
			Round	Hexagon	Square
1/8	.1250	3.175	.014	.016	.018
5/32	.1563	3.969	.023	.025	.029
3/16	.1875	4.763	.032	.036	.041
7/32	.2188	5.556	.044	.049	.056
1/4	.2500	6.350	.058	.064	.074
9/32	.2813	7.144	.073	.081	.093
5/16	.3125	7.938	.090	.099	.115
11/32	.3438	8.731	.109	.120	.139
3/8	.3750	9.525	.130	.143	.165
13/32	.4063	10.319	.152	.168	.194
7/16	.4375	11.113	.177	.195	.225
15/32	.4688	11.906	.203	.224	.258
1/2	.5000	12.700	.231	.255	.294
17/32	.5313	13.494	.261	.287	.332
9/16	.5625	14.288	.292	.322	.372
19/32	.5938	15.081	.326	.359	.415
5/8	.6250	15.875	.361	.398	.459
21/32	.6563	16.669	.398	.438	.507
11/16	.6875	17.463	.437	.481	.556
23/32	.7188	18.256	.477	.526	.608
3/4	.7500	19.050	.520	.573	.662
25/32	.7813	19.844	.564	.621	.718
13/16	.8125	20.638	.610	.672	.776
27/32	.8438	21.431	.658	.725	.837
7/8	.8750	22.225	.707	.779	.900
29/32	.9063	23.019	.759	.836	.966
15/16	.9375	23.813	.812	.895	1.034
31/32	.9688	24.606	.867	.955	1.104
1	1.0000	25.400	.924	1.018	1.176
1-1/16	1.0625	26.988	1.043	1.149	1.328
1-1/8	1.1250	28.575	1.169	1.288	1.488
1-3/16	1.1875	30.163	1.303	1.435	1.658
1-1/4	1.2500	31.750	1.444	1.591	1.838
1-5/16	1.3125	33.338	1.592	1.754	2.026
1-3/8	1.3750	34.925	1.747	1.925	2.223
1-7/16	1.4375	36.513	1.909	2.104	2.430
1-1/2	1.5000	38.100	2.079	2.291	2.646
1-9/16	1.5625	39.688	2.256	2.485	2.871
1-5/8	1.6250	41.275	2.440	2.688	3.105
1-11/16	1.6875	42.863	2.631	2.899	3.345
1-3/4	1.7500	44.450	2.830	3.118	3.602
1-13/16	1.8125	46.038	3.035	3.344	3.863
1-7/8	1.8750	47.625	3.248	3.579	4.134
1-15/16	1.9375	49.213	3.469	3.821	4.415
2	2.0000	50.800	3.696	4.072	4.704
2-1/16	2.0625	52.388	3.931	4.330	5.003
2-1/8	2.1250	53.975	4.172	4.597	5.310
2-3/16	2.1875	55.563	4.421	4.871	5.627
2-1/4	2.2500	57.150	4.678	5.154	5.954
2-5/16	2.3125	58.738	4.941	5.444	6.289
2-3/8	2.3750	60.325	5.212	5.742	6.633
2-7/16	2.4375	61.913	5.490	6.048	6.987
2-1/2	2.5000	63.500	5.775	6.363	7.350
2-5/8	2.6250	66.675	6.367	7.015	8.103
2-3/4	2.7500	69.850	6.988	7.699	8.894
2-7/8	2.8750	73.025	7.637	8.414	9.720
3	3.0000	76.200	8.316	9.162	10.584
3-1/8	3.1250	79.375	9.023	9.941	11.484
3-1/4	3.2500	82.550	9.760	10.753	12.422
3-3/8	3.3750	85.725	10.525	11.596	13.395
3-1/2	3.5000	88.900	11.319	12.471	14.406
3-5/8	3.6250	92.075	12.142	13.377	15.453
3-3/4	3.7500	95.250	12.994	14.316	16.538
3-7/8	3.8750	98.425	13.874	15.286	17.658
4	4.0000	101.600	14.784	16.288	18.816

Brass rectangular bars (Imperial measure)—weight in lb/ft

THICKNESS

INS.	$\frac{1}{16}$	$\frac{3}{32}$	$\frac{1}{8}$	$\frac{5}{32}$	$\frac{3}{16}$	$\frac{7}{32}$	$\frac{1}{4}$	$\frac{9}{32}$	$\frac{5}{16}$	$\frac{11}{32}$	$\frac{3}{8}$	$\frac{13}{32}$	$\frac{7}{16}$	$\frac{15}{32}$	$\frac{1}{2}$	$\frac{17}{32}$	$\frac{9}{16}$	$\frac{19}{32}$	$\frac{5}{8}$	INS.
$\frac{3}{32}$	.0215																			$\frac{3}{32}$
$\frac{1}{8}$	.0287	.0431																		$\frac{1}{8}$
$\frac{5}{32}$	.0359	.0538	.0717																	$\frac{5}{32}$
$\frac{3}{16}$	.0430	.0646	.0861	.1076																$\frac{3}{16}$
$\frac{7}{32}$	.0502	.0754	.1004	.1256	.1506															$\frac{7}{32}$
$\frac{1}{4}$	.0574	.0861	.1148	.1435	.1721	.2009														$\frac{1}{4}$
$\frac{9}{32}$	.0646	.0964	.1291	.1614	.1937	.2260	.2582													$\frac{9}{32}$
$\frac{5}{16}$	.0717	.1076	.1434	.1794	.2151	.2512	.2869	.3228												$\frac{5}{16}$
$\frac{11}{32}$	.0789	.1184	.1578	.1973	.2367	.2762	.3156	.3551	.3945											$\frac{11}{32}$
$\frac{3}{8}$	.0861	.1292	.1721	.2152	.2582	.3013	.3443	.3874	.4303	.4734										$\frac{3}{8}$
$\frac{13}{32}$	.0932	.1399	.1865	.2332	.2797	.3264	.3730	.4197	.4662	.5129	.5595									$\frac{13}{32}$
$\frac{7}{16}$	.1004	.1507	.2008	.2511	.3012	.3515	.4016	.4519	.5020	.5523	.6024	.6527								$\frac{7}{16}$
$\frac{15}{32}$	.1076	.1615	.2152	.2691	.3228	.3766	.4304	.4842	.5379	.5918	.6455	.6994	.7531							$\frac{15}{32}$
$\frac{1}{2}$	.1148	.1722	.2295	.2870	.3443	.4017	.4590	.5165	.5738	.6132	.6885	.7460	.8033	.8607						$\frac{1}{2}$
$\frac{17}{32}$	.1219	.1830	.2439	.3049	.3658	.4269	.4877	.5488	.6097	.6707	.7316	.7927	.8535	.9146	.9755					$\frac{17}{32}$
$\frac{9}{16}$	.1291	.1937	.2582	.3228	.3873	.4519	.5164	.5810	.6455	.7101	.7746	.8392	.9037	.9683	1.033	1.097				$\frac{9}{16}$
$\frac{19}{32}$	.1363	.2045	.2626	.3408	.4088	.4771	.5451	.6133	.6814	.7496	.8177	.8859	.9539	1.022	1.090	1.158	1.226			$\frac{19}{32}$
$\frac{5}{8}$	.1434	.2153	.2869	.3587	.4303	.5021	.5738	.6456	.7172	.7890	.8606	.9325	1.004	1.076	1.148	1.219	1.291	1.363		$\frac{5}{8}$
$\frac{21}{32}$	.1506	.2260	.3012	.3767	.4519	.5273	.6025	.6778	.7531	.8285	.9037	.9791	1.054	1.130	1.205	1.280	1.356	1.431	1.506	$\frac{21}{32}$
$\frac{11}{16}$	.1578	.2368	.3156	.3946	.4733	.5524	.6311	.7101	.7889	.8679	.9467	1.026	1.104	1.183	1.262	1.341	1.420	1.499	1.578	$\frac{11}{16}$
$\frac{23}{32}$	.1650	.2576	.3299	.4125	.4949	.5775	.6599	.7425	.8248	.9074	.9898	1.072	1.155	1.237	1.320	1.402	1.485	1.567	1.650	$\frac{23}{32}$
$\frac{3}{4}$	.1721	.2583	.3443	.4305	.5164	.6026	.6885	.7747	.8606	.9468	1.033	1.119	1.205	1.291	1.377	1.463	1.549	1.635	1.721	$\frac{3}{4}$
$\frac{25}{32}$	.1793	.2691	.3586	.4484	.5379	.6277	.7172	.8070	.8965	.9863	1.076	1.166	1.255	1.345	1.434	1.524	1.614	1.704	1.793	$\frac{25}{32}$
$\frac{13}{16}$	.1865	.2799	.3729	.4663	.5594	.6528	.7459	.8393	9323	1.026	1.119	1.212	1.305	1.399	1.492	1.585	1.678	1.772	1.865	$\frac{13}{16}$
$\frac{27}{32}$	.1937	.2906	.3873	.4843	.5810	.6779	.7746	.8716	.9683	1.065	1.162	1.259	1.356	1.453	1.459	1.646	1.743	1.840	1.937	$\frac{27}{32}$
$\frac{7}{8}$	.2008	.3014	.4016	.5022	.6024	.7030	.8033	.9038	1.004	1.105	1.205	1.305	1.406	1.506	1.607	1.707	1.807	1.908	2.008	$\frac{7}{8}$
$\frac{29}{32}$	.2080	.3122	.4160	.5202	.6240	.7281	.8320	.9361	1.040	1.144	1.248	1.352	1.456	1.560	1.664	1.768	1.872	1.976	2.080	$\frac{29}{32}$
$\frac{15}{16}$	.2152	.3229	.4303	.5381	.6455	.7532	.8606	.9684	1.076	1.184	1.291	1.399	1.506	1.614	1.721	1.829	1.936	1.044	2.152	$\frac{15}{16}$
$\frac{31}{32}$	.2223	.3337	.4447	.5560	.6670	.7784	.8894	1.001	1.112	1.223	1.334	1.445	1.556	1.668	1.779	1.890	2.001	2.112	2.223	$\frac{31}{32}$
1	.2295	.3444	.4590	.5739	.6885	.8034	.9180	1.033	1.148	1.262	1.377	1.492	1.607	1.721	1.836	1.950	2.066	2.180	2.295	1
$1\frac{1}{8}$	.2582	.3875	.5164	.6457	.7746	.9039	1.033	1.162	1.291	1.420	1.549	1.678	1.807	1.937	2.066	2.195	2.324	2.453	2.582	$1\frac{1}{8}$
$1\frac{1}{4}$	.2869	.4305	.5738	.7174	.8606	1.004	1.148	1.291	1.434	1.578	1.721	1.865	2.008	2.152	2.295	2.439	2.582	2.726	2.869	$1\frac{1}{4}$
$1\frac{3}{8}$	.3156	.4736	.6311	.7892	.9467	1.105	1.262	1.429	1.578	1.736	1.893	2.051	2.209	2.367	2.525	2.683	2.840	2.998	3.156	$1\frac{3}{8}$
$1\frac{1}{2}$	.3443	.5167	.6885	.8609	1.033	1.205	1.377	1.549	1.721	1.894	2.066	2.238	2.410	2.582	2.754	2.926	3.098	3.270	3.443	$1\frac{1}{2}$
$1\frac{5}{8}$	.3729	.5597	.7459	.9326	1.119	1.306	1.492	1.679	1.865	2.051	2.238	2.424	2.611	2.797	2.984	3.170	3.356	3.543	3.729	$1\frac{5}{8}$
$1\frac{3}{4}$	.4016	.6028	.8033	1.004	1.205	1.406	1.607	1.808	2.008	2.209	2.410	2.611	2.811	3.013	3.213	3.414	3.615	3.816	4.016	$1\frac{3}{4}$
$1\frac{7}{8}$	.4303	.6458	.8606	1.076	1.291	1.506	1.721	1.937	2.152	2.367	2.582	2.797	3.012	3.228	3.443	3.658	3.873	4.088	4.303	$1\frac{7}{8}$
2	.4590	.6889	.9180	1.148	1.377	1.607	1.836	2.066	2.295	2.525	2.754	2.984	3.213	3.443	3.672	3.902	4.131	4.361	4.590	2
$2\frac{1}{4}$	.5164	.7750	1.033	1.291	1.549	1.808	2.066	2.324	2.582	2.840	3.098	3.357	3.615	3.873	4.131	4.390	4.647	4.906	5.164	$2\frac{1}{4}$
$2\frac{1}{2}$	.5738	.8611	1.148	1.435	1.721	2.009	2.295	2.582	2.869	3.156	3.443	3.730	4.016	4.304	4.590	4.877	5.164	5.451	5.738	$2\frac{1}{2}$
$2\frac{3}{4}$	.6311	.9472	1.262	1.578	1.893	2.209	2.525	2.841	3.156	3.472	3.787	4.103	4.418	4.734	5.049	5.365	5.680	5.996	6.311	$2\frac{3}{4}$
3	.6885	1.033	1.377	1.722	2.066	2.410	2.754	3.099	3.443	3.787	4.131	4.476	4.820	5.164	5.508	5.853	6.197	6.541	6.885	3
$3\frac{1}{4}$	.7459	1.119	1.492	1.865	2.238	2.611	2.984	3.357	3.729	4.103	4.475	4.849	5.221	5.595	5.967	6.341	6.713	7.086	7.459	$3\frac{1}{4}$
$3\frac{1}{2}$	.8033	1.206	1.607	2.009	2.410	2.812	3.213	3.615	4.016	4.419	4.820	5.222	5.623	6.025	6.426	6.828	7.229	7.632	8.033	$3\frac{1}{2}$
$3\frac{3}{4}$	.8606	1.292	1.721	2.152	2.582	3.013	3.443	3.874	4.303	4.734	5.164	5.595	6.024	6.455	6.885	7.316	7.746	8.177	8.606	$3\frac{3}{4}$
4	.9180	1.378	1.836	2.296	2.754	3.214	3.672	4.132	4.590	5.050	5.508	5.968	6.426	6.886	7.344	7.804	8.262	8.722	9.180	4

THICKNESS

THICKNESS

WIDTH INS.	21/32	11/16	23/32	3/4	25/32	13/16	27/32	7/8	29/32	15/16	31/32	1	1⅛	1¼	1⅜	1½	1⅝	1¾	1⅞	2	INS. WIDTH
3/32																					3/32
1/8																					1/8
5/32																					5/32
3/16																					3/16
7/32																					7/32
1/4																					1/4
9/32																					9/32
5/16																					5/16
11/32																					11/32
3/8																					3/8
13/32																					13/32
7/16																					7/16
15/32																					15/32
1/2																					1/2
17/32																					17/32
9/16																					9/16
19/32																					19/32
5/8																					5/8
21/32																					21/32
11/16	1.657																				11/16
23/32	1.732	1.815																			23/32
3/4	1.807	1.893	1.980																		3/4
25/32	1.883	1.972	2.062	2.152																	25/32
13/16	1.958	2.051	2.145	2.238	2.331																13/16
27/32	2.033	2.131	2.227	2.324	2.420	2.517															27/32
7/8	2.109	2.209	2.310	2.410	2.510	2.611	2.711														7/8
29/32	2.184	2.288	2.392	2.496	2.600	2.704	2.808	2.912													29/32
15/16	2.259	2.367	2.474	2.582	2.690	2.797	2.905	3.012	3.120												15/16
31/32	2.335	2.446	2.557	2.668	2.779	2.890	3.002	3.113	3.224	3.335											31/32
1	2.410	2.525	2.639	2.754	2.869	2.984	3.098	3.213	3.328	3.443	3.557										1
1⅛	2.711	2.840	2.969	3.098	3.228	3.356	3.486	3.618	3.744	3.873	4.002	4.131									1⅛
1¼	3.102	3.156	3.299	3.443	3.586	3.729	3.873	4.016	4.160	4.303	4.447	4.590	5.164								1¼
1⅜	3.314	3.472	3.629	3.787	3.945	4.102	4.260	4.418	4.576	4.733	4.891	5.049	5.680	6.311							1⅜
1½	3.615	3.787	3.959	4.131	4.303	4.475	4.648	4.820	4.992	5.164	5.336	5.508	6.197	6.885	7.574						1½
1⅝	3.916	4.102	4.289	4.475	4.662	4.848	5.035	5.221	5.408	5.594	5.781	5.967	6.713	7.459	8.205	8.951					1⅝
1¾	4.217	4.418	4.619	4.820	5.021	5.221	5.422	5.623	5.824	6.024	6.226	6.426	7.229	8.033	8.836	9.639	10.442				1¾
1⅞	4.519	4.733	4.949	5.164	5.379	5.594	5.810	6.024	6.240	6.455	6.670	6.885	7.746	8.606	9.467	10.328	11.188	12.049			1⅞
2	4.820	5.049	5.279	5.508	5.738	5.967	6.197	6.426	6.656	6.885	7.115	7.344	8.262	9.180	10.098	11.016	11.934	12.852	13.770		2
2¼	5.422	5.680	5.939	6.197	6.455	6.713	6.970	7.229	7.488	7.746	8.004	8.262	9.295	10.328	11.360	12.393	13.426	14.459	15.491	16.524	2¼
2½	6.025	6.311	6.599	6.885	7.172	7.459	7.746	8.033	8.320	8.606	8.894	9.180	10.328	11.475	12.623	13.770	14.918	16.065	17.213	18.360	2½
2¾	6.627	6.942	7.258	7.574	7.890	8.205	8.520	8.836	9.152	9.467	9.783	10.098	11.360	12.623	13.885	15.147	16.409	17.672	18.934	20.196	2¾
3	7.230	7.574	7.918	8.262	8.607	8.951	9.295	9.639	9.984	10.328	10.672	11.016	12.393	13.770	15.147	16.524	17.901	19.278	20.655	22.032	3
3¼	7.832	8.205	8.578	8.951	9.324	9.696	10.070	10.442	10.816	11.188	11.562	11.934	13.426	14.918	16.409	17.901	19.393	20.885	22.376	23.868	3¼
3½	8.435	8.836	9.238	9.639	10.041	10.442	10.845	11.246	11.648	12.049	12.451	12.852	14.459	16.065	17.672	19.278	20.885	22.491	24.098	25.704	3½
3¾	9.037	9.467	9.898	10.328	10.759	11.188	11.619	12.049	12.480	12.909	13.340	13.770	15.491	17.213	18.934	20.655	22.376	24.098	25.819	27.540	3¾
4	9.640	10.098	10.558	11.016	11.476	11.934	12.394	12.852	13.312	13.770	14.230	14.688	16.524	18.360	20.196	22.032	23.868	25.704	27.540	29.376	4
INS.	21/32	11/16	23/32	3/4	25/32	13/16	27/32	7/8	29/32	15/16	31/32	1	1⅛	1¼	1⅜	1½	1⅝	1¾	1⅞	2	INS. WIDTH

THICKNESS

Brass rod (B.A. sizes)—weight in lb/ft

B.A. No.*	ROUND		HEXAGON	
	Diameter of Head (in.)	Weight (lb.) per foot	Width Across Flats (in.)	Weight (lb.) per foot
0	.413	.4920	.413	.5425
1	.366	.3864	.365	.4237
2	.319	.2935	.324	.3339
3	.283	.2310	.282	.2529
4	.252	.1832	.248	.1957
5	.221	.1409	.220	.1539
6	.194	.1086	.193	.1185
7	.173	.0863	.172	.0941
8	.157	.0711	.152	.0736
9	.128	.0473	.131	.0546
10	.112	.0362	.117	.0436
11	.110	.0349	.103	.0338
12	.095	.0261	.090	.0258
13	.081	.0190	.083	.0220
14	.064	.0119	.069	.0151
15	.064	.0119	.062	.0122
16	.058	.0097	.056	.0100

* The particulars given in these columns are abstracted from B.S.57:1951, 'B.A. Screws, Bolts, Nuts and Plain Washers', and are reproduced by courtesy of the British Standards Institution.

Brass wire (in s.w.g.)—weight in lb/100 ft

Gauge number	Diameter inches	Weight (lb) PER 100 FEET	Gauge number	Diameter inches	Weight (lb.) PER 100 FEET
7/0	.500	72.34	16	.064	1.190
6/0	.464	62.30	17	.056	0.908
5/0	.432	54.00	18	.048	0.668
4/0	.400	46.29	19	.040	0.464
3/0	.373	40.04	20	.036	0.375
2/0	.348	35.04	21	.032	0.297
0	.324	30.38	22	.028	0.227
1	.300	26.04	23	.024	0.167
2	.276	22.04	24	.022	0.140
3	.252	18.37	25	.020	0.116
4	.232	15.57	26	.018	0.0939
5	.212	13.00	27	.0164	0.0779
6	.192	10.67	28	.0148	0.0635
7	.176	8.96	29	.0136	0.0536
8	.160	7.41	30	.0124	0.0445
9	.144	6.00	31	.0116	0.0389
10	.128	4.74	32	.0108	0.0338
11	.116	3.89	33	.0100	0.0290
12	.104	3.13	34	.0092	0.0245
13	.092	2.45	35	.0084	0.0205
14	.080	1.85	36	.0076	0.0167
15	.072	1.50			

Steel and wood pillars—simple approximate formulae

NB Safety factors should be added

Long, solid, circular section pillars:

where L = pillar length in feet; d = diameter in inches.

Maximum loads: Steel — $\dfrac{45d^4}{L^2}$

Oak — $\dfrac{2d^4}{L^2}$

Pine — $\dfrac{2 \cdot 5d^4}{L^2}$

Long, hollow, circular section pillars:

Maximum load: $\dfrac{kt^2}{(1 + 6 \cdot 5\frac{L^2 t}{d^3})}$

where t = thickness of tube, d = mean diameter,
k = 2300 (steel), 100 (oak), 130 (pine)

Short pillars:

Maximum load (tons) $= \dfrac{\text{Sectional area (sq. in)} \times j}{1 + \frac{1}{q}\left(\frac{CS}{t} + \frac{L^2}{p^2}\right)}$

where j = 36 for steel; 3·2 for wood
q = 4000 for steel; 750 for wood
CS = Coefficient of Shape
= 500 for circular pillar; 600 for square; 700 for I-section; 0 for solid pillar
t = thickness of material (wall)
L = length in inches (unsupported both ends)
= length $\times \sqrt{\frac{1}{2}}$ (one end fixed)
= length $\times \frac{1}{2}$ (both ends fixed)
p = least radius of gyration of cross-section in inches

Long pillars where $\frac{L}{p}$ is greater than 140

ie. if L is more than about 38 diameters and the pillar is circular.

Maximum load (tons) $= \dfrac{\text{Sectional area (sq. in)} \times \pi^2 E}{\frac{CS \cdot p}{t} + \frac{L^2}{p^2}}$

where E = Modulus of Elasticity

45

Circular hollow sections (mild steel)—dimensions and strength

To save calculating the correct size of the pillar the following tables give the loading that can be carried by different sizes and length of pillar. Where a single pillar is inadequate two or four may be used. Alternatively some sections are available in High Yield Stress steel to B.S.968.1962.

Interpolation should be used for intermediate lengths and diameters of pillars. Extrapolation (figures beyond those quoted) should be used with great caution.

Outside Diameter	mm	26·9	33·7	42·4
	in	1·062	1·344	1·688
Thickness	mm	3·2	3·2	3·2
	in	0·128	0·128	0·128
Weight	kg/m	1·89	2·42	3·11
	lb/ft	1·27	1·63	2·09
Area	sq cm	2·43	3·15	4·05
	sq in	0·376	0·489	0·627
I	cm⁴	1·75	3·79	7·99
	in⁴	0·042	0·091	0·192
Z	cm³	1·28	2·23	3·72
	in³	0·078	0·136	0·227
S	cm³	1·84	3·11	5·11
	in³	0·112	0·190	0·312
r	cm	0·846	1·10	1·40
	in	0·333	0·432	0·553

		26·9	33·7	42·4
Axial tension (tonnef)		3·84	4·98	6·40
Axial compression (tonnef) for effective lengths (metres)				
	1·5 m	0·73 tonnef	1·54 tonnef	2·95 tonnef
	2·0 m	0·42 ,,	0·91 ,,	1·82 ,,
	2·5 m	0·27 ,,	0·59 ,,	1·21 ,,
Axial tension (tonf)		3·77	4·91	6·29
Axial compression (tonf) for effective lengths (feet)				
	5 ft	0·70 tonf	1·47 tonf	2·85 tonf
	7 ft	0·37 ,,	0·79 ,,	1·60 ,,
	9 ft	0·22 ,,	0·48 ,,	1·00 ,,

46

in tension and compression

Tonf means tons force and *Tonnef* means metric tonnes force.

Outside Diameter	mm	48·3	60·3	76·1	88·9	114·3
	in	1·906	2·375	3·0	3·5	4·5
Thickness	mm	4·0	4·0	4·5	4·0	4·5
	in	0·160	0·160	0·176	0·160	0·176
Weight	kg/m	4·41	5·59	7·92	8·43	12·1
	lb/ft	2·96	3·76	5·32	5·66	8·13
Area	sq cm	5·66	7·16	10·1	10·8	15·4
	sq in	0·878	1·11	1·56	1·68	2·39
I	cm⁴	14·0	28·6	64·9	97·8	233·0
	in⁴	0·337	0·686	1·56	2·35	5·60
Z	cm³	5·80	9·47	17·0	22·0	40·8
	in³	0·354	0·578	1·04	1·34	2·49
S	cm³	8·01	12·9	23·1	29·3	53·9
	in³	0·489	0·786	1·41	1·79	3·29
r	cm	1·57	1·99	2·54	3·00	3·89
	in	0·620	0·785	1·00	1·18	1·53

Axial tension (tonnef)	8·95	11·32	15·96	17·07	24·34
Axial compression (tonnef) for effective lengths (metres)					
1·5 m	4·87 tonnef	7·97 tonnef	13·01 tonnef	14·68 tonnef	21·92 tonnef
2·0 m	3·11 ,,	5·74 ,,	10·82 ,,	13·11 ,,	20·78 ,,
2·5 m	2·09 ,,	4·03 ,,	8·34 ,,	10·94 ,,	19·08 ,,

Axial tension (tonf)	8·81 tonf	11·14 tonf	15·66 tonf	16·86 tonf	23·99 tonf
Axial compression (tonf) for effective lengths (feet)					
6 ft	3·58 ,,	6·39 ,,	11·43 ,,	13·55 ,,	20·92 ,,
8 ft	2·16 ,,	4·16 ,,	8·47 ,,	11·08 ,,	19·03 ,,
10 ft	1·42 ,,	2·80 ,,	6·03 ,,	8·41 ,,	16·32 ,,

Rectangular hollow sections (mild steel)—dimensions and strength in tension and compression

Dimensions	mm	50·8 × 25·4		63·5 × 38·1		76·2 × 50·8	
	in	2·0 × 1·0		2·5 × 1·5		3·0 × 2·0	
Thickness	mm	3·2		4·0		4·0	
	in	0·128		0·160		0·160	
Weight	kg/m	3·51		5·89		7·52	
	lb/ft	· 2·36		3·96		5·05	
Area	sq cm	4·48		7·55		9·61	
	sq in	0·695		1·17		1·49	
Axis		X–X	Y–Y	X–X	Y–Y	X–X	Y–Y
I	cm⁴	13·6	4·33	37·8	16·4	73·7	38·5
	in⁴	0·327	0·104	0·909	0·394	1·77	0·924
Z	cm³	5·36	3·39	11·9	8·62	19·3	15·1
	in³	0·327	0·207	0·727	0·526	1·18	0·924
S	cm³	6·96	4·15	15·1	10·4	23·9	17·9
	in³	0·425	0·253	0·924	0·635	1·46	1·09
r	cm	1·74	0·980	2·24	1·48	2·77	2·00
	in	0·687	0·386	0·883	0·582	1·09	0·789
Axial Tension (tonnef)		7·08		11·93		15·19	
Axial compression (tonnef) for effective lengths (metres)							
1·5 m		4·37	1·78	9·14	5·98	12·77	10·74
2·0 m		2·93	1·03	7·08	3·75	11·06	7·76
2·5 m		1·99	0·67	5·17	2·49	8·89	5·46
Axial Tension (tonf)		6·98		11·74		14·95	
Axial compression (tonf) for effective lengths (feet)							
5 ft							
6 ft		3·33	1·21	7·70	4·30	11·54	8·64
7 ft							
8 ft		2·06	0·69	5·30	2·57	9·01	5·63
9 ft							
10 ft		1·37	0·45	3·65	1·68	6·62	3·80

Tonf means tons force and *Tonnef* means metric tonnes force.

Square hollow sections (mild steel)

127.0 × 76.2 5.0 × 3.0	25.4 × 25.4 1.0 × 1.0	38.1 × 38.1 1.5 × 1.5	50.8 × 50.8 2.0 × 2.0	63.5 × 63.5 2.5 × 2.5	76.2 × 76.2 3.0 × 3.0
6.3 0.250	2.0 0.104	3.2 0.128	4.0 0.160	4.0 0.160	4.0 0.160
18.6 12.6	1.86 1.25	3.51 2.36	5.89 3.96	7.52 5.05	9.14 6.14
24.0 3.72	2.37 0.368	4.48 0.695	7.55 1.17	9.61 1.49	11.7 1.81
X–X Y–Y 499 221 / 12.0 5.30	2.04 0.049	8.99 0.216	27.1 0.652	56.2 1.35	101 2.42
78.8 57.8 / 4.81 3.53	1.59 0.097	4.72 0.288	10.7 0.652	17.7 1.08	26.4 1.61
98.5 68.2 / 6.01 4.16	2.00 0.122	5.82 0.355	13.1 0.799	21.3 1.30	31.5 1.92
4.57 3.02 / 1.80 1.19	0.952 0.364	1.42 0.558	1.90 0.748	2.42 0.953	2.95 1.16
37.93	3.75	7.08	11.93	15.19	18.49
34.71 32.68 / 33.53 29.24 / 31.80 24.49	0.84 0.49 0.32	3.34 2.07 1.37	8.07 5.66 3.93	12.12 9.82 7.41	15.84 14.06 11.64
37.33	3.69	6.98	11.74	14.95	18.17
33.46 30.12 / 31.55 24.73 / 28.67 18.85	0.81 0.43 0.26	3.20 1.80 1.13	7.82 5.04 3.28	10.51 7.56 5.31	14.49 11.73 8.84

Pitch pine pillars—safe working loads

The approximate safe working load is given in tons or tonnes which are almost the same for the purpose of this table. One tonne equals 0·9842 tons. The safety factor is five times.

For rectangular columns having sides X and Y, where X is the smaller, the safe load equals (load for X) $\times \dfrac{Y}{X}$. For example, a column of 1·8 metres, 100 millimetres by 150 millimetres has a safe load of $5·3 \times \dfrac{150}{100} = 7·5$ tonnes.

For round columns take the side as equal to the diameter and multiply by 0·75. For example, a round column ten feet long and six inches diameter has a safe load of $11·5 \times 0·75 = 8·6$ tons.

For oak take 90% of the load; for spruce take 80% of the load.

LENGTH METRES / FEET	DIMENSIONS OF SIDES								
	MM 100 / 4 INS.	MM 130 / 5 INS.	MM 150 / 6 INS.	MM 180 / 7 INS.	MM 200 / 8 INS.	MM 230 / 9 INS.	MM 250 / 10 INS.	MM 280 / 11 INS.	MM 300 / 12 INS.
0·6 / 2	6·8	10·9	15·8	21·6	28·3				
1·2 / 4	6·2	10·0	14·9	20·8	27·3	34·1	43·4	52·6	63·0
1·8 / 6	5·3	9·1	13·8	19·5	26·1	33·5	42·0	51·3	61·5
2·4 / 8	4·6	8·2	12·5	18·1	24·6	31·9	40·2	49·3	59·7
3·1 / 10	4·0	7·2	11·5	16·8	23·0	30·3	38·4	47·5	57·6
3·7 / 12	3·5	6·6	10·4	15·4	21·3	28·4	36·5	45·3	55·3
4·3 / 14	3·1	5·8	9·4	14·1	19·9	26·5	34·6	44·0	53·0
4·9 / 16	2·7	5·2	8·6	13·0	18·4	25·2	32·7	41·1	50·5
5·5 / 18		4·8	7·9	12·3	17·2	23·4	30·7	38·9	47·7
6·1 / 20		4·2	7·2	11·0	16·0	22·0	28·8	36·8	45·9
6·7 / 22			6·6	10·5	15·0	20·9	27·3	34·9	43·7
7·3 / 24			6·1	9·6	13·9	19·4	25·8	33·1	41·6
7·9 / 26				8·9	13·0	18·2	24·4	31·5	39·6
8·5 / 28				8·3	12·2	17·3	23·1	30·1	37·8
9·1 / 30					11·5	16·2	21·8	28·3	36·2

Stock timber sizes

When ordering timber it is almost always better to buy stock sections both for quick delivery and economy. Not every timber merchant will stock all these sizes. 40 mm thickness in particular might be described as 'semi non-standard'.

   Allowance will have to be made for planing when ordering timber. By its nature the material expands with varying moisture content, so these dimensions are no more than a valuable buyer's guide and are not an engineer's exact specification.

   It is always advisable to check stocks before designing and certainly before ordering.

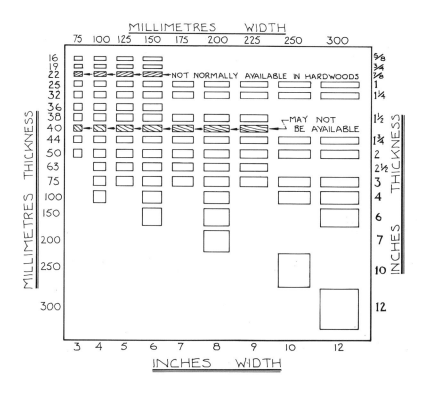

Mechanical properties of woods

WOOD	WEIGHT			TEARING FORCE	
	SPECIFIC GRAVITY	KGS PER CUBE METRE	POUNDS PER CUBE FOOT	KGS PER SQ CENTIMTR	POUNDS PER SQ. INCH
ASH	0·75	750	47.0	1190	17,000
BEECH	0·70	700	43·8	800	11,500
BIRCH	0·75	750	46·9	1050	15,000
CEDAR	0·49	492	30·8	800	11,400
ELM	0·54	540	33·8	945	13,490
GREENHEART	1·00	999	62·5		
LARCH	0·50	496	31·0	720	10,200
LIGNUM VITAE	1·33	1330	83·2	835	11,800
MAHOGANY, HONDURAS	0·56	559	35·0		
MAHOGANY, SPANISH	0·85	848	53·2	1530	21,800
OAK, BRITISH	0·93	929	58·3	700	10,000
OAK, RIGA	0·68	687	43·0		
OAK, RED	1·02	1021	64·4	720	10,250
PINE, RED	0·58	576	36·1	1010	14,300
PINE, PITCH	0·66	658	41·2	550	7,820
PINE, YELLOW	0·46	460	28·8		
SPRUCE	0·51	511	32·0	700	10,000
TEAK INDIAN	0·88	879	55·0	1050	15,000
TEAK AFRICAN	0·93	934	61·3	1470	21,000
WALNUT	0·67	667	41·8	570	8,130

CRUSHING FORCE		BREAKING FORCE		MODULUS OF ELASTICITY	
KGS PER SQ CENTIMTR	POUNDS PER SQ. INCH	KGS PER SQ CENTIMTR	POUNDS PEO SQ INCH	KGS PER SQUARE CENTIMETRE	POUNDS PER SQUARE INCH
632	9,000	855	12,200	115,500	1,645,000
658	9,360	657	9,340	950,000	1,354,000
450	6,400	820	11,670	115,500	1,645,000
412	5,860	522	7,420	34,200	486,000
725	10,330	427	6,080	49,200	700,000
		1160	16,550	186,000	2,656,000
392	5,570	417	5,940	957,000	1,363,000
647	9,920	800	11,400	39,000	558,000
		810	11,480	110,000	1,593,000
576	8,200	531	7,560	882,000	1,255,000
700	10,000	700	10,000	102,000	1,451,000
		905	12,890	113,000	1,610,000
421	5,990	745	10,600	142,500	2,149,000
378	5,380	621	8,840	102,500	1,458,000
		688	9,790	861,000	1,226,000
383	5,450			112,300	1,600,000
457	6,500	865	12,350	126,500	1,804,000
		1030	14,600	197,000	2,800,000
656	9,320	1050	14,980	161,500	2,305,000
467	6,650	562	8000		

Mechanical properties of balsa wood

Weight — kg/m² and lbs/cu ft.	96·1	6	176·2	11	258·3	15½
Specific gravity	0·0962		0·176		0·248	
Compressive strength in kilonewtons per square metre and pounds per square inch						
1. Parallel to grain (end grain)						
(a) Stress at proportional limit	3,440	500	10,000	1,450	15,900	2,310
(b) Maximum crushing strength	5,160	750	13,200	1,910	20,400	2,950
(c) Modulus of elasticity	2,280,000	330,000	5,290,000	768,000	8,000,000	1,164,000
2. Perpendicular to grain (flat grain)						
(a) Stress at proportional limit						
(i) High Strength Value	580	84	990	144	1,370	198
(ii) Low Strength Value	345	50	690	100	1,000	145
(b) Modulus of elasticity						
(i) High Strength Value	110,000	16,000	254,000	37,000	380,000	55,000
(ii) Low Strength Value	35,200	5,100	90,000	13,000	131,000	19,000
Tensile strength in kilonewtons per meter and pounds per square inch						
1. Parallel to grain (end grain)						
Maximum	9,450	1,375	21,000	3,050	31,200	4,525
2. Perpendicular to grain (flat grain)						
Maximum						
(i) High Strength Value	770	112	1,170	170	1,530	223
(ii) Low Strength Value	500	72	810	118	1,070	156
Bending strength in kilonewtons per square metre and pounds per square inch						
Static bending						
(a) Stress at proportional limit	5,680	825	11,900	1,725	17,500	2,535
(b) Modulus of rupture	9,460	1,375	21,000	3,050	31,200	4,525
(c) Modulus of elasticity	1,930,000	280,000	4,300,000	625,000	6,360,000	925,000

	96·1	6	176·2	11	258·3	15½
Weight – kg/m² and lbs/cu ft	96·1	6	176·2	11	258·3	15½
Specific gravity	0·0962		0·176		0·248	
Toughness in millimetre/ kilogram per specimen and inch/pound per specimen						
(i) High Strength Value	860	125	2,140	310	3,270	475
(ii) Low Strength Value	830	120	1,840	267	2,760	400
Shear in kilonewtons per square metre and pounds per square inch						
(i) High Strength Value	1,240	180	2,480	360	3,600	522
(ii) Low Strength Value	1,090	158	2,050	298	2,920	425
Hardness Load required to embed a 11·1 mm (0·444 inch) ball to one half its diameter kilogrammes/pounds						
1. Parallel to grain (end grain)	46	102	114	250	175	386
2. Perpendicular to grain (flat grain)						
(i) High Strength Value	23	50	54	120	85	186
(ii) Low Strength Value	21	47	47	103	69	151
Cleavage in kilogrammes per metre width and pounds per inch width Load to cause splitting						
(i) High Strength Value	1,000	56	1,250	70	1,550	87
(ii) Low Strength Value	660	37	1,130	63	1,530	86

Based on an average strength at 12% moisture content.
Figures are from Balsa Equador Lumber Corporation, to whom acknowledgement is made.

Bending marine plywood

Thickness (mm)	4	5	6	6*	8	9	12	15	18
Radius of curvature along the grain (metres)	0·38	0·455	0·61	0·685	0·76	0·99	1·52	1·83	2·74
(inches)	15	18	24	27	30	39	60	72	108
Radius of curvature across the grain (metres)	0·23	0·305	0·51	0·61	0·76	0·99	1·14	1·52	2·74
(inches)	9	12	20	24	30	39	45	60	108

* three equal thickness plies.

The above are approximate minimum radii to which marine ply can be bent with a standard moisture content of about 10%. Some plywood can be bent more if it is of low grade and, when wet, plywood boards can be bent to tighter curves than given above.

Bending should be done slowly while reducing the radius of curvature evenly. Straps on the convex side of the curve will help to keep the curvature even which will also reduce breakages. A creaking sound from the ply is an indication that it is about to fail.

To form tight bends it is often advisable to make a former and build up a lamination of layers of thin ply glued together. This technique is especially recommended where the final thickness is considerable because ply over about 12 mm needs considerable force to coax it into a curve.

Natural seasoning of timber

Thickness	mm	12	18	25	50	75	100
Thickness	Inches	$\frac{1}{2}$	$\frac{3}{4}$	1	2	3	4
Time needed to season	Months	13	16	24	36	46	52

Paint—efficiency in preventing moisture absorption

	28-day efficiency
Enamel (two applications of commercial undercoat, one top coat of enamel)	58%
Oil paint (three coats as for lead paint)	44 to 56%
Lead paint (one coat pink primer, second coat of mixed primer and finishing, third coat exterior lead paint)	45%
Shellac (two coats)	31%
Copal varnish (two coats)	20%
Spar varnish (two coats)	17%
Pink primer (one coat)	14%
Wax polish (two coats of beeswax and turps over cellulose grain sealer)	3%
Boiled oil and turps (two brushed coats)	Low efficiency
Raw linseed oil (one rubbed coat)	Low efficiency

Moisture content of timber

Any wood used in boat or ship construction should have the correct moisture content to allow paint or polish to go on, and stay on, efficiently. Moisture content is also important to reduce the movement of timber, and ensure that rot preservative fluids work in as deeply as possible.

Particular note should be taken of timber components which are to be used in heated cabins, or near warm, or even hot, components like exhaust pipes.

It is important to select the right timber for a given job and then get it down to the right moisture content before working it. Just as vital, the timber should be kept at the correct moisture content by protecting it properly, both from the weather, from rain, and from variations in temperature.

Wood should be used so that the smallest movement occurs in the most important direction. An obvious example of this is decking, which should always be radial sawn, sometimes called rift sawn, so that the grain is vertical. This is not only to minimise shrinkage athwartships but also to give the best wear.

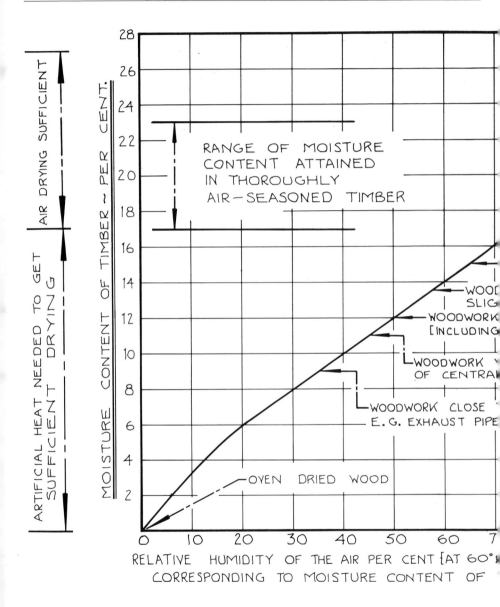

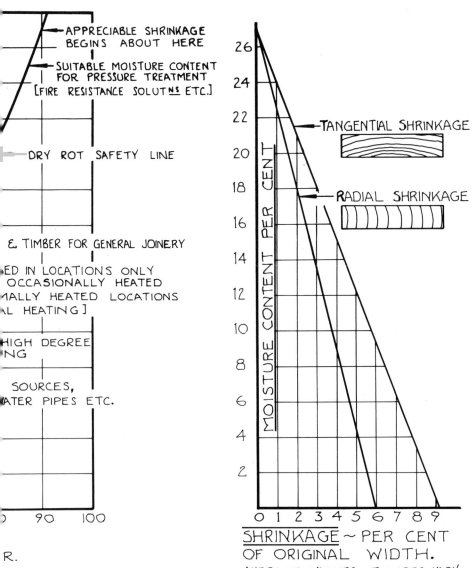

APPRECIABLE SHRINKAGE
BEGINS ABOUT HERE

SUITABLE MOISTURE CONTENT
FOR PRESSURE TREATMENT
[FIRE RESISTANCE SOLUTNS ETC.]

DRY ROT SAFETY LINE

E. TIMBER FOR GENERAL JOINERY

ED IN LOCATIONS ONLY
OCCASIONALLY HEATED
MALLY HEATED LOCATIONS
L HEATING]

HIGH DEGREE
NG

SOURCES,
ATER PIPES ETC.

90   100

R.

TANGENTIAL SHRINKAGE

RADIAL SHRINKAGE

MOISTURE CONTENT PER CENT

SHRINKAGE ~ PER CENT
OF ORIGINAL WIDTH.
AVERAGE VALUES ~ FIGURES VARY
WITH DIFFERENT WOODS.

59

Light weight materials—mechanical properties

Material	Weight at 12% Moisture Content kg/m³	lbs/ cu. ft	Specific Gravity	Crushing Strength Max – parallel to Grain kN/m³	p.s.i.	Stress at proportional limit perpendicular to Grain kN/m³	p.s.i.	Compress Modulus of elasticity parallel to Grain kN/m²	p.s.i.
Light weight Balsa	96	6	0·0962	5,160	750	344– 580	50– 84	2,270,000	330,00
Medium weight Balsa	176	11	0·176	13,400	1,910	690– 990	100– 144	5,280,000	768,00
Heavy type Balsa	248	15½	0·248	20,300	2,950	1,000	145– 198	8,020,000	1,164,00
C.C.A. Foam	64–144	4–9	0·064– 0·144	520– 2,070	75– 300	510– 2,070	75– 300	9,300– 24,100	1,350– 3,500
Styrene Foam	16–32	1–2	0·016– 0·032	138– 276	20– 40	138– 276	20– 40	5,850	850
Extra dense Styrene Foam	80–112	5–7	0·080– 0·112	760– 1,380	110– 200	760– 1,380	110– 200	48,200– 68,950	7,000– 10,000
Polyurethane Foam	16	2	0·032	110,300	16– 43			8,900	1,300
Extra dense Polyurethane Foam	96	6	0·096	1,030	150			38,600	5,600
Aspen (Populus tremuloides)	416	26	0·380	29,200	4,250	3,160	460	8,930,000	1,298,00
Western Red Cedar (Thuja plicata)	368	23	0·330	34,600	5,020	4,200	610	8,490,000	1,232,00

ength Modulus of elasticity erpendicular to Grain /m²	p.s.i.	Tensile Strength Maximum parallel to Grain kN/m²	p.s.i.	Maximum perpendicular to Grain kN/m²	p.s.i.	Bending Strength Modulus of Rupture kN/m²	p.s.i.	Modulus of elasticity kN/m²	p.s.i.
100– ,000	5,100– 16,000	9,460	1,375	496– 770	72– 112	9,460	1,375	1,925,000	280,000
500– ,000	13,000– 37,000	21,000	3,050	815– 1,170	118– 170	21,000	3,050	4,300,000	625,000
000– 000	19,000– 55,000	31,100	4,525	1,070– 1,530	156– 223	31,400	4,525	6,360,000	925,000
00– 100	1,350– 3,500	2,140	310	2,140	310				
350	850	276– 552	40– 80	276– 552	40– 80				
200– 950	7,000– 10,000	1,380– 2,400	200– 350	1,380– 2,400	200– 350				
30	600	250	36	200	29			4,130– 8,950	600– 1,300
		1,310	190					38,500	5,600
000– 000	64,900– 129,800	57,900	8,400	1,790	260	57,814	8,400	8,120,000	1,180,000
000– 000	61,600– 123,200	53,000	7,700	1,510	220	53,000	7,700	7,710,000	1,120,000

Typical marine laminates (glass-fibre)—physical properties

From T & R Bulletin 2–12 to which acknowledgement is made.

Note: These properties are from short term loading tests—wet conditions. Composite and woven roving values are for the warp direction. The physical properties were tested in accordance with ASTM Standard Specification or equivalent Federal Standard LP-406b.

The composite laminate is based on typical alternate plies of 610 g/m² (2 oz/sq. ft) mat and 820 g/m² (24 oz/sq. yd) woven roving.

Physical Properties			Chopped Strand Mat Laminate Low Glass Content	
Percentage Glass by weight			25–30	
Specific Gravity			1·40–1·50	
Flexural Strength kN/m² × 10³	and	p.s.i. × 10³	124–172	18–25
Flexural Modulus kN/m² × 10⁶	and	p.s.i. × 10⁶	5·5–8·3	0·8–1·2
Tensile Strength kN/m² × 10³	and	p.s.i. × 10³	76–103	11–15
Tensile Modulus kN/m² × 10⁶	and	p.s.i. × 10⁶	6·2–8·3	0·9–1·2
Compressive Strength kN/m² × 10³	and	p.s.i. × 10³	117–145	17–21
Compressive Modulus kN/m² × 10⁶	and	p.s.i. × 10⁶	6·2–9·0	0·9–1·3
Shear Strength Perpendicular kN/m² × 10³	and	p.s.i. × 10³	69–90	10–13
Shear Strength Parallel kN/m² × 10³	and	p.s.i. × 10³	69–83	10–12
Shear Modulus Parallel kN/m² × 10⁶	and	p.s.i. × 10⁶	2·75	0·4

Composite Laminate Medium Glass Content		Woven Roving Laminate High Glass Content	
30–40 1·50–1·65		40–45 1·65–1·80	
172–206	25–30	206–240	30–35
7·6–10·3	1·1–1·5	10·3–15·1	1·5–2·2
124–172	18–25	193–220	28–32
6·9–9·7	1·0–1·4	10·3–13·8	1·5–2·0
117–145	17–21	117–145	17–22
6·9–11	1·0–1·6	11·7–16·5	1·7–2·4
76–97	11–14	90–103	13–15
62–83	9–12	55–76	8–11
3·1	0·45	3·44	0·5

Reinforced plastic laminates—thickness (average figures)

LAY UP

KILOS PER SQ. METRE	OZ. PER SQ YD	MATERIAL
0·039	1·5	MAT
0·052	2	MAT
0·26	10	CLOTH
0·42	16	WOVEN ROVING
0·62	24	WOVEN ROVING

Mechanical properties of laminates—compared with other

	GLASS CONTENT		SPECIFIC GRAVITY	TENSILE STRENGTH		TENSILE MODULUS	
	% WEIGHT	% VOLUME		$\frac{N}{MM^2}$	$\frac{Lbf}{INS.^2}$	$\frac{KN}{MM^2}$	$\frac{Lbf}{INS.^2}$
RANDOM R P	30	17	1·4	110	16 000	7·6	1,100,000
UNI-DIRECTIONAL R P	75	59	2·0	828	120000	27·6	4,000,000
MILD STEEL			7·8	862	125000	207	30,000,000
LIGHT ALLOY			2·8	450	65000	69	10,000,000

NUMBER OF PLIES

MM 1 INS	MM 2 INS	MM 3 INS	MM 4 INS	MM 5 INS
1·1 / 0·044	2·2 / 0·081	3·3 / 0·131	4·5 / 0·178	5·7 / 0·224
1·5 / 0·058	2·9 / 0·116	4·4 / 0·175	6·0 / 0·237	7·6 / 0·299
0·4 / 0·016	0·8 / 0·032	1·2 / 0·048	1·6 / 0·064	2·0 / 0·080
0·6 / 0·024	1·2 / 0·048	1·9 / 0·074	2·4 / 0·098	3·1 / 0·123
0·9 / 0·036	1·8 / 0·071	2·8 / 0·109	3·7 / 0·147	4·7 / 0·185

materials

COMPRESSIVE STRENGTH		IMPACT STRENGTH		SPECIFIC STRENGTH		SPECIFIC MODULUS	
$\frac{N}{MM^2}$	$\frac{Lbf}{INS.^2}$	N METRE	ft lb f	$\frac{N}{MM^2}$	$\frac{Lbf}{INS.^2}$	$\frac{KN}{MM^2}$	$\frac{Lbf}{INS.^2}$
138	20 000	20	15	79	11,400	5·5	800,000
345	50 000	68	50	414	60,000	14	2,000,000
193	28 000	13·5	10	110	16,000	25·5	3,000,000
83	12 000	7	5	160	23,000	25	3,600,000

Fresh water—allowance and measurements

Normal allowance per man per day is $\frac{1}{2}$ gallon ($2\frac{1}{4}$ litres).

1 litre	weighs	1 kilogram
1 gallon	weighs	10 lbs
1 cubic metre	weighs	1000 kilograms
1 cubic foot	weighs	62·4 lbs
1 cubic metre	is	1000 litres
1 cubic foot	is	6·23 gallons
1 ton	occupies	35·96 cubic feet
1 ton	is	224 gallons (Imperial)

Sail cloth weights—comparative figures

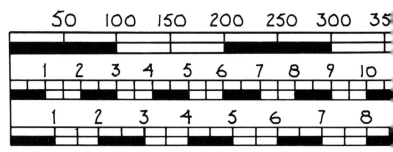

Tank materials

Tank material	Uses	Advantages	Treatment
Mild steel	Fuel	Cheap. May be built into steel craft.	Paint outside.
Galvanised Steel	Fresh water. Sewage.	Cheap.	Cement wash or treat with 'Water Tank Black' or similar paint inside. Paint outside.
Stainless Steel	Fresh water. Sewage. Fuels.	Long lasting. Easily Maintained.	
Aluminium Alloys Sea water resisting	Fresh water. Fuels.	Long lasting. Light weight.	If used for water the inside may need painting.
Glass/Polyester	Fresh water. Sewage.	Cheap. Long lasting. May be built in.	
Flexible materials such as rubberised cloth	Fresh water. Sewage.	Cheap when installation costs are included. Light weight. Fits irregular and inaccessible spaces.	The space containing the tank must be free from sharp projections.

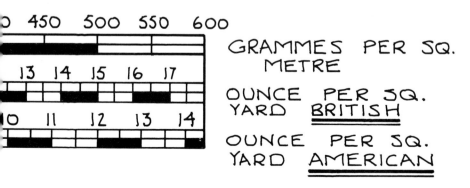

GRAMMES PER SQ. METRE

OUNCE PER SQ. YARD BRITISH

OUNCE PER SQ. YARD AMERICAN

Paint—container sizes and covering properties

Paint is sold in the following size containers in European and many other countries.

Metric Paint Container Sizes.

100 ml	=	0·022 gal
250 ml	=	0·055 gal
500 ml	=	0·11 gal
1 litre	=	0·22 gal
2·5 litres	=	0·55 gal
5 litres	=	1·1 gal
10 litres	=	2·2 gal
20 litres	=	4·4 gal

Paint Conversion Table

sq ft/gallon	sq yds/gallon	sq m/litre
90	10	1·84
100	11·1	2·04
150	16·7	3·07
200	22·2	4·09
250	27·8	5·11
300	33·4	6·13
350	38·9	7·15
400	44·4	8·17
450	50	9·19
500	55·6	10·2
550	61·2	11·2
600	66·7	12·3
650	72·3	13·3
700	77·8	14·3
750	83·3	15·3
800	89	16·3
850	94·5	17·4
900	100	18·4
1000	111	20·1

These figures are a rough guide. The covering ability of paint varies from one brand to another, also it varies with different methods of application, and depends on the skill of the painter. The temperature and the surface being painted also have different effects.

Primers	sq m/litre	sq yds/gallon
Pink Priming	10·2	55
Metallic Pink Wood Primer	11	60
Bare Plate Primer	7	35
Glass Fibre Primer	18·5	100
Metal Primer	12	66
Light Alloy Primer	10·2	55
Self etch Primer for light alloy and galvanized steel	13	70
Primer for ferro-cement	8·2	44
Primer for polystyrene	13	70

Undercoats & Enamels		
Undercoating	10	55
Enamel	10	55
One-Pot Polyurethane	10	55
Two-Pot Polyurethane	11	60

Varnish		
Polyurethane Varnish	10	55
Marine Varnish	13	70

Underwater paint		
Underwater Undercoat	10	55
Antifouling — normal	10	55
— heavy (e.g. Kobe)	7	35
Boot-top	8·5	45

Miscellaneous materials		
Anti-condensation paint (contains granulated cork)	7·0	35
Non-slip deck paint	7·2	38
Ordinary deck paint	8·2	44

Metal	CORRODED END	Approx. Voltage
Magnesium Alloy		−1·6
Galvanised Iron		−1·05
Zinc		−1·03
Aluminium 3003		−0·94
Cadmium		−0·80
Aluminium		−0·75
Carbon Steel		−0·61
Grey Iron		−0·61
Lead		−0·55
Type 304 Stainless Steel (active) 18/8		−0·53
Copper		−0·36
Admiralty Brass		−0·29
Manganese Bronze		−0·27
70/30 Copper–Nickel		−0·25
Copper		−0·24
Nickel 200		−0·20
Silicon Bronze		−0·18
Type 316 Stainless Steel (active) 18/10/3		−0·18
INCONEL (Inco Registered Trademark) alloy 600		−0·17
Titanium		−0·15
Silver		−0·13
Type 304 Stainless Steel (passive) 18/8		−0·08
MONEL (Inco Registered Trademark)		−0·08
Type 316 Stainless Steel (passive) 18/10/3		−0·05

INCREASING NOBILITY →

PROTECTED END

To prevent corrosion in the presence of seawater the voltage difference between two dissimilar metals should not exceed 0·20 volts. The *less* noble metal corrodes away fastest.

The stainless steels are normally passive in atmospheric conditions because they are protected by a layer of oxide. However, this is liable to penetration and stainless steels are not recommended for use below or near the waterline.

Where dissimilar metals must be used, make sure the *less* noble one has a much larger *area* and volume than the nobler one so that corrosion will be negligible. If the volume alone is large but the exposed area is small there will be intense corrosion on the small area open to attack.

SECTION 3 — **Fastenings**

Hexagonal bolts, nuts and screws—ISO metric sizes

STANDARD DIAMETERS M.M.	PITCH OF THREADS	MAXᴹ WIDTH ACROSS FLATS	MAXᴹ WIDTH ACROSS CORNERS	MAXᴹ HEIGHT OF HEAD	MAXᴹ THICKNESS OF NUT.
5	0·8	8	9·2	3·88	4·38
6	1	10	11·5	4·38	5·38
8	1·25	13	15·0	5·88	6·88
10	1·5	17	19·6	7·45	8·45
12	1·75	19	21·9	8·45	10·45
16	2	24	27·7	10·45	13·55
20	2·5	30	34·6	13·90	16·55
[22]	2·5	32	36·9	14·90	18·55
24	3	36	41·6	15·90	19·65
[27]	3	41	47·3	17·90	22·65
30	3·5	46	53·1	20·05	24·65
[33]	3·5	50	57·7	22·05	26·65
36	4	55	63·5	24·05	29·65
[39]	4	60	69·3	26·05	31·80
42	4·5	65	75·1	27·05	34·80
45	4·5	70	80·8	29·05	36·80
48	5	75	86·6	31·05	38·80
[52]	5	80	92·4	34·25	42·80
56	5·5	85	98·1	36·25	45·80
[60]	5·5	90	103·9	39·25	48·80
64	6	95	109·7	41·25	51·95
68	6	100	115·5	44·25	54·95

Screw threads per inch

These tables are particularly useful for identifying a bolt or nut.

B.S.W. = British Standard Whitworth.
B.S.F. = British Standard Fine.
U.N.C. = Unified Screw Threads – Coarse.
U.N.F. = Unified Screw Threads – Fine.
B.A. = British Association.
B.S.P. = British Standard Pipe & Whitworth Pipe.
N.B. for pipes the diameter is the bore diameter.

Diameter		Threads per inch (25·4 mm).				
mm	in	B.S.W.	B.S.F.	U.N.C.	U.N.F.	B.S.P.
3·2	$\frac{1}{8}$	40				28
4·8	$\frac{3}{16}$	24	32			
5·6	$\frac{7}{32}$		28			
6·4	$\frac{1}{4}$	20	26	20	28	19
7·1	$\frac{9}{32}$		26			
7·9	$\frac{5}{16}$	18	22	18	24	
9·5	$\frac{3}{8}$	16	20	16	24	19
11·1	$\frac{7}{16}$	14	18	14	20	
12·7	$\frac{1}{2}$	12	16	13	20	14
14·3	$\frac{9}{16}$	12	16	12	18	
15·9	$\frac{5}{8}$	11	14	11	18	14
17·5	$\frac{11}{16}$	11	14			
19·1	$\frac{3}{4}$	10	12	10	16	14
20·6	$\frac{13}{16}$		12			
22·2	$\frac{7}{8}$	9	11	9	14	14
25·4	1	8	10	8	12	11
28·6	$1\frac{1}{8}$	7	9	7	12	11 for each size to 6″
31·8	$1\frac{1}{4}$	7	9	7	12	
34·9	$1\frac{3}{8}$	6	8	6	12	
38·1	$1\frac{1}{2}$	6	8	6	12	
44·5	$1\frac{3}{4}$	5	7	5		
50·8	2	$4\frac{1}{2}$	7	$4\frac{1}{2}$		

B.A.

No.	0	1	2	3	4	5	6	7	8	9	10
Diameter in mm	6·0	5·3	4·7	4·1	3·6	3·2	2·8	2·5	2·2	1·9	1·7
inches	·236	·209	·185	·161	·142	·126	·110	·098	·087	·075	·067
Threads per inch	25·4	28·2	31·4	34·8	38·5	43·1	47·9	52·9	59·1	65·1	72·6

Bolts in wood—failing loads

These curves are for a constant load applied equally at the two ends of the bolt. For a constant load at one end take half the figure given on the graph.

The loads given apply to two or more bolts, or one bolt and several screws. For an isolated bolt take two thirds the given value.

When working in lb/ft², Load = 4500 × diameter × length.
Above 16 diameters   Load = 4800 × diameter × length.

NB. These are failing loads and a safety factor must be used in practice.

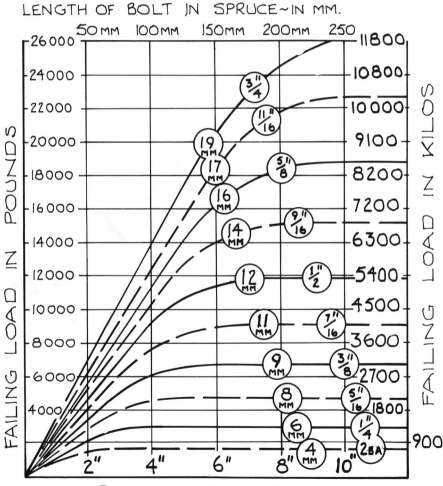

LENGTH OF BOLT IN SPRUCE~IN MM.

FAILING LOAD IN POUNDS

FAILING LOAD IN KILOS

LENGTH OF BOLT IN SPRUCE~IN INCHES

Breaking loads of bolts

To find the strength of a bolt, select from the left hand columns the size of bolt of the correct thread type. Read across horizontally to the appropriate curve, and then down to the Breaking Load.

In practice the majority of bolts are 25 tonf/in² (385 MN/m²), and only the high tensile ones are up to the higher strength standards. Common brass bolts are about $\frac{1}{3}$ or $\frac{1}{4}$ the strength of 25 tonf/in² steel and bronze.

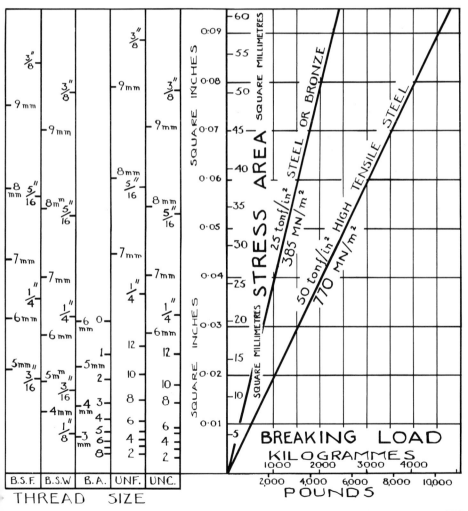

Wood screws—weight in pounds per 1000

Brass, counter-sunk head

LENGTH INS	\	\	\	\	\	SCREW	GAUGE	\	\	\	\	\	\	\	\	\
	0	1	2	3	4	5	6	7	8	9	10	12	14	16	18	20
1/4	·201	·243	·333	·486	·688											
3/8	·299	·319	·479	·694	·896	1·23	1·50		2·24							
1/2		·403	·611	·931	1·16	1·54	1·92	2·31	2·85		4·22					
5/8			·715	1·06	1·41	1·83	2·36	2·80	3·47		4·88					
3/4			·819	1·24	1·62	2·19	2·68	3·29	4·10	4·92	5·74	7·08				
7/8					1·85	2·56	3·13	3·79	4·70	5·65	6·48	8·33				
1				1·64	2·17	2·83	3·58	4·29	5·29	6·35	7·29	9·51	11·94			
1 1/4					2·63	3·44	4·40	5·22	6·49	7·71	8·96	11·67	15·21	18·54		
1 1/2					3·18	4·10	5·25	6·24	7·71	8·89	10·56	13·61	17·85	21·88	27·85	
1 3/4							6·11	7·15	8·89	10·35	12·08	15·69	20·56			
2							6·94	8·13	10·07	11·74	13·75	18·19	23·19	28·68	36·81	42·92
2 1/4									11·25	14·31	15·49	20·07	25·90			
2 1/2							8·68		12·57		17·15	22·22	28·61	35·42	45·83	
2 3/4									13·68			24·17				
3									14·86		20·28	26·32	33·96	42·22	54·86	63·26
3 1/2											21·81	30·49	39·31	49·03		
4											26·94	34·93	44·72	55·14		83·54

Note: The tables are for brass screws. For silicone bronze multiply these weights by 1·062. For aluminium alloy divide these weights by three.

The tables also show the available gauge sizes for different screw lengths. In practice, on small craft, only even number screw gauge sizes are used.

Wood screws—weight in pounds per 1000

Brass, round head

LENGTH INS.						SCREW GAUGE							
	1	2	3	4	5	6	7	8	9	10	12	14	16
1/4	·319												
3/8	·410	·486	·715	·896									
1/2	·507	·597	·847	1·15	1·62	2·13		3·49					
5/8		·736	1·04	1·39	1·88	2·55		4·04		6·07	7·92		
3/4		·896	1·23	1·63	2·23	2·96	3·62	4·59	5·96	6·87	9·03		
7/8		1·06	1·40	1·87	2·49	3·38	4·06	5·15		7·64	10·14		
1				2·10	3·21	3·74	5·15	5·69		8·40	12·01	15·97	
1 1/4				2·37		4·19	6·18	6·25	8·68	9·24	14·03	18·54	
1 1/2				2·81		5·00		7·36	10·14	10·76	16·25	21·04	
1 3/4				3·36		5·63		8·40	11·53	12·43	18·40		27·71
2						6·65		9·51		14·03	20·49	28·38	
2 1/4						7·43		10·63	14·31	15·56	22·5	31·74	
2 1/2								12·92		18·75	24·58		
3								15·07		21·94	28·89	37·15	

Note: The tables are for brass screws. For silicone bronze multiply these weights by 1·062. For aluminium alloy divide these weights by three.

The tables also show the available gauge sizes for different screw lengths. In practice, on small craft, only even number screw gauge sizes are used.

Coach screws or lag bolts—lengths and diameters

Steel

Length / *Available diameters*

Diameter unit labels: first three mm diameters **6·4 8 9·5**; further mm diameters **12·7 15·9 19·1**; inch diameters **$\frac14$ $\frac{5}{16}$ $\frac38$ $\frac12$ $\frac58$ $\frac34$**. A "⟂" mark below denotes an available size (shown as ,, ditto marks in the original).

Length mm	inches	6·4	8	9·5	12·7	15·9	19·1	$\frac14$	$\frac{5}{16}$	$\frac38$	$\frac12$	$\frac58$	$\frac34$
25·4	1	6·4	8	9·5				$\frac14$	$\frac{5}{16}$	$\frac38$			
32	$1\frac14$	,,	,,	,,				,,	,,	,,			
38	$1\frac12$	,,	,,	,,	12·7			,,	,,	,,	$\frac12$		
45	$1\frac34$	,,	,,	,,	,,			,,	,,	,,	,,		
51	2	,,	,,	,,	,,	15·9		,,	,,	,,	,,	$\frac58$	
57	$2\frac14$	,,	,,	,,	,,	,,		,,	,,	,,	,,	,,	
64	$2\frac12$	,,	,,	,,	,,	,,	19·1	,,	,,	,,	,,	,,	$\frac34$
70	$2\frac34$	,,	,,	,,	,,	,,	,,	,,	,,	,,	,,	,,	,,
76	3	,,	,,	,,	,,	,,	,,	,,	,,	,,	,,	,,	,,
83	$3\frac14$	,,	,,	,,	,,	,,	,,	,,	,,	,,	,,	,,	,,
89	$3\frac12$	,,	,,	,,	,,	,,	,,	,,	,,	,,	,,	,,	,,
95	$3\frac34$	,,	,,	,,	,,	,,	,,	,,	,,	,,	,,	,,	,,
102	4	,,	,,	,,	,,	,,	,,	,,	,,	,,	,,	,,	,,
114	$4\frac12$	,,	,,	,,	,,	,,	,,	,,	,,	,,	,,	,,	,,
127	5				,,	,,	,,				,,	,,	,,
140	$5\frac12$				,,	,,	,,				,,	,,	,,
152	6				,,	,,	,,				,,	,,	,,
165	$6\frac12$				,,	,,	,,				,,	,,	,,
178	7				,,	,,	,,				,,	,,	,,
191	$7\frac12$				,,	,,	,,				,,	,,	,,
203	8				,,	,,	,,				,,	,,	,,
216	$8\frac12$				,,	,,	,,				,,	,,	,,
229	9				,,	,,	,,				,,	,,	,,
241	$9\frac12$				,,	,,	,,				,,	,,	,,
254	10				,,	,,	,,				,,	,,	,,
267	$10\frac12$				,,	,,	,,				,,	,,	,,
279	11				,,	,,	,,				,,	,,	,,
292	$11\frac12$				,,	,,	,,				,,	,,	,,
305	12				,,	,,	,,				,,	,,	,,

Bronze Bronze coach screws are becoming difficult to obtain and may have to be specially made when required. In Britain these fastenings will continue to be made to Imperial measure for the foreseeable future (November 1975). This does not affect the user since they are screwed into wood.

Length	mm/ins	$64/2\frac12$	76/3	$89/3\frac12$	102/4
Available diameters	mm/ins	$8/\frac{5}{16}$	$8/\frac{5}{16}$ $9·5/\frac38$	$12·7/\frac12$	$12·7/\frac12$

Barbed ring nails

These nails have barbed rings along the length to give them particularly effective holding power in all types of wood. They have various trade names including 'Gripfast' and 'Anchorfast'. They cost less per fastening than screws both to buy and to fix. They are hammered in, like ordinary nails, which is far quicker than drilling, counter-sinking and screwing for a wood screw. However a little of the time and cost advantage is off-set by the need to put in more barbed nails than screws for a given measure of strength.

The makers recommend that the 14 and 16 gauge sizes do not need pilot holes, but some experienced shipwrights make pilot holes for all sizes which should be half the nail diameter. These nails are available countersunk or with flat heads. They can easily be punched below the surface or they can be driven flat and varnished over.

Barbed ring nails have good corrosion resistance, being made of such materials as silicon bronze or stainless steel. They can therefore be used to replace the ferrous nails (which rust) fitted in various types of electric cable clip.

Thickness			Available lengths					
mm	*swg*	*Inches*	*mm/Inches*					
4	8	·160	34 $1\frac{1}{2}$	44·5 $1\frac{3}{4}$	51 2	57 $2\frac{1}{4}$	63·5 $2\frac{1}{2}$	76 3
3·3	10	·128	25·4 1	32 $1\frac{1}{4}$	38 $1\frac{1}{2}$	44·5 $1\frac{3}{4}$	50·8 2	57 $2\frac{1}{4}$
2·6	12	·104	19 $\frac{3}{4}$	22 $\frac{7}{8}$	25·4 1	32 $1\frac{1}{4}$	38 $1\frac{1}{2}$	50·8 2
2	14	·80	19 $\frac{3}{4}$	22 $\frac{7}{8}$	25·4 1	32 $1\frac{1}{4}$		
1·6	16	·064	16 $\frac{5}{8}$	19 $\frac{3}{4}$	22 $\frac{7}{8}$	25·4 1		

Note: In Britain these fastenings will continue to be made to Imperial measure for the foreseeable future.

Pilot hole sizes—wood screws

Screw Gauge	P	Hard Woods			Soft Woods		
		Pilot Hole Dia.	Drill Sizes Fraction	mm	Pilot Hole Dia.	Drill Sizes Fraction	mm
3	1/8″	·057		1·45	No Pilot Hole necessary for these sizes		
4	1/8″	·066		1·70			
5	5/32″	·073		1·85			
6	5/32″	·082		2·10	·059		1·50
7	3/16″	·091	3/32″	2·30	·066		1·70
8	7/32″	·097		2·50	·071		1·80
9	1/4″	·103		2·65	·078	5/64″	2·00
10	1/4″	·108	7/64″	2·75	·084		2·15
12	5/16″	·124	1/8″	3·15	·097		2·50
14	11/32″	·140	9/64″	3·60	·108	7/64″	2·75

Hole approx. equal to Nominal Screw Diameter

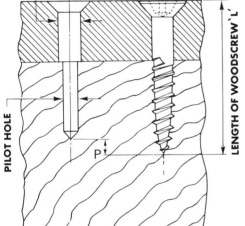
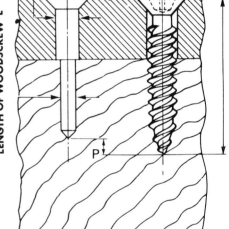

PILOT HOLE

LENGTH OF WOODSCREW 'L'

P

P

Screw Gauge	P	Hard Woods High Density Boards			Soft Woods Low Density Boards		
		Pilot Hole Dia.	Drill Sizes Fraction	mm	Pilot Hole Dia.	Drill Sizes Fraction	mm
3	·100	·063	1/16″		·035		0·90
4	·125	·070		1·80	·049		1·25
5	·136	·082		2·10	·057		1·45
6	·150	·093	3/32″		·062	1/16″	
7	·166	·106		2·70	·065		1·65
8	·166	·116		2·95	·076		1·95
10	·200	·125	1/8″		·089		2·25
12	·231	·142		3·60	·102		2·60
14	·250	·166		4·20	·116		2·95

Pilot hole sizes—nails and copper clenches

NAIL GAUGE AND CLENCH DIAMETER	DRILL SIZE HARD WOOD	DRILL SIZE SOFT WOOD	ROOVE SIZE
14 g	MM 2 / $\frac{1}{16}$ INS.	MM 1 / $\frac{3}{64}$ INS.	MM 8 / $\frac{5}{16}$ INS.
13 g	MM 2 / $\frac{5}{64}$ INS.	MM 2 / $\frac{1}{16}$ INS.	MM 10 / $\frac{3}{8}$ INS.
12 g	MM 2 / $\frac{5}{64}$ INS.	MM 2 / $\frac{1}{16}$ INS.	MM 11 / $\frac{7}{16}$ INS.
11 g	MM 2·5 / $\frac{3}{32}$ INS.	MM 2 / $\frac{5}{64}$ INS.	MM 13 / $\frac{1}{2}$ INS.
10 g	MM 2·5 / $\frac{3}{32}$ INS.	MM 2 / $\frac{5}{64}$ INS.	MM 13 / $\frac{1}{2}$ INS.
8 g	MM 3 / $\frac{1}{8}$ INS.	MM 2·5 / $\frac{3}{32}$ INS.	MM 13 / $\frac{1}{2}$ INS.
4·88 MM $\frac{3}{16}$ INS.	MM 4·5 / $\frac{3}{16}$ INS.	MM 4 / $\frac{11}{64}$ INS.	MM 15 / $\frac{9}{16}$ INS.
6·4 MM $\frac{1}{4}$ INS.	MM 6·4 / $\frac{1}{4}$ INS.	MM 6 / $\frac{15}{64}$ INS.	MM 16 / $\frac{5}{8}$ INS.
7·9 MM $\frac{5}{16}$ INS.	MM 7·9 / $\frac{5}{16}$ INS.	MM 7 / $\frac{9}{32}$ INS.	MM 19 / $\frac{3}{4}$ INS.
9·5 MM $\frac{3}{8}$ INS	MM 9·5 / $\frac{3}{8}$ INS.	MM 9 / $\frac{11}{32}$ INS.	MM 22 / $\frac{7}{8}$ INS.

SECTION THROUGH COPPER NAIL

For hardwood: drill diam $= \dfrac{D}{2}$

For softwood: drill diam $= \dfrac{A}{2}$

Pipe clips—sizes

Not all manufacturers use the same scale for their size numbers. For marine use stainless steel pipe clips are recommended, especially in awkward locations. Galvanizing on mild steel clips is sometimes thin and often scratched and, as a result, the corrosion rate is high.

On exhaust pipes the clips should be in pairs at each end. Extra large sizes, not listed here, are available from mast makers, who use them to secure mast coats.

Inside diameter

mm	Inches	Size No.	B.S.3628 No.
9– 13	$\frac{3}{8}- \frac{1}{2}$	000	050
9– 16	$\frac{3}{8}- \frac{5}{8}$	M00	062
13– 19	$\frac{1}{2}- \frac{3}{4}$	00	075
16– 22	$\frac{5}{8}- \frac{7}{8}$	0	087
19– 25	$\frac{3}{4}-1$	0X	100
22– 28	$\frac{7}{8}-1\frac{1}{8}$	1A	112
25– 35	$1 -1\frac{3}{8}$	1	137
28– 41	$1\frac{1}{8}-1\frac{5}{8}$	1X	162
32– 48	$1\frac{1}{4}-1\frac{7}{8}$	2A	187
38– 54	$1\frac{1}{2}-2\frac{1}{8}$	2	212
44– 60	$1\frac{3}{4}-2\frac{3}{8}$	2X	237
50– 70	$2 -2\frac{3}{4}$	3	275
60– 80	$2\frac{3}{8}-3\frac{1}{8}$	3X	312
70– 90	$2\frac{3}{4}-3\frac{1}{2}$	4	350
82–100	$3\frac{1}{4}-4$	4X	400
95–115	$3\frac{3}{4}-4\frac{1}{2}$	5	450
105–125	$4\frac{1}{8}-5$	6	500
125–146	$5 -5\frac{3}{4}$	6X	575
133–158	$5\frac{1}{4}-6\frac{1}{4}$	7	625

Split pins—sizes

BOLT DIAMETER		SPLIT PIN			
		LENGTH OVERALL		DIAMETER	
MM	INCHES	MM	INCHES	MM	INCHES
	2 BA	19	3/4	1·5	1/16
6	1/4	19	3/4	1·5	1/16
8	5/16	25	1	1·5	1/16
10	3/8	25	1	1·5	1/16
11	7/16	32	1 1/4	2·5	3/32
12	1/2	32	1 1/4	2·5	3/32
14	9/16	32	1 1/4	2·5	3/32
16	5/8	38	1 1/2	3·5	1/8
17·5	11/16	45	1 3/8	3·5	1/8
19	3/4	45	1 3/4	4·0	5/32
20	13/16	45	1 3/4	4·0	5/32
22	7/8	50	2	4·0	5/32
24	15/16	50	2	4·0	5/32
25	1	57	2 1/4	5·0	3/16
29	1 1/8	57	2 1/4	5·0	3/16
33	1 1/4	65	2 1/2	6·5	1/4
35	1 3/8	75	3	6·5	1/4
38	1 1/2	75	3	6·5	1/4
41	1 5/8	75	3	7·0	9/32
45	1 3/4	75	3	7·0	9/32
50	2	90	3 1/2	10	3/8

SECTION 4 — Spars and rigging

Aluminium alloy masts—general guide

This scale is a rough guide to mast dimensions which is quick and conveniently useful. For long range cruising go up one or two sizes. Except where stated the dimensions do not include mast track.

Acknowledgement is made to Ian Proctor Metal Masts Ltd for assistance.

YACHT SIZE APPROX WATERLINE LENGTH		TYPICAL MAST SECTION		WALL THICKNESS		APPROX MAST WEIGHT	
METRES	FEET	MM	INCHES	MM	INCHES	KILO/M	LB/FT
5·5	18	105×75	4×3	INTEGRAL TRACK		2·15	1·44
5·5	18	115×75	4·5×3	2	0·08	1·7	1·15
5·8	19	120×80	4·8×3·2	2·	0·08	1·8	1·21
6·4	21	130×85	5·2×3·9	2·3	0·09	2·25	1·51
6·7	22	140×92	5·5×3·6	2·6	0·10	2·7	1·81
6·7	22	153×92	6×3·6	2·6	0·10	2·93	1·97
7·3	24	140×108	5·5×4·25	3·2	0·13	3·44	2·3
7·3	24	125×90	4·8×3·5	INTEGRAL TRACK		3·2	2·15
7·9	26	160×120	6·3×4·8	3·2	0·13	3·68	2·47
8·5	28	205×115	8×4·5	3·2	0·13	4·38	2·94
9·1	30	200×140	7·8×5·5	4·1	0·16	5·46	3·67
10	33	205×170	8×6·6	4·1	0·16	6·47	4·35
10·7	35	240×165	9·5×6·5	4·1	0·16	7·29	4·9
13·7	45	270×190	10·5×7·5	5·4	0·21	9·9	6·7
15·2	50	305×205	12×8	6·4	0·25	14·5	9·7
25	80	360×250	14×10	6·4	0·25	16·4	11·5

Aluminium alloy masts—size selection graph

To find the diameter and wall thickness of a mast given:
1) The yacht's waterline length
2) The height of the fore-triangle

Items 1) and 2) are first added. If they are in metric units use the left hand side of the graph. If in imperial units use the right hand side. The plotting method is shown below in the small graph.

Where the sum of items 1) and 2) intercepts the type of rig, read vertically down for the area of the rectangle which will enclose the mast tube. Read on further down for the mast wall thickness.

When using this type of graph, it is important to make adjustments according to the type of yacht. For long range cruising in severe weather conditions increase the mast size by one or two steps.

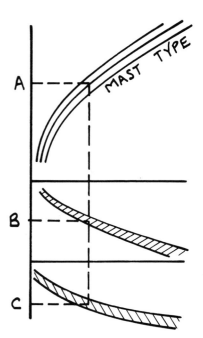

Example: An ocean racer having a waterline length plus fore-triangle height added together to give a total of 22 m with a single spreader mast head rig:

The mast section would be something approaching 27×10^3 sq. mm in area. The section might be 190 mm × 145 mm or 180 mm × 150 mm. Its wall thickness would be of the order of 4 mm.

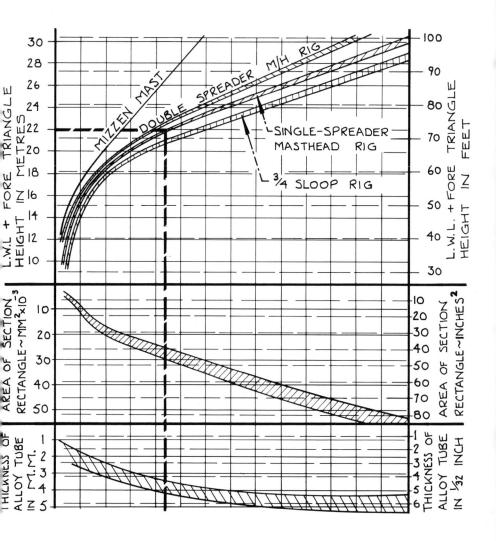

Boom dimensions

The graph for boom diameter against overall length is drawn in metric figures (left and bottom scales with solid lines) and also in feet and inches (top and right hand scales with dotted lines).

The graph is an approximate guide. For long range cruising an increase of at least 10% would be usual. For inshore racing special considerations apply but the diameter might be reduced.

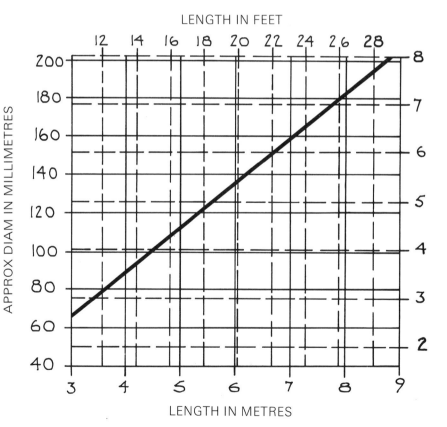

Spinnaker boom dimensions

The graph is for the maximum spinnaker boom diameter and is marked in metric figures (left hand side and bottom scales with solid lines) and also in feet and inches (right hand side and upper scale with dotted lines). These booms normally taper considerably at each end, though some of the smaller or cheaper ones are parallel.

The graph is an approximate guide. For extended cruising, particularly when using twin running headsails, these dimensions may well be increased. However, the larger the overall diameter of a boom, the more difficult it is to grasp in the hand. About 75 mm (3 in) is the biggest convenient diameter for most people. This fact may influence a choice towards a thinner maximum section with a thicker wall.

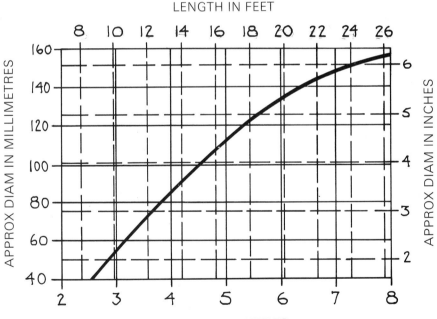

LENGTH IN FEET

APPROX DIAM IN MILLIMETRES

APPROX DIAM IN INCHES

LENGTH IN METRES

Rigging screw pins, forks and standard ends

Since rigging screws break far more often than the wire, the screw should be $1\frac{1}{2}$ times as strong as the shroud it is connected to. For ocean racing the factor should be 3. However where standard components are used, the correct standing rigging screw must be bought to fit the standard rigging terminal, standard chain plate, toggle etc.

Note: Ropes of sizes other than those listed should be associated with the next maximum size above it in the table. The working depth l_1 indicates the limit of parallelism of the facing sides of the fork slot. The threaded length of shaft (l_2)

Dimensions are in mm.

MAXIMUM DIAMETER OF WIRE ROPE	SIZE OF RIGGING SCREW	DESIGNATION OF SCREW THREAD OF SHANK	DIAMT OF PIN d_1	DIAMT OF EYE d_2	WORKING DEPTH OF FORK END l_1	WIDTH OF FORK SLOT $[d_2 \pm 5\%]b_2$		THICKNESS OF EYE	
						MIN	MAX	MIN	MAX
3	6	6×1×8g	5	6·5	10	6·3	6·7	4·5	5·3
4	8	8×1·25×8g	7	8	12	7·5	8·5	6·5	7·5
5	10	10×1·5×8g	8	10	15	9·5	10·5	7·5	8·5
7	12	12×1·75×8g	11	13	20	12·3	13·7	10·5	11·5
10	16	16×2×8g	14	16	24	15·2	16·8	13·3	14·7
12	20	20×2·5×8g	18	20	30	19·0	21·0	17·0	19·0
16	24	24×3×8g	22	25	38	23·7	26·3	21·0	23·0

Shackles—safe working loads

is to be not less than the diameter of the screw thread.
Limits of tolerance of ±0·3 mm are allowable on dimensions d_1 and d_2, plus 1·0 mm on dimension l_1.

Safe working load is approximately a quarter of the distortion load.

DIAMETER OF PIN		STAINLESS STEEL			GALVANIZED TESTED	
		NORMAL D SHAPE	NARROW D SHAPE	HARP OR BOW	D SHAPE	HARP OR BOW
MM	INCHES	KGS / LBS	KGS / LBS	KGS / LBS	KGS / LBS	KGS / LBS
3	1/8	140 / 310		130 / 290		
4	5/32	320 / 700				
5	3/16	380 / 840		190 / 420		
6	1/4	510 / 1120		200 / 450		
8	5/16		790 / 1700	410 / 900	200 / 450	190 / 420
10	3/8	1400 / 3080		510 / 1120	310 / 670	292 / 645
11	7/16		1660 / 3650			
13	1/2	2350 / 5200		760 / 1680	410 / 900	360 / 780
16	5/8				610 / 1350	610 / 1350
19	3/4				1120 / 2480	1010 / 2240
22	7/8				1620 / 3580	1520 / 3360
25	1				2260 / 5000	2020 / 4480
29	1 1/8				3060 / 6750	2260 / 5000

Stainless steel flexible wire—breaking load and weight of running rigging

NOMINAL DIAM. MM	APPROX. DIAM. INCHES	APPROX. CIRCUM. INCHES	CONSTRUCTION	NOMINAL BREAKING LOAD KGS	LBS	APPROX. WEIGHT KG PER 100 M.	LBS PER 100 FT.
2	5/64	1/4	6×7	270	600	1·5	1·0
2·5	3/32	5/16	7×12	410	900	2·4	1·6
3	1/8	3/8	7×12	640	1400	3·7	2·5
4	5/32	1/2	7×19	950	2100	5·8	3·9
5	3/16	5/8	7×19	1500	3300	8·2	5·5
6	1/4	3/4	7×19	2100	4800	15·3	10·3
7	9/32	7/8	7×19	2900	6500	19·1	12·8
8	5/16	1	7×19	3800	8500	23·6	15·9

Stainless steel wire rope—breaking load and weight of standing rigging

NOMINAL DIAM. MM	APROX DIAM. INCHES	APROX CIRCUM. INCHES	1 × 19 NOMINAL BREAKING LOAD KGS	1 × 19 NOMINAL BREAKING LOAD LBS	1 × 19 WEIGHT KGS PER 100 M	1 × 19 WEIGHT LBS PER 100 FT	7 × 7 NOMINAL BREAKING LOAD KGS	7 × 7 NOMINAL BREAKING LOAD LBS	7 × 7 WEIGHT KGS PER 100 M	7 × 7 WEIGHT LBS PER 100 FT
2	5/64	1/4	320	700	2.0	1.4	290	650	1.8	1.2
2.5	3/32	5/16	530	1165	3.1	2.1	400	900	2.5	1.7
3	1/8	3/8	760	1680	4.0	2.7	660	1470	3.7	2.5
4	5/32	1/2	1350	3000	7.3	4.9	970	2150	5.7	3.8
5	3/16	5/8	2100	4650	11.3	7.6	1600	3700	8.5	5.7
6	1/4	3/4	3000	6700	16.5	11.1	2300	5200	15.5	10.4
7	9/32	7/8	4150	9150	22.5	15.1				
8	5/16	1	5400	11950	32.7	22.0				
9	3/8	1 1/8	6400	14140	40.9	27.5				
10	13/32	1 1/4	8400	18600	47.5	32.0				
12	15/32	1 1/2	12200	26800	82.0	55.0				
14	9/16	1 3/4	16600	36600	100.1	68.0				
16	5/8	2	21700	47750	132.0	89.0				

Galvanized steel flexible wire—breaking load and weight of running rigging

NOMINAL DIAM MM	APROX DIAM INCHES	APROX CIRCMF INCHES	CONSTRUCTION	NOMINAL BREAKING LOAD KGS	NOMINAL BREAKING LOAD LBS	APROX. WEIGHT KGS PER 100 M	APROX. WEIGHT LBS PER 100 FT
2·5	3/32	5/16	7 × 12	340	750	2·3	1·5
3	1/8	3/8	7 × 12	525	1160	3·8	2·5
4	5/32	1/2	7 × 12	880	1940	6·3	4·2
5	3/16	5/8	7 × 12	1130	2510	8·1	5·4
6	1/4	3/4	7 × 19	2180	4890	15·1	10·1
7	9/32	7/8	7 × 19	2820	6280	19·2	12·8
8	5/16	1	7 × 19	3400	7560	23·8	15·9
10	13/32	1¼	7 × 19	4930	10900	32·2	21·5

Galvanized steel wire rope—breaking load and weight of standing rigging

NOMINAL DIAM. MM	APROX DIAM. INCHES	APROX CIRCUM INCHES	1 × 19				7 × 7			
			NOMINAL BREAKING LOAD KGS	LBS	WEIGHT KGS PER 100 M	LBS PER 100 FT	NOMINAL BREAKING LOAD KGS	LBS	WEIGHT KGS PER 100 M	LBS PER 100 FT
2	5/64	1/4					224	490	1·5	1·0
2·5	3/32	5/16	530	1165	3·1	2·1	322	705	2·3	1·5
3	1/8	3/8	760	1680	4·0	2·7	530	1160	3·8	2·5
4	5/32	1/2	1350	3000	7·3	4·9	1140	2500	5·9	3·9
5	3/16	5/8	2100	4650	11·3	7·6	1810	3950	9·3	6·2
6	1/4	3/4	3000	6700	16·5	11·1	2580	5650	13·4	8·9
7	9/32	7/8	4150	9150	22·5	15·1	3520	7700	18·3	12·2
8	5/16	1	5400	11950	32·7	22·0	4610	10100	23·8	15·9
10	13/32	1¼	8400	18600	47·5	32·0	7180	15700	37·2	24·8
12	15/32	1½	12200	26800	82·0	55·0	10300	22600	79·8	53·2

Ropes of man-made fibres—diameter, circumference, breaking

Terylene/Dacron. 3-strand (Polyester multifilament)

SIZE DIAMETER MM.	SIZE DIAMETER INCHES	SIZE CIRCUMFERENCE INCHES	STRENGTH KGS	STRENGTH LBS	WEIGHT KGS PER 100 M	WEIGHT LBS PER 100 FT
2	3/32	1/4	140	300	0·37	0·25
4	3/16	1/2	290	650	1·46	0·98
6	1/4	3/4	560	1250	3·0	1·95
8	5/16	1	1020	2240	5·1	3·5
10	3/8	1 1/4	1590	3500	8·1	5·5
12	1/2	1 1/2	2270	5000	11·6	7·8
14	9/16	1 3/4	3180	7000	15·7	10·6
16	5/8	2	4000	9000	20·5	13·8
18	3/4	2 1/4	5000	11200	26·0	17·6
20	13/16	2 1/2	6300	14000	32·0	21·6
22	7/8	2 3/4	7600	17000	38·4	25·9
24	1	3	9000	20000	46·0	31·0
28	1 3/16	3 1/2	12200	27000	63·0	42·3
32	1 3/8	4	15700	35000	82·0	55·0
36	1 1/2	4 1/2	19300	42500	104·0	70·0
40	1 11/16	5	23900	52500	128·0	86·0

Nylon 3-strand (Polyamide multifilament)

SIZE DIAMETER MM	SIZE DIAMETER INS	SIZE CIRCUMFERE INS	STRENGTH KGS	STRENGTH LBS	WEIGHT KGS PER 100 M	WEIGHT LBS PER 100 FT
4	3/16	1/2	320	700	1·1	0·7
6	1/4	3/4	750	1600	2·37	1·67
8	5/16	1	1350	2900	4·2	2·85
10	3/8	1 1/4	2000	4500	6·5	4·38
12	1/2	1 1/2	3000	6600	9·4	6·4
14	9/16	1 3/4	4000	9000	12·8	8·7
16	5/8	2	5300	11600	16·6	11·3

oad, weight

Nylon (continued)

SIZE			STRENGTH		WEIGHT	
DIAMETER		CIRCUMFERE			KGS PER	LBS PER
MM	INS.	INS.	KGS	LBS	100 M	100 FT
18	3/4	2 1/4	6,700	14,700	21·0	14·2
20	13/16	2 1/2	8,300	18,000	26·0	17·5
22	7/8	2 3/4	10,000	21,900	31·5	21·3
24	1	3	12,000	26,400	37·5	25·3
28	1 3/16	3 1/2	15,800	34,600	51·0	34·4
32	1 3/8	4	20,000	43,900	66·5	44·8
36	1 1/2	4 1/2	24,800	54,400	84	56·6
40	1 11/16	5	30,000	66,100	104	70

Ulstron/Courlene 3-strand (Polypropylene multifilament).

SIZE			STRENGTH		WEIGHT	
DIAM.	DIAM	CIRCUME	KGS	LBS	KGS PER	LBS PER
MM.	INS.	INS.			100 M	100 FT
4	3/16	1/2	250	550	0·93	0·63
6	1/4	3/4	500	1100	1·9	1·3
8	5/16	1	900	2000	3·4	2·3
10	3/8	1 1/4	1350	3000	5·2	3·5
12	1/2	1 1/2	1900	4200	7·5	5·0
14	9/16	1 3/4	2600	5700	10·2	6·9
16	5/8	2	3300	7300	13·2	8·9
18	3/4	2 1/4	4300	9500	16·9	11·3
20	13/16	2 1/2	5350	11700	20·6	13·9
22	7/8	2 3/4	6000	13400	25	16·7
24	1	3	7500	16800	30	20·0
28	1 3/16	3 1/2	10000	22400	41	27·3
32	1 3/8	4	12500	28000	53	35·5
36	1 1/2	4 1/2	16000	36000	67	45
40	1 11/16	5	19200	42500	83	56

Polyester ropes—recommended sizes for running rigging

Note: All rope sizes are diameters.
For ocean cruising use one or two sizes larger.

Length Overall	Up to 5·5 m Up to 18 ft	5·5–7·3 m 18–24 ft	7·3–9 m 24–30 ft
Thames Tonnage	Dinghies and Dayboats	2–4 tons	4–8 tons
Halyards – Mainsails and Masthead jibs	6·5 mm $\frac{1}{4}$ in 3 strand	8 mm $\frac{5}{16}$ in 3 strand	10 mm $\frac{3}{8}$ in 3 strand
Halyards – Staysails and Mizzen	6·5 mm $\frac{1}{4}$ in 3 strand	8 mm $\frac{5}{16}$ in 3 strand	8 mm $\frac{5}{16}$ in 3 strand
Topping Lift – Main boom	5 mm $\frac{3}{16}$ in Plaited	6·5 mm $\frac{1}{4}$ in Plaited	6·5 mm $\frac{1}{4}$ in Plaited
Topping Lift – Mizzen	5 mm $\frac{3}{16}$ in Plaited	5 mm $\frac{3}{16}$ in Plaited	6·5 mm $\frac{1}{4}$ in Plaited
Burgee Halyard	2 mm $\frac{1}{16}$ in Plaited	3 mm $\frac{1}{8}$ in Plaited	3 mm $\frac{1}{8}$ in Plaited
Sheets – Mainsail and Headsails	11 mm $\frac{7}{16}$ in Plaited	11 mm $\frac{7}{16}$ in Plaited	13 mm $\frac{1}{2}$ in Plaited
Sheets – Mizzen and Spinnakers	6·5 mm $\frac{1}{4}$ in Plaited	10 mm $\frac{3}{8}$ in Plaited	11 mm $\frac{7}{16}$ in Plaited
Spinnaker Sheets – Light weather	5 mm $\frac{3}{16}$ in Plaited	6·5 mm $\frac{1}{4}$ in Plaited	6·5 mm $\frac{1}{4}$ in Plaited

–11 m 0–36 ft	11–13·5 m 36–44 ft	13·5–16·5 m 44–54 ft	16·5–20 m 54–66 ft	20–25 m 66–80 ft
–12 tons	12–18 tons	18–30 tons	30–55 tons	55–90 tons
3 mm in strand	13 mm $\frac{1}{2}$ in 3 strand	13 mm $\frac{1}{2}$ in 3 strand	16 mm $\frac{5}{8}$ in 3 strand	21 mm $\frac{13}{16}$ in 3 strand
0 mm in strand	13 mm $\frac{1}{2}$ in 3 strand	13 mm $\frac{1}{2}$ in 3 strand	13 mm $\frac{1}{2}$ in 3 strand	16 mm $\frac{5}{8}$ in 3 strand
0 mm in laited	10 mm $\frac{3}{8}$ in Plaited	13 mm $\frac{1}{2}$ in Plaited	13 mm $\frac{1}{2}$ in Plaited	16 mm $\frac{5}{8}$ in Plaited
5 mm in laited	10 mm $\frac{3}{8}$ in Plaited	10 mm $\frac{3}{8}$ in Plaited	13 mm $\frac{1}{2}$ in Plaited	13 mm $\frac{1}{2}$ in Plaited
mm in laited	3 mm $\frac{1}{8}$ in Plaited	5 mm $\frac{3}{16}$ in Plaited	5 mm $\frac{3}{16}$ in Plaited	6·5 mm $\frac{1}{4}$ in Plaited
3 mm in laited	16 mm $\frac{5}{8}$ in Plaited	16 mm $\frac{5}{8}$ in Plaited	19 mm $\frac{3}{4}$ in Plaited	22 mm $\frac{7}{8}$ in Plaited
3 mm in laited	13 mm $\frac{1}{2}$ in Plaited	13 mm $\frac{1}{2}$ in Plaited	16 mm $\frac{5}{8}$ in Plaited	19 mm $\frac{3}{4}$ in Plaited
0 mm in laited	10 mm $\frac{3}{8}$ in Plaited	10 mm $\frac{3}{8}$ in Plaited	11 mm $\frac{7}{16}$ in Plaited	11 mm $\frac{1}{2}$ in Plaited

Standing rigging sizes

The thickness of standing rigging on a boat depends on her purpose, her beam, the mast height, sail area, the intended cruising ground and similar factors.

The graph gives a good working average, but for ocean cruising the sizes should be increased *at least* one step on the scale. For inshore racing the sizes might be reduced by one step.

Since rigging is relatively cheap but a dismasting is expensive, it is better to fit one size too large than one too small. Even when racing it is worth remembering that in order to win it is necessary to finish.

On the left side of the graph are the metric sizes; on the right are imperial. The base is in tonnes or tons, which for the purposes of this graph are closely similar.

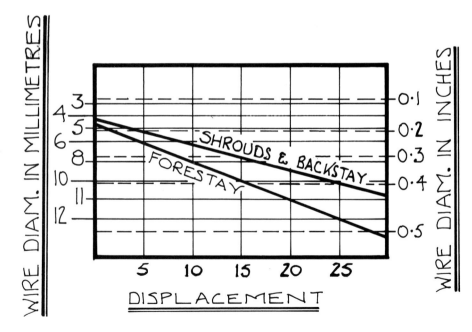

Sheave sizes—for rope cordage

ROPE SIZE		RECOMMENDED SHEAVE DIAMETER		MINIMUM SHEAVE DIAMETER	
MM.	INCHES	MM	INCHES	MM	INCHES
2 & 3	$1/16$ & $1/8$	25	1	16	$5/8$
5	$3/16$	38	$1\frac{1}{2}$	25	1
6·5	$1/4$	45	$1\frac{3}{4}$	25	1
8	$5/16$	50	2	29	$1\frac{1}{8}$
10	$3/8$	57	$2\frac{1}{4}$	32	$1\frac{1}{4}$
11	$7/16$	64	$2\frac{1}{2}$	45	$1\frac{3}{4}$
13	$1/2$	70	$2\frac{3}{4}$	57	$2\frac{1}{4}$
14	$9/16$	83	$3\frac{1}{4}$	67	$2\frac{5}{8}$
16	$5/8$	90	$3\frac{1}{2}$	73	$2\frac{7}{8}$

Note: *Rope sizes are diameters*

Colour code—for running rigging

Though not yet universally accepted the following colours are recommended by Lloyds:

Main halyards and general use, *white*; genoa sheets and halyards, *blue*; headsails, *gold*; spinnakers, *red*.
Topping lifts do not have a designated colour but it is suggested that *green* be used.

Running rigging—typical lengths for dinghies

Class	Sheets Mainsails Metres	Sheets Mainsails Ft	No. of Sheaves	Sheets Foresails Metres	Sheets Foresails Ft	Halyards Mainsails Metres	Halyards Mainsails Ft	Halyards Foresails Metres	Halyards Foresails Ft
Albacore	7·35	24	4	9·15	30	13·40	44	9·15	30
Bobcat	14·65	48	4	9·15	30	20·15	66	18·30	60
Cadet	6·40	21	2	6·10	20	10·35	34	8·25	27
Enterprise	7·95	26	2	7·35	24	12·80	42	9·45	31
Finn	8·25	27	3			14·65	48		
Fireball	7·65	25	3	7·65	25	14·65	48	10·70	35
Firefly	6·70	22	2	6·75	22	13·70	45	10·05	33
5.0.5.	10·70	35	4	9·15	30	14·05	46	10·40	34
Fleetwind	6·40	21	2	5·50	18	12·20	40	7·65	25
Flying Dutchman	9·15	30	4	14·02	46	14·65	48	11·00	36
Flying 15	7·35	24	5	7·35	24				
470	9·75	32	4	8·85	29	14·05	46	10·40	34
G.P.14	7·95	26	2	7·35	24	13·75	45	10·10	33
Graduate	7·35	24	2	7·35	24	11·00	36	7·95	26
Heron	7·35	24	2	6·10	20	7·95	26	7·95	26
Hornet	9·75	32	4	7·05	23	13·75	45	8·85	29
Jollyboat	11·00	36	5	8·25	27	9·75	32	13·75	45
Merlin Rocket	7·95	26	4	6·75	22	14·65	48	10·70	35
National 12 ft	7·65	25	2	6·75	22	13·75	45	11·00	36
O.K.	8·55	28	2			11·00	36		
Shearwater	9·15	30	4	9·15	30	14·65	48	7·95	26
Signet	7·35	24	2	5·50	18	11·00	36	8·55	28
Silhouette	12·20	40	3	7·95	26	12·20	40	13·45	44
Snipe	7·95	26	3	8·55	28	11·90	39		
Solo	11·00	36	3			11·90	39		
Tempest	10·05	33	5	12·20	40	16·30	55	14·65	48
Vagabond	7·35	24	2	6·1	20	7·95	26	7·95	26
Wayfarer	12·80	42	3	9·75	32	14·05	46	10·70	35

SECTION 5 — Engines and powering

Fuel tank design

For small craft all fuel tanks should be made in accordance with the principles shown here. Though this sketch is based on British official recommendations, similar rules apply in other countries.

Key: 1 The deck filler must be fully watertight and sealed all round so that:
a) There is no chance of rain or spray getting into the fuel and,
b) There is no chance that spillage will get below decks.
2 Stainless steel hose clips.
3 Short length of oil resistant hose.
4 Electric conductor between the engine and tank.

Note: The fuel feed pipe is normally made the same size as the connection on the engine.

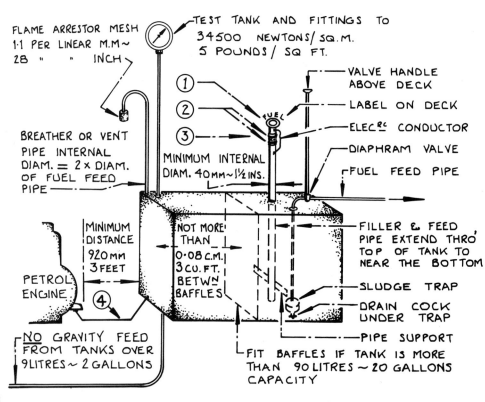

FLAME ARRESTOR MESH
1·1 PER LINEAR M.M~
28 "   "   INCH

TEST TANK AND FITTINGS TO
34500 NEWTONS/SQ.M.
5 POUNDS/SQ FT.

VALVE HANDLE ABOVE DECK

LABEL ON DECK

ELEC ʳᶜ CONDUCTOR

DIAPHRAM VALVE

FUEL FEED PIPE

BREATHER OR VENT
PIPE INTERNAL
DIAM. = 2 x DIAM.
OF FUEL FEED
PIPE

MINIMUM INTERNAL
DIAM. 40mm~1½ INS.

MINIMUM DISTANCE
920mm
3 FEET

NOT MORE THAN
0·08 C.M.
3 CU. FT.
BETWⁿ BAFFLES

FILLER & FEED
PIPE EXTEND THRO'
TOP OF TANK TO
NEAR THE BOTTOM

SLUDGE TRAP

PETROL ENGINE

DRAIN COCK
UNDER TRAP

PIPE SUPPORT

NO GRAVITY FEED
FROM TANKS OVER
9 LITRES ~ 2 GALLONS

FIT BAFFLES IF TANK IS MORE
THAN 90 LITRES ~ 20 GALLONS
CAPACITY

Engine room exhaust system

A particularly attractive way of sucking hot, foul air from an engine room is to use the power of the engine exhaust. The ejector type of combined exhaust and ventilator must be carefully proportioned if it is to work well. Two alternative layouts are shown here, based on recommendations by Caterpillar Diesels Limited.

Key: 1 The exhaust pipe with a gently sweeping elbow.
2 The ejector mixing section.
3 The ejector entrance.
4 The funnel or exhaust stack, with hot air from the engine room rising up outside the engine exhaust pipe. The cross-sectional area of the funnel should exceed $(4D)^2$.
5 Exhaust pipe extension. Minimum length $= D$.
6 Partial bell-mouth formed by the end piece cut at 45° and added to lower end of ejector mixing section.
7 Water drains formed by transverse slots cut in the under side of the pipe. Edges of slot bent as shown. Transverse length of slot $= D/2$.

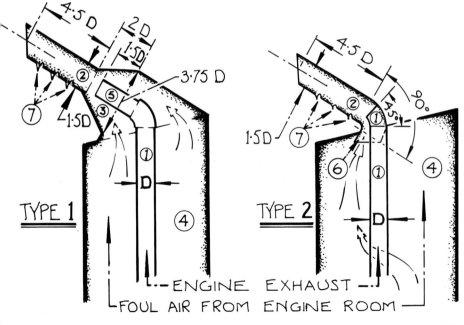

Fuel—consumption, weight, tankage

Consumption	Litres B.H.P. × Hours	Pints B.H.P. × Hours
High speed diesel engines	0·23	0·4
Low speed diesel engines	0·21	0·37
Petrol engines	0·34	0·6
T.V.O. (kerosene or paraffin)	0·40	0·7

Weight	One litre weighs	One gallon weighs
Diesel	0·84 kilograms	8·5 pounds
Petrol	0·73 kilograms	7·4 pounds
T.V.O. (kerosene or paraffin)	0·81 kilograms	8·2 pounds

Tankage	1 tonne is approx.	1 ton is approx.
Diesel	1180 litres	1200 litres 264 galls
Petrol	1340 litres	1360 litres 300 galls
T.V.O. (kerosene or paraffin)	1250 litres	1270 litres 280 galls

Fuel and gas piping

Fuel and bottled gas pipes should have the minimum number of joins. If possible pipes should be run in one unbroken length from the tank to the units served. Junctions, taps etc should be accessible. Seamless annealed copper piping should always be used, except where flexible piping is essential.

Flexible piping should be as short as possible and protected from sharp edges and from rubbing with the craft's movement.

Bottled gas flexible piping should be to B.S.S. 3212:1960 or the equivalent.

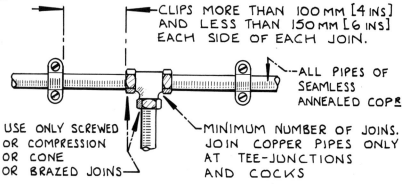

CLIPS MORE THAN 100 mm [4 INS] AND LESS THAN 150 mm [6 INS] EACH SIDE OF EACH JOIN.

ALL PIPES OF SEAMLESS ANNEALED COPR

USE ONLY SCREWED OR COMPRESSION OR CONE OR BRAZED JOINS

MINIMUM NUMBER OF JOINS. JOIN COPPER PIPES ONLY AT TEE-JUNCTIONS AND COCKS

Electric cables—current capacity

Wire specification for rubber insulated twin and single core cables.

CURRENT RATING IN AMPERES	CABLE
5	1/.044 OR 3/.029
10	1/.064 OR 3/.036
15	7/.029
24	7/.036
31	7/.044
37	7/.052
46	7/.064
53	19/.044
64	19/.052
83	19/.064
118	19/.083

Fuse wire—current capacity

DIAMETER		S.W.G.	CURRENT CAPACITY IN AMPS
MILLIMETRES	INCHES		
0·213	0·0084	35	5
0·345	0·0136	29	10
0·510	0·020	25	15
0·610	0·024	23	20
0·815	0·033	21	30
1·02	0·040	19	38
1·43	0·056	17	65
1·83	0·072	15	77
2·03	0·080	14	100

Speed/horsepower—launches and workboats (1)

These speeds are reduced, often considerably, by head winds, rough seas, damaged propeller blades, a weed-covered under-body and so on.

Graph **A** is for boats 9·1 metres, 30 ft, on the waterline

Graph **B** is for boats 7·9 metres, 26 ft, on the waterline

Graph **C** is for boats 6·7 metres, 22 ft, on the waterline

Graph **D** is for boats 5·5 metres, 18 ft, on the waterline

Graph **E** is for boats 4·3 metres, 14 ft, on the waterline

$$\textcircled{M} = 4\cdot7 = \frac{L}{\triangle^{\frac{1}{3}}}$$

L = Length on waterline
$\triangle$ = Immersed volume
$SHP = 0\cdot9 \times BHP$
$\dfrac{THP}{SHP}$ = Propeller efficiency

Propeller efficiency = 0·43 for 1:1 ratio reduction gearing
Propeller efficiency = 0·53 for 2:1 ratio reduction gearing
Propeller efficiency = 0·59 for 3:1 ratio reduction gearing

See also the following pages.
This and subsequent graphs are by courtesy of R. A. Lister & Co. Ltd.

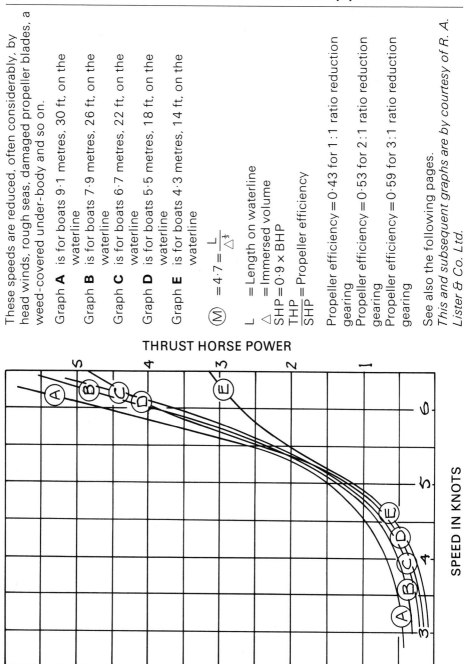

THRUST HORSE POWER

SPEED IN KNOTS

Speed/horsepower—launches and workboats (2)

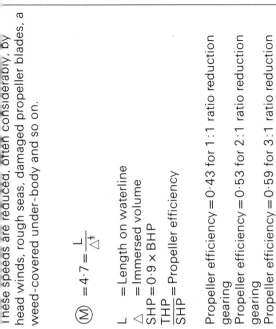

These speeds are reduced, often considerably, by head winds, rough seas, damaged propeller blades, a weed-covered under-body and so on.

$$\textcircled{M} = 4 \cdot 7 = \frac{L}{\triangle^{\frac{1}{3}}}$$

L = Length on waterline
$\triangle$ = Immersed volume
SHP = $0 \cdot 9 \times$ BHP
$\frac{\text{THP}}{\text{SHP}}$ = Propeller efficiency

Propeller efficiency = $0 \cdot 43$ for 1:1 ratio reduction gearing
Propeller efficiency = $0 \cdot 53$ for 2:1 ratio reduction gearing
Propeller efficiency = $0 \cdot 59$ for 3:1 ratio reduction gearing

See also the previous and following pages.

THRUST HORSE POWER

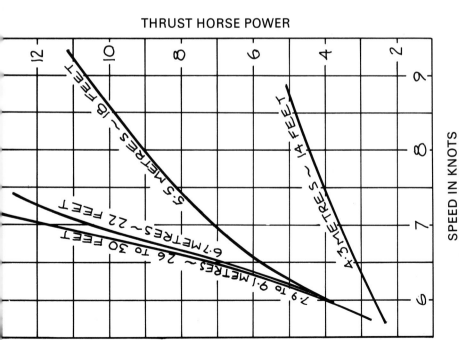

SPEED IN KNOTS

109

These speeds are reduced, often considerably, by head winds, rough seas, damaged propeller blades, a weed-covered under-body and so on.

$$\text{\textcircled{M}} = 4 \cdot 7 = \frac{L}{\triangle^{\frac{1}{3}}}$$

L = Length on waterline
△ = Immersed volume
SHP = 0·9 × BHP
$\frac{THP}{SHP}$ = Propeller efficiency

Propeller efficiency = 0·43 for 1:1 ratio reduction gearing
Propeller efficiency = 0·53 for 2:1 ratio reduction gearing
Propeller efficiency = 0·59 for 3:1 ratio reduction gearing

See also the previous and following pages.

THRUST HORSE POWER

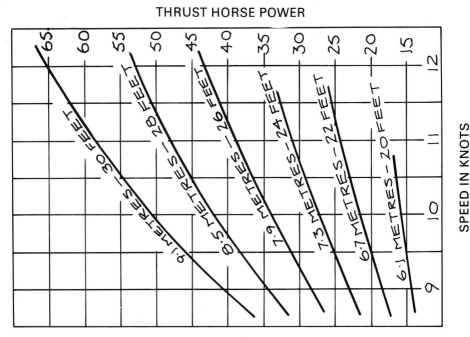

SPEED IN KNOTS

Speed/horsepower—auxiliary yachts (1)

Graph P is for boats 9·1 metres, 30 ft, on the waterline

Graph Q is for boats 7·9 metres, 26 ft, on the waterline

Graph R is for boats 7·3 metres, 24 ft, on the waterline

Graph S is for boats 6·7 metres, 22 ft, on the waterline

Graph T is for boats 6·1 metres, 20 ft, on the waterline

Graph U is for boats 5·5 metres, 18 ft, on the waterline

Graph V is for boats 4·9 metres, 16 ft, on the waterline

$$(M) = 4\cdot7 = \frac{L}{\triangle^{\frac{1}{3}}}$$

L = Length on waterline
△ = Immersed volume
SHP = 0·9 × BHP
$\frac{THP}{SHP}$ = Propeller efficiency

Propeller efficiency = 0·43 for 1:1 ratio reduction gearing
Propeller efficiency = 0·53 for 2:1 ratio reduction gearing
Propeller efficiency = 0·59 for 3:1 ratio reduction gearing

See also the previous and following pages.

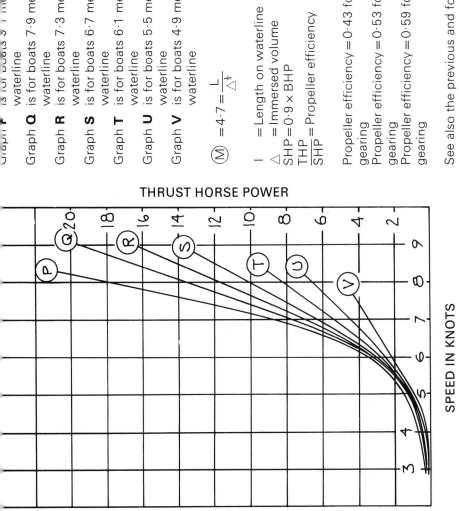

THRUST HORSE POWER

SPEED IN KNOTS

Speed/horsepower—auxiliary yachts (2)

These speeds are reduced, often considerably, by head winds, rough seas, damaged propeller blades, a weed-covered under-body and so on.

Graph **F** is for boats 15·2 metres, 50 ft, on the waterline

Graph **G** is for boats 13·7 metres, 45 ft, on the waterline

Graph **H** is for boats 12·2 metres, 40 ft, on the waterline

Graph **J** is for boats 10·7 metres, 35 ft, on the waterline

Graph **K** is for boats 9·1 metres, 30 ft, on the waterline

$$\text{M} = 4·7 = \frac{L}{\triangle^{\frac{1}{3}}}$$

L = Length on waterline
△ = Immersed volume
SHP = 0·9 × BHP
$\frac{THP}{SHP}$ = Propeller efficiency

Propeller efficiency = 0·43 for 1:1 ratio reduction gearing
Propeller efficiency = 0·53 for 2:1 ratio reduction gearing
Propeller efficiency = 0·59 for 3:1 ratio reduction gearing

See also the previous and following pages.

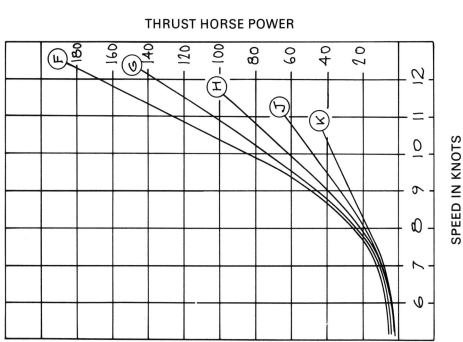

THRUST HORSE POWER

SPEED IN KNOTS

Outboard engines (1)—for small power craft

Maximum Safe Power. Before using this type of power make sure that the transom is strong enough. Weak points are usually along the top edge and at the junction with the topsides.

Power of this order will be expensive on fuel and more than is needed for general cruising or water skiing.

Minimum Planing Power. Should be exceeded for planing types of craft, especially for water skiing. For rough water use, too, some extra power is needed to overcome the additional resistance.

On the graph the upper scale and the dotted vertical lines represent *Length* in feet (L) × *Transom width* in feet (T).

The bottom scale and the solid vertical lines represent *Length* in metres (L) × *Transom width* in metres (T).

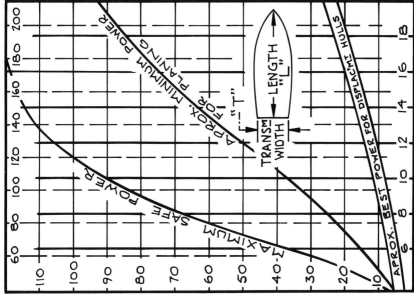

Outboard engines (2)—for inflatable boats

The speed to be expected from an inflatable boat depends on the horse power of the engine, the number of people and the amount of luggage to be carried, the weather conditions etc. This graph shows typical speeds against loading for inflatable craft between 2·7 metres (9 ft) and 5 metres (16 ft 6 in). To get the best speed the inflatable must be pumped up hard and the outboard engine has to be in first class condition, using the correct fuel and the right propeller.

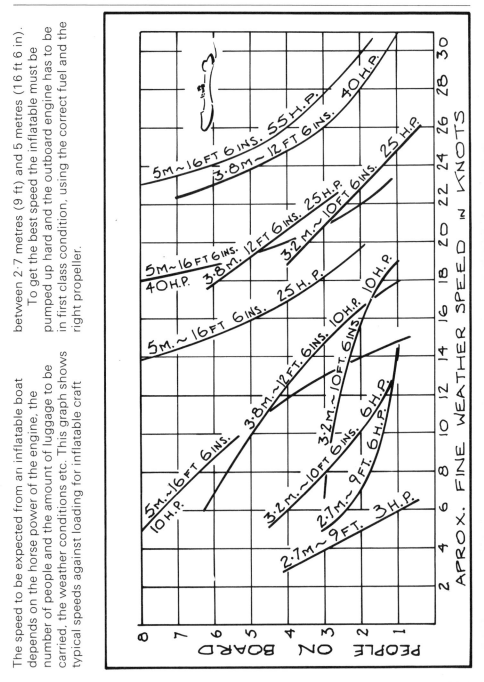

Outboard engines (3)—power for 10 kph (6 mph)

This graph is for small sailing boats, day boats and centreboard dinghies.
The following conditions apply:
1 The waterline length is the basis.
2 A 50% overload has been allowed for.
3 With headwinds or steep seas the speed will drop. In very severe conditions double the horse power shown may be scarcely adequate to maintain way.
4 This graph is a guide only. Easily driven hulls and those lightly laden may need less power. Heavy boats with deeply immersed transoms and a lot of windage are likely to need more power.

The graph is based on the Manual of the BIA, Chicago, to whom acknowledgement is made.

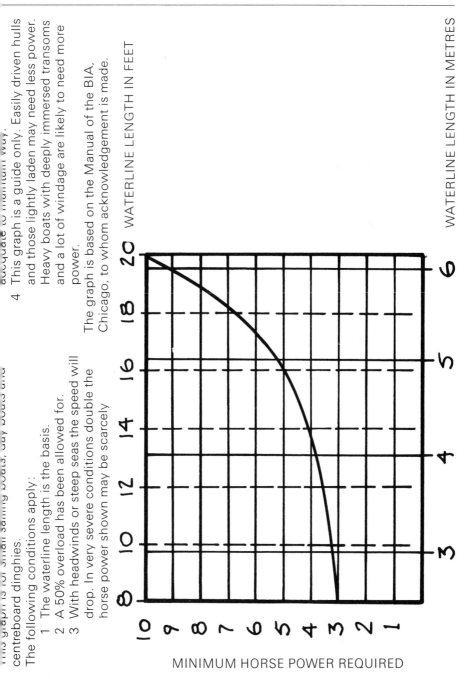

WATERLINE LENGTH IN FEET

WATERLINE LENGTH IN METRES

MINIMUM HORSE POWER REQUIRED

115

Outboard engines (4)—speed-v-weight in runabouts

The speed of an outboard runabout very largely depends on the weight of the craft, when under way, and the horse power of the engine. With the accompanying graph a probable speed for a typical boat of about 4 m (13 ft) can be predicted.

Alternatively a boat with a known weight and engine which does not achieve something like the indicated speed is likely to be suffering from a defect such as a poor bottom shape, or marine growth fouling, or the engine may not be putting out its advertised horse power.

This example shows how the graph is used:

	Kgs	Pounds
Boat weight	270	600
40 h.p. engine	86	190
Battery weight	20	45
Portable fuel tank	45	100
One man (typical average weight)	68	150
Total weight	489	1085

From the graph—the speed should be about 23 knots.

TOTAL WEIGHT OF BOAT & ENGINE, CREW, ETC.

Outboard engine weights

TYPICAL WEIGHTS OF ENGINES AND EQUIPMENT

ENGINE HORSE POWER	ENGINE AND CONTROLS KGS	LBS	BATTERY KGS	LBS	PORTABLE FUEL TANK KGS	LBS
UP TO 3½	16	35				
4 TO 5	25	55			11	25
5½ TO 10	32	70	9	20	23	50
10½ TO 30	48	105	20	45	23	50
30½ TO 50	86	190	20	45	45	100
50½ TO 75	110	240	20	45	45	100
75½ TO 140	140	300	20	45	45	100

Lead/acid batteries

BATTERY CONDITION —Specific Gravity

CHARGE CONDITION	TEMPERATURE 43°C 110°F	38°C 100°F	32°C 90°F	27°C 80°F	21°C 70°F	16°C 60°F	10°C 50°F
	READING ON HYDROMETER						
FULLY DISCHARGED	1·094	1·098	1·102	1·106	1·110	1·114	1·118
HALF DISCHARGED	1·184	1·188	1·192	1·196	1·200	1·204	1·208
CHARGED FULLY	1·264	1·268	1·272	1·276	1·280	1·284	1·288

Propeller graphs—medium and slow speed craft

The graphs, which can be used in a number of ways, are first approximation guides for propellers on small craft. They should not be taken as precise, but then the selection of propellers for boats only approaches an exact science on racing and other very high-speed power boats.

To find the right propeller for a given boat:

1 Decide on the wake factor. This will be between 30% and zero. This depends mainly on the location of the propeller relative to the hull. A sailing cruiser with a propeller well sheltered behind a wide stern-post, or a heavy displacement hull-form with full aft sections, will have wake factors equal to about 30% of the vessel's speed. A power boat with a propeller well exposed below the whole hull should have a very small wake factor.

2 Add the boat's speed to the wake factor
For example if the craft is designed for 10 knots and the wake factor is 20%:
   20% of 10 knots = 2 knots.
   10 plus 2 = 12 knots.
   Select the graph for 12 knots 'water-past-propeller' speed.

3 Determine the propeller r.p.m. at the vessel's full speed. If the engine achieves a peak of 2,800 r.p.m. and there is a 2:1 reduction gear the propeller r.p.m. is
$$\frac{2,800}{2} = 1,400 \text{ r.p.m.}$$

4 Select the *Diameter* curve relating to *shaft* horse power (see note in later section) and work along it until it crosses the correct r.p.m. axis.
Read across to get the correct Diameter (left side in mm, right side in inches).

5 Then select the *Pitch* curve relating to the *shaft* horse power and work along it until it crosses the correct r.p.m. axis.
Read across for the correct Pitch (left side for mm, right side for inches).

6 The resulting figures will be a first approximation. The diameter figure should suffice for determining such matters as propeller aperture size allowing for tip clearance. This latter should be 15% of the diameter, and never less than 8%. The diameter figure should also be adequate for making a propeller cost estimate.

The graphs can also be used to discover if a fitted propeller is correct. For instance, knowing the propeller on the boat, if the speed seems inadequate it is easy to discover if the fault is due to the wrong pitch or diameter. To do this:

1. Determine the actual diameter and pitch of the propeller. As the figures stamped on the boss are not always correct the propeller should be measured.
2. Determine the true boat speed by running accurately over a measured mile. Correct this for the 'speed-past-propeller' by adding the wake factor.
3. Select the graphs corresponding to the calculated speed of water past the propeller. (One graph for *diameter*, one for *pitch*.)
4. On the graphs select the horse power curve relating to the shaft horse power of the engine (see note re shaft horse power).
5. On the vertical ordinate of the propeller r.p.m. (not the same as the engine r.p.m. if a reduction gear is fitted) read off the recommended propeller diameter, or pitch on the respective graph.
6. Compare the recommended diameter and pitch with the actual measurements of the propeller. Any serious difference suggests that the wrong propeller is fitted.

If the true propeller size agrees with the charts then the indications are that there is some reason not connected with the propeller which is causing the loss of speed.

In practice a loss of speed is often caused by more than one factor. The propeller may be partly to blame, but the hull may also be covered with marine growth, extra weights may have been added since the boat was built, there may be shaft wear, poor trim, and so on, which can all contribute.

Above all it must be appreciated that these graphs are preliminary guides and not final selection recommendations.

Note: Shaft horse power.

The published output of an engine will normally be the horse power of the engine with its auxiliaries, such as water-pump and alternator, coupled up. But as some manufacturers still publish the output without the load from these essential components, the horse power figures should be checked with the maker. The shaft horse power is the actual horse power delivered to the propeller. It will be less than the published figure since there are losses at the stern gland, stern bearing, in

continued overleaf

Propeller graphs—for 6 knots water velocity past propeller

the gear-box, due to vibration, at plummer blocks and so on. The losses are greater if the engine is not properly aligned. It is usual for the shaft horse power in small craft to be between 90% and 70% of the published horse power. A bad installation or an abused engine may result in greater losses. Naturally the assumption must be that the engine is in reasonable and fairly new condition.

Propeller diameter
This graph is for 6 knots water velocity past the propeller.

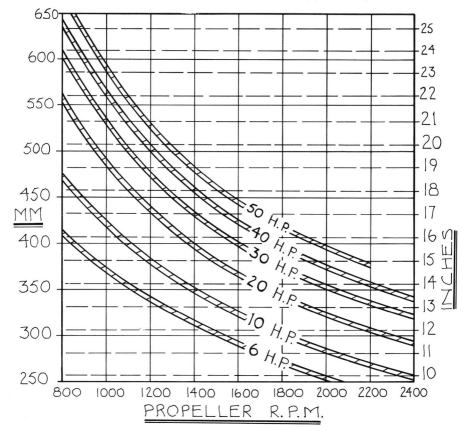

Propeller pitch

This graph is for 6 knots water velocity past the propeller.

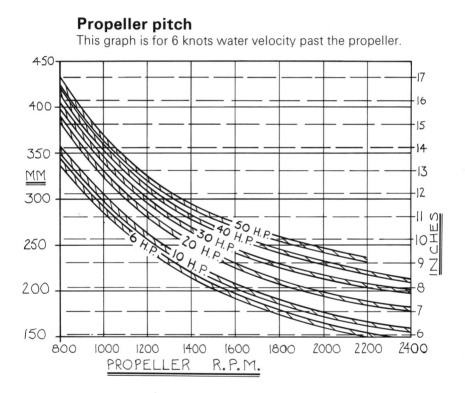

Propeller graphs—for 8 knots water velocity past propeller

Propeller diameter

This graph is for 8 knots water velocity past the propeller.

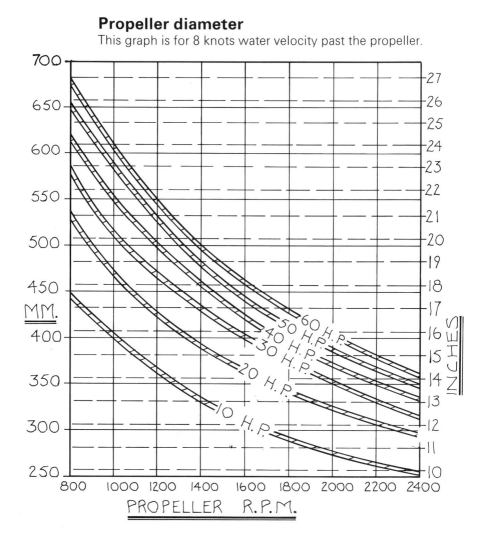

Propeller pitch

This graph is for 8 knots water velocity past the propeller.

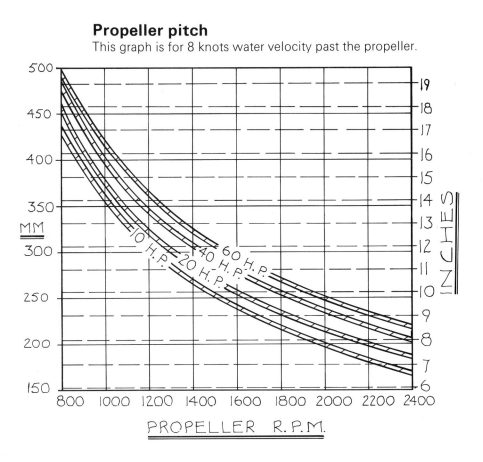

Propeller diameter

This graph is for 10 knots water velocity past the propeller.

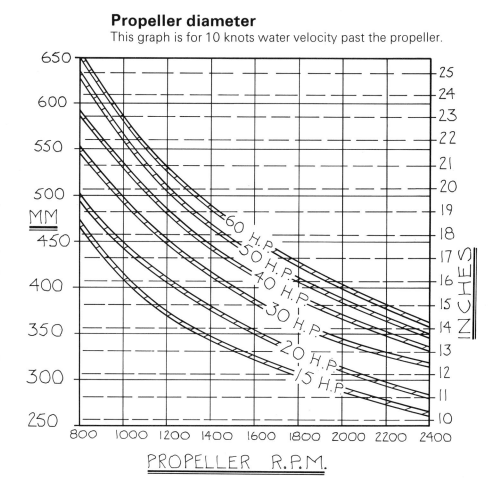

PROPELLER R.P.M.

Propeller pitch

This graph is for 10 knots water velocity past the propeller.

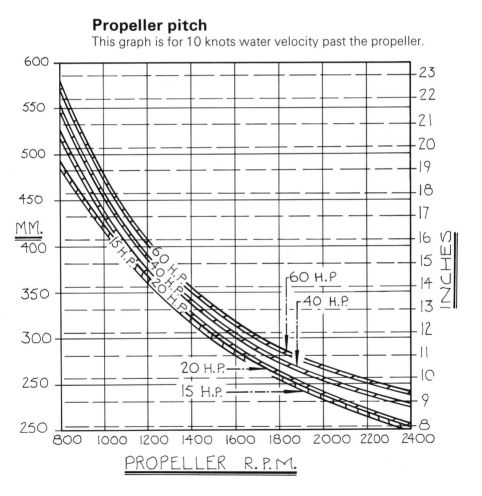

Propeller diameter

This graph is for 12 knots water velocity past the propeller.

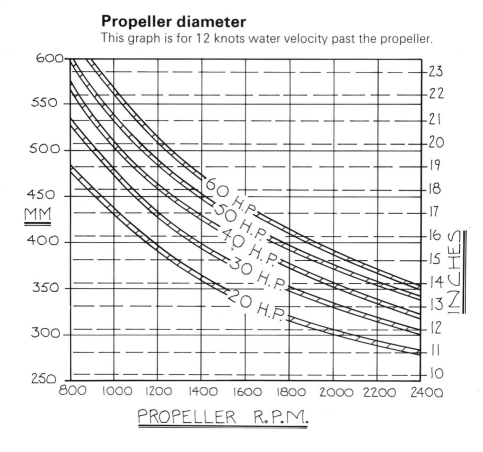

Propeller pitch
This graph is for 12 knots water velocity past the propeller.

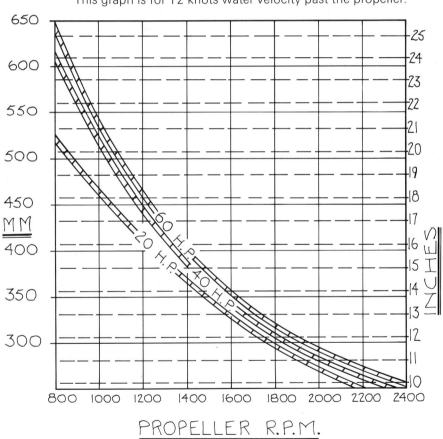

Propeller diameter
This graph is for 14 knots water velocity past the propeller.

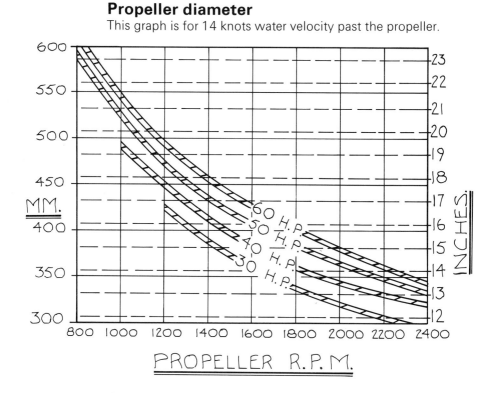

Propeller pitch

This graph is for 14 knots water velocity past the propeller.

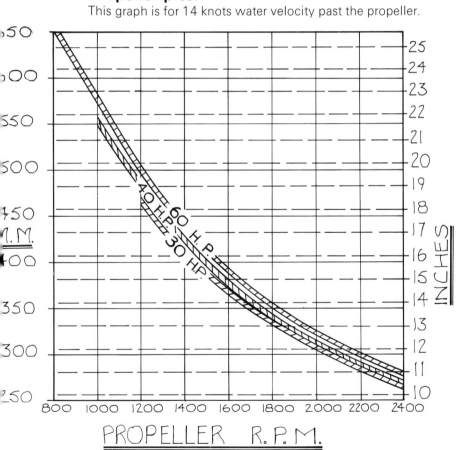

PROPELLER R.P.M.

Stern gear—propeller shafts, glands, stern tubes etc.

The proportions and sizes of flanges etc vary according to the manufacturer. When designing, planning, ordering and fitting it is often desirable, and sometimes essential, to know how much space to allow.

The table gives a guidance to typical manufacturing sizes and proportions and is based on common small craft usage but is not suitable for racing power craft.

Information supplied by courtesy of J. M. Macdonald and Co. Glasgow.

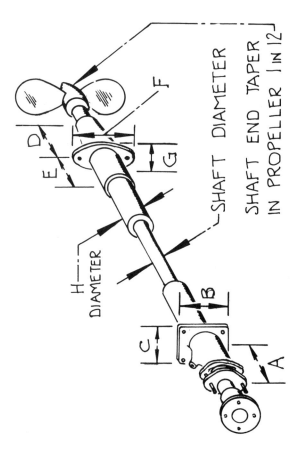

SHAFT DIAMETER

SHAFT END TAPER
IN PROPELLER 1 IN 12

SHAFT DIA. MM	SHAFT DIA. INCHES	A MM	A INCHES	B MM	B INCHES	C MM	C INCHES	D MM	D INCHES	E MM	E INCHES	F MM	F INCHES	G MM	G INCHES	H MM	H INCHES
15·9	⅝	95·3	3¾	79·4	3⅛	50·8	2	69·9	2¾			79·4	3⅛	69·9	2¾	28·6	1⅛
19·1	¾	95·3	3¾	79·4	3⅛	50·8	2	69·9	2¾			79·4	3⅛	69·9	2¾	28·6	1⅛
25·4	1	108	4¼	101·6	4	55·6	2³⁄₁₆	108	4¼			101·6	4	82·6	3¼	38·1	1½
28·6	1⅛	108	4¼	101·6	4	55·6	2³⁄₁₆	108	4¼			101·6	4	82·6	3¼	38·1	1½
31·8	1¼	101·6	4	88·9	3½ DIA.			95·3	3¾	63·5	2½	114·3	4½	69·9	2¾	44·5	1¾
34·9	1⅜	114·3	4½	114·3	4½ DIA.			114·3	4½	76·2	3	139·7	5½	82·6	3¼	50·8	2
38·1	1½	114·3	4½	114·3	4½ DIA.			114·3	4½	76·2	3	139·7	5½	82·6	3¼	50·8	2
41·3	1⅝	109·5	4⁵⁄₁₆	114·3	4½	88·9	3½	152·4	6	76·2	3	165·1	6½	101·6	4	63·5	2½
44·5	1¾	109·5	4⁵⁄₁₆	114·3	4½	88·9	3½	152·4	6	76·2	3	165·1	6½	101·6	4	63·5	2½
50·8	2	139·7	5½	139·7	5½	101·6	4	152·4	6	114·3	4½	177·8	7	120·7	4¾	76·2	3
57·2	2¼	177·8	7	165·1	6½ DIA.			190·5	7½	120·7	4¾	203·2	8	133·4	5¼	88·9	3½
63·5	2½	177·8	7	165·1	6½ DIA.			190·5	7½	120·7	4¾	203·2	8	133·4	5¼	88·9	3½

Propeller shafts—sizes-v-b.h.p. and r.p.m.

R. P. M.

B.H.P	3000	2000	1500	1000	500
3	12	14	15·5	17·5	22
6	15·5	17·5	19·5	22	28
10	18	21	23	26·5	33
20	23	26·5	29	33	42
30	26·5	30	33	38	48
40	29	33	36·5	42	53
50	31	35·5	39·5	45	56·5
75	35·5	41	45	51·5	65
100	39·5	45	49·5	56·5	71·5
125	42·5	48·5	53	61	77
150	45	51·5	56·5	65	82
200	49·5	56·5	62·5	71·5	90
250	53	61	67	77	97
300	56·5	65	71·5	82	103
350	59·5	68·5	75	86	108
400	62·5	71·5	78·5	90	113
500	67·5	77	85	97	122

SHAFT DIAMETER in M.M.

R. P. M.

B.H.P.	3000	2000	1500	1000	500
3	1/2	9/16	5/8	11/16	7/8
6	5/8	11/16	3/4	7/8	1 1/8
10	11/16	13/16	7/8	1 1/16	1 5/16
20	7/8	1 1/16	1 1/8	1 5/16	1 5/8
30	1 1/16	1 3/16	1 5/16	1 1/2	1 7/8
40	1 1/8	1 5/16	1 7/16	1 5/8	2 1/16
50	1 1/4	1 3/8	1 9/16	1 3/4	2 1/4
75	1 3/8	1 5/8	1 3/4	2	2 9/16
100	1 9/16	1 3/4	1 15/16	2 1/4	2 13/16
125	1 11/16	1 15/16	2 1/16	2 3/8	3
150	1 3/4	2	2 1/4	2 9/16	3 1/4
200	1 15/16	2 1/4	2 7/16	2 13/16	3 9/16
250	2 1/16	2 3/8	2 5/8	3	3 13/16
300	2 1/4	2 9/16	2 13/16	3 1/4	4 1/16
350	2 5/16	2 11/16	2 15/16	3 3/8	4 1/4
400	2 7/16	2 13/16	3 1/16	3 9/16	4 7/16
500	2 11/16	3	3 5/16	3 13/16	4 13/16

SHAFT DIAMETER IN INCHES

Rubber shaft bearings

Water lubricated. Recommended especially for use in shallow and gritty waters.

SHAFT DIAMETER		OUTSIDE DIAMT		LENGTH	
MM.	INS.	MM.	INS.	MM.	INS.
19·1	¾	31·8	1¼	76·2	3
22·2	⅞	34·9	1⅜	88·9	3½
25·4	1	38·1	1½	101·6	4
28·6	1⅛	41·3	1⅝	114·3	4½
31·8	1¼	44·5	1¾	127	5
34·9	1⅜	47·6	1⅞	139·7	5½
38·1	1½	50·8	2	152·4	6
41·3	1⅝	54	2⅛	165·1	6½
44·5	1¾	60·3	2⅜	177·8	7
47·6	1⅞	66·7	2⅝	190·5	7½
50·8	2	66·7	2⅝	203·2	8
57·2	2¼	76·2	3	228·6	9
60·3	2⅜	79·4	3⅛	241·3	9½
63·5	2½	82·6	3¼	254	10
63·5	2½	85·7	3⅜	254	10
66·7	2⅝	88·9	3½	266·7	10½
69·9	2¾	88·9	3½	279·4	11
69·9	2¾	95·3	3¾	279·4	11
76·2	3	95·3	3¾	304·8	12
76·2	3	101·6	4	304·8	12

Propeller shaft bearings—spacing

To find the spacing of propeller shaft bearings:

1 Rule a line from the shaft size on scale 2 to modulus on scale 4.
2 Rule a line from point of intersection on scale 3 to connect with propeller Revs per Minute on scale 1.
3 Extend this last line to scale 5 and read off the answer.

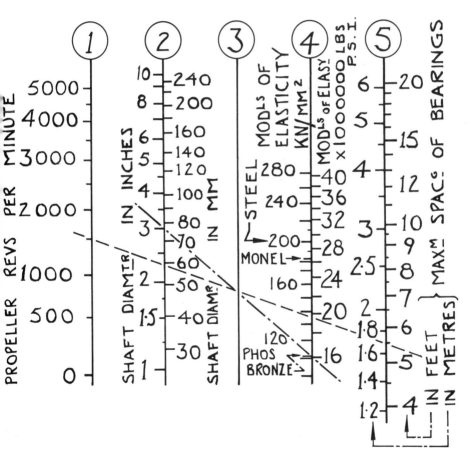

SECTION 6 — Design

The human figure—space required

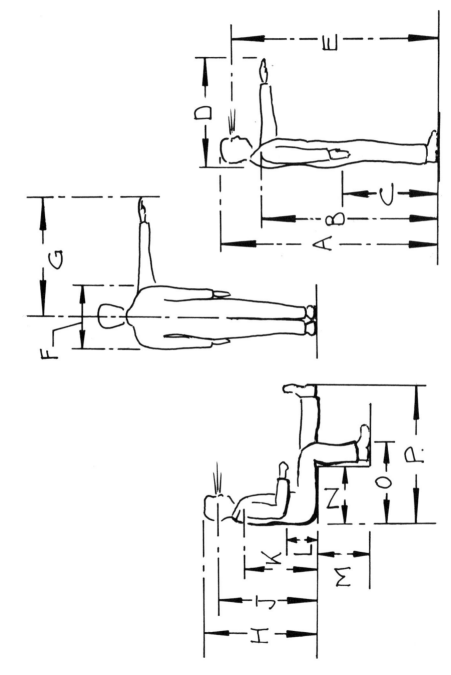

Key Dimensions & Typical Use

		Tall Man		Average Man		Small Woman	
		mm	ft & in	mm	ft & in	mm	ft & in
A	Headroom*	1880	6 — 2	1740	5 — 8½	1455	4 — 9¼
B	Shoulder height — for restricted or shaped doorways	1435	4 — 8½	1400	4 — 7	1200	3 — 11¼
C	Hand height — for tiller when standing	840	2 — 9	740	2 — 5	655	2 — 1¾
D	Reach forward — Engine controls from helmsman's seat†	925	3 — 0½	845	2 — 9¼	600	1 — 11½
E	Eye height standing — window level	1745	5 — 8¾	1630	5 — 4¼	1340	4 — 4¾
F	Shoulder width — Narrow or shaped doorways	505	1 — 7¾	465	1 — 6¼	375	1 — 2¾
G	Side reach — Instrument controls beside chart table†	925	3 — 0½	885	2 — 11	765	2 — 6
H	Headroom above seat — settees under side deck*	960	3 — 1¾	900	2 — 11½	740	2 — 5¼
J	Eye height above seat — deckhouse saloon windows	845	2 — 9¼	730	2 — 4¾	620	2 — 0½
K	Shoulder above seat — Back rests behind seats	640	2 — 1¼	580	1 — 10¾	480	1 — 7
L	Elbow above seat — Arm rest above seat	270	10¾	220	8¾	145	5¾
M	Seat above sole level — Seat heights	470	1 — 6½	420	1 — 4½	365	1 — 2¼
N	Thigh length — Seat width	520	1 — 8½	480	1 — 7	420	1 — 4½
O	Back to knee — Helmsman's seat space above toe space	660	2 — 0½	590	1 — 11¼	520	1 — 8½
P	Back to outstretched foot — Cockpit well width	1185	3 — 10¾	1060	3 — 5¾	890	2 — 11

*Allow 100 mm (4 in) for Hats etc.
†Reduce by about 150 mm (6 in) for full grasp

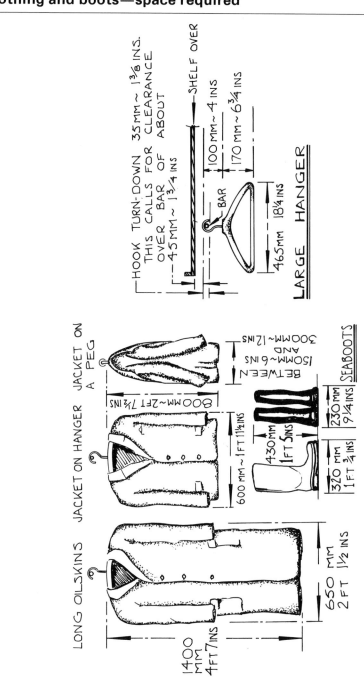

HOOK TURN-DOWN 35mm ~ 1⅜ INS.
THIS CALLS FOR CLEARANCE OVER BAR OF ABOUT 45mm ~ 1¾ INS

SHELF OVER

BAR

100 mm ~ 4 INS

170 mm ~ 6¾ INS

465mm 18¼ INS

LARGE HANGER

JACKET ON A PEG

JACKET ON HANGER

LONG OILSKINS

800 mm ~ 2FT 7½ INS

600 mm ~ 1FT 11½ INS

1400 MM
4FT 7INS

650 MM
2 FT 1½ INS

BETWEEN 150MM ~ 6 INS AND 300MM ~ 12 INS

SEABOOTS

430MM
1FT 5INS

230 MM
9¼ INS

320 MM
1FT ¾ INS

Bunk sizes

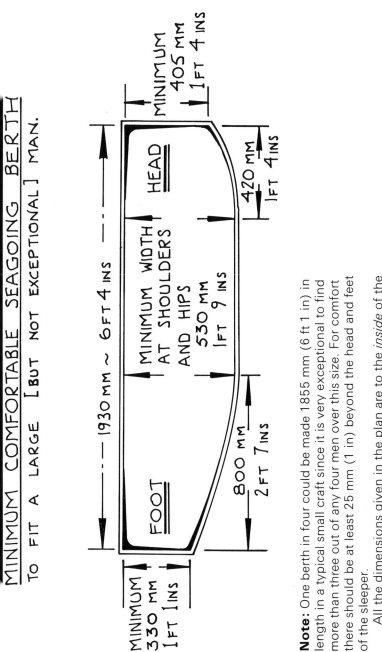

MINIMUM COMFORTABLE SEAGOING BERTH
TO FIT A LARGE [BUT NOT EXCEPTIONAL] MAN.

1930 MM ~ 6FT 4 INS

MINIMUM WIDTH AT SHOULDERS AND HIPS
530 MM
1FT 9 INS

HEAD

MINIMUM 405 MM 1FT 4 INS

420 MM 1FT 4 INS

FOOT

800 MM
2 FT 7 INS

MINIMUM 330 MM 1 FT 1 INS

Note: One berth in four could be made 1855 mm (6 ft 1 in) in length in a typical small craft since it is very exceptional to find more than three out of any four men over this size. For comfort there should be at least 25 mm (1 in) beyond the head and feet of the sleeper.

All the dimensions given in the plan are to the *inside* of the berth. Where the ship's side slopes out, the width dimensions can be reduced a little.

Chart table, chair—recommended sizes

Especially in boats under about 10 metres (32 ft) it is often hard to fit in a proper chart table and seat. The dimensions here are the minimum practicable. If the seat has to be lowered it will probably be best to lower the chart table almost the same amount, and extra foot-room should be worked in.

Chart table. Big charts may be 1300 mm (4 ft 3 in) when opened out, so the table top should be at least this size where possible.

Chart drawer. Folded charts require a drawer in excess of 712 mm (28 in) by 535 mm (21 in). The depth and number of drawers depends on how many charts are to be carried. 25 folded charts make a pile 12 mm ($\frac{1}{2}$ in) thick.

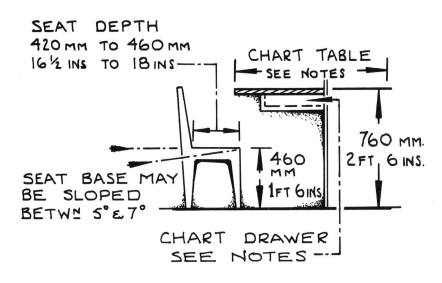

SEAT DEPTH
420 mm TO 460 mm
16½ INS TO 18 INS

CHART TABLE
SEE NOTES

760 mm.
2 FT 6 INS.

460 MM
1 FT 6 INS

SEAT BASE MAY
BE SLOPED
BETWⁿ 5° & 7°

CHART DRAWER
SEE NOTES

Desk or dressing table
The height of a desk or dressing table should not be varied just because there is less headroom over it, or because the cabin space round it is limited. There have been fashions for lower levels for these working surfaces, but they tend to conflict with convenience and comfort.

Desk, dressing table, stool—sizes

    If necessary desks can be much smaller than the one shown in the plan view. In large yachts' engine rooms, for example, an under-size desk is better than none. However the dimensions given here should not be under-cut without good reason.

    Likewise the seat size of 250 mm (10 in) wide by 150 mm (6 in) deep at the top can be reduced, especially if there is good padding. But small seats become uncomfortable sooner than large ones.

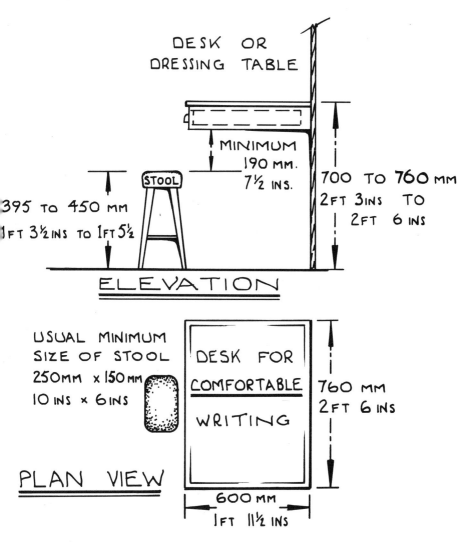

DESK OR DRESSING TABLE

MINIMUM 190 MM. 7½ INS.

700 TO 760 MM 2FT 3INS TO 2FT 6 INS

STOOL

395 TO 450 MM 1FT 3½ INS TO 1FT 5½

ELEVATION

USUAL MINIMUM SIZE OF STOOL 250MM x 150MM 10 INS × 6 INS

DESK FOR COMFORTABLE WRITING

760 MM 2FT 6 INS

PLAN VIEW

600 MM 1FT 11½ INS

Upholstery, bookcase—sizes

Upholstery thicknesses – plastic and rubber materials

Thickness	As mattress or cushion	As backrest
25 mm/1 in	For use on cot or root berths and other berths where there is a canvas or cloth base	Scarcely comfortable. May be used where weight saving is important
50 mm/2 in	For use on dished, radiussed or scooped out bases	Used to save space, weight and cost. Fairly common in very small craft
75 mm/3 in	In general use on very small craft, and inexpensive boats. Adequately comfortable	Widespread. Fully comfortable
100 mm/4 in	Much preferred to 75 mm. General in quality craft	Widespread. Very comfortable
150 mm/6 in	Sumptuous but may be too deep for hot climates. Note that full headroom is still needed over the top surface	May be inconveniently thick and may look wrong on craft under 12 m (40 ft)

Book case, book rack design notes

For an average book allow 38 mm ($1\frac{1}{2}$ in) width.
For a paper-back book allow 16 mm ($\frac{5}{8}$ in) width.
For large books and magazines allow 300 mm ($11\frac{3}{4}$ in) height, H_1.
For paper-back books allow 185 mm ($7\frac{1}{4}$ in) height, H_2.
For large books and magazines allow 215 mm ($8\frac{1}{2}$ in) depth, D_1.
For paper-back books allow 115 mm ($4\frac{1}{2}$ in) depth, D_2.

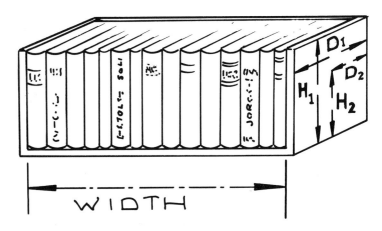

Tables and seats—minimum area

Tables and seats

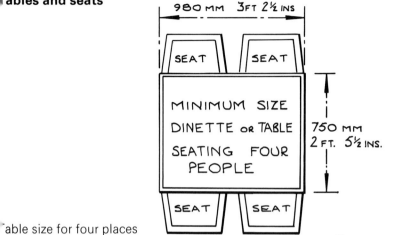

Table size for four places

This should be considered the minimum to allow adequate comfort and space for crockery etc, at least in harbour.

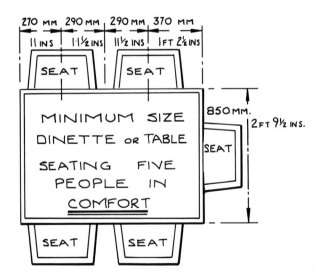

Table size for five or more places

For comfortable meals in harbour, or in a large boat at sea, the dimensions shown are a minimum.

The size of table needed for seven, nine, eleven etc can be worked out from the drawing.

Galley—recommended dimensions

ELEVATION

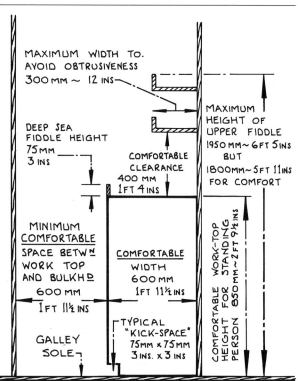

MAXIMUM WIDTH TO. AVOID OBTRUSIVENESS 300 mm ~ 12 INS

DEEP SEA FIDDLE HEIGHT 75 mm 3 INS

MAXIMUM HEIGHT OF UPPER FIDDLE 1950 mm ~ 6 FT 5 INS BUT 1800 mm ~ 5 FT 11 INS FOR COMFORT

COMFORTABLE CLEARANCE 400 mm 1 FT 4 INS

MINIMUM COMFORTABLE SPACE BETW^N WORK TOP AND BULKH^D 600 mm 1 FT 11½ INS

COMFORTABLE WIDTH 600 mm 1 FT 11½ INS

COMFORTABLE WORK-TOP HEIGHT FOR STANDING PERSON 850 mm ~ 2 FT 9½ INS

GALLEY SOLE

TYPICAL "KICK-SPACE" 75 mm x 75 mm 3 INS. x 3 INS

PLAN VIEW

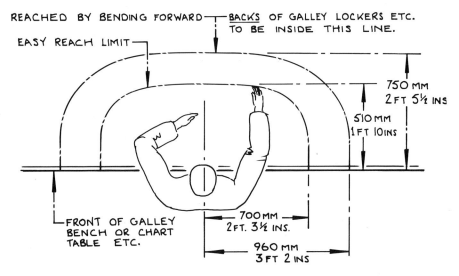

REACHED BY BENDING FORWARD — BACKS OF GALLEY LOCKERS ETC. TO BE INSIDE THIS LINE.

EASY REACH LIMIT

750 mm 2 FT 5½ INS

510 mm 1 FT 10 INS

FRONT OF GALLEY BENCH OR CHART TABLE ETC.

700 mm 2 FT. 3½ INS.

960 mm 3 FT 2 INS

Gas cylinders—size and weight

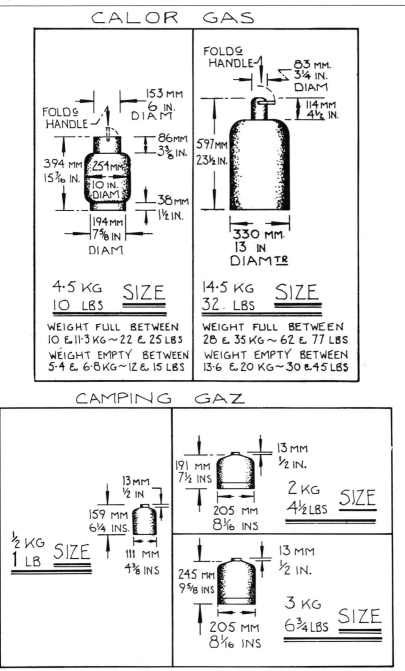

CALOR GAS

FOLDS HANDLE

153 MM
6 IN. DIAM

86 MM
3⅜ IN.

394 MM
15⁷⁄₁₆ IN.

254 MM

10 IN. DIAM

38 MM
1½ IN.

194 MM
7⅝ IN DIAM

4·5 KG
10 LBS   SIZE

WEIGHT FULL BETWEEN
10 & 11·3 KG ~ 22 & 25 LBS
WEIGHT EMPTY BETWEEN
5·4 & 6·8 KG ~ 12 & 15 LBS

FOLDS HANDLE

83 MM
3¼ IN. DIAM

114 MM
4½ IN.

597 MM
23½ IN.

330 MM
13 IN DIAMTR

14·5 KG
32 LBS   SIZE

WEIGHT FULL BETWEEN
28 & 35 KG ~ 62 & 77 LBS
WEIGHT EMPTY BETWEEN
13·6 & 20 KG ~ 30 & 45 LBS

CAMPING GAZ

13 MM
½ IN

159 MM
6¼ INS

111 MM
4⅜ INS

½ KG
1 LB   SIZE

191 MM
7½ INS

13 MM
½ IN.

205 MM
8¹⁄₁₆ INS

2 KG
4½ LBS   SIZE

245 MM
9⅝ INS

13 MM
½ IN.

205 MM
8¹⁄₁₆ INS

3 KG
6¾ LBS   SIZE

147

Crockery, glassware, bottles—standard dimensions

The dimensions given here are the maximum sizes for normal crockery. Lockers and shelves built to these sizes will take any normal set of crockery and glassware.

Note that dimension A is the height of one plate. B is the increment for further stacking plates.

Handle thicknesses are given because cups and mugs may be stowed in special racks or lockers with slots to take the handles. These slots should be extended well down as some handles protrude from near the bottom of the cup and mug body.

Traditionally the crockery was bought before the galley was made so that the galley racks could be designed round the crockery. Nowadays it is advisable to check that the crockery intended for a particular boat will fit the galley, which is likely to be a mass-produced compartment with standard fittings.

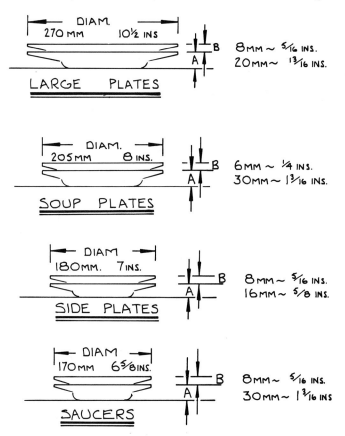

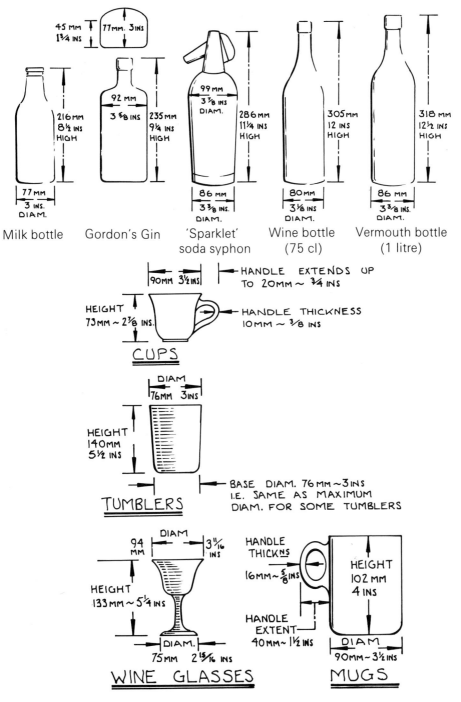

45 mm 1¾ INS   77 mm. 3 INS

216 mm 8½ INS HIGH

77 MM 3 INS. DIAM.

Milk bottle

92 mm 3⅝ INS   235 mm 9¼ INS HIGH

Gordon's Gin

99 mm 3⅞ INS DIAM.   286 mm 11¼ INS HIGH

86 MM 3⅜ INS. DIAM.

'Sparklet' soda syphon

305 mm 12 INS HIGH

80 MM 3⅛ INS DIAM.

Wine bottle (75 cl)

318 MM 12½ INS HIGH

86 MM 3⅜ INS. DIAM.

Vermouth bottle (1 litre)

90 MM 3½ INS   HANDLE EXTENDS UP TO 20 MM ~ ¾ INS

HEIGHT 73 MM ~ 2⅞ INS.   HANDLE THICKNESS 10 MM ~ ⅜ INS

CUPS

DIAM 76 MM 3 INS

HEIGHT 140 MM 5½ INS

BASE DIAM. 76 MM ~ 3 INS I.E. SAME AS MAXIMUM DIAM. FOR SOME TUMBLERS

TUMBLERS

94 MM   DIAM 3¹¹⁄₁₆ INS

HEIGHT 133 MM ~ 5¼ INS

DIAM. 75 MM 2¹³⁄₁₆ INS

WINE GLASSES

HANDLE THICKNS 16 MM ~ ⅝ INS

HEIGHT 102 MM 4 INS

HANDLE EXTENT 40 MM ~ 1½ INS

DIAM 90 MM ~ 3½ INS

MUGS

149

Small power boat seats

Maximum allowable impaired vision forward

Metric

Boat length	Distance ahead at water level
5 m	14·6
6 m	17·4
7 m	20·2
9 m	25·8

Imperial

Boat length	Distance ahead at water level
16 ft	47
20 ft	58
24 ft	69
28 ft	80

The wheel rim, windshield framing or other structure should not obstruct forward vision.

EYE LEVEL

USE THIS HEIGHT TO CALCULATE IMPAIRED VISION DISTANCE

760 MM 30 INS

LEVEL OF TOP OF COMPRESSED CUSHION

UNDER STEERING WHEEL TO TOP OF CUSHION BETWEEN 190mm ~ 7½ INS & 280mm ~ 11 ins

CENTRE OF WHEEL TO BACKREST BETW'N 585 MM ~ 23 INS. & 635mm ~ 25 INS.

LINE OF VISION OVER BOW

WATER-LINE

IMPAIRED VISION

Sail covers—measurement plan

It is possible to make a sail cover without a drawing but in practice the best approach is to make a sail cover drawing and this means putting the sail on its boom. It should be stowed in the normal way, with the battens in and the slides on the mast track if this is the owner's practice.

Coloured chalk is used to mark off the locations of the girths (distances round the sail-and-boom or, in the case of GE, GF and GH, distance round sail-and-mast).

All dimensions prefixed G on the diagram are girths. Their locations are based on ordinates (distances off) from the fore side of the mast, in line with the under side of the boom.

Halliard winches are located by height and if they are not exactly on the fore side, or exactly athwartships, this must be shown. The diameter (shown as X) and the distance off the mast (shown as Z) must be detailed.

Other obstructions like spinnaker boom cups must be marked in, with their size and exact location.

A sail cover needs to be cut full, in fact slightly baggy, so that water on a wet sail will drain away and the bottom should be sufficiently open to allow a circulation of air to dry up surface moisture. But the cover must not be cut so full that it flaps in the breeze and destroys itself in a season.

A cover should extend along the boom at least 75 mm (3 in) beyond the extreme aft end of the sail. If the boom diameter is more than 125 mm (5 in), the cover should extend the boom's diameter beyond the sail.

At the top the cover must extend up the mast beyond the sail for enough to allow the lashing to be secured tightly round the mast. This will normally be of the order of 50 mm (2 in) but the dimension depends partly on the lashing method used.

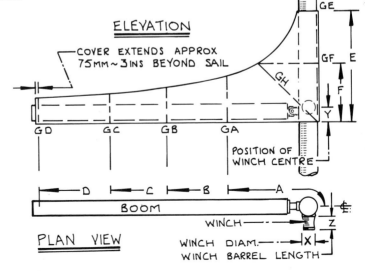

Seacock sizes

Seacocks are measured by the bore of the pipe to which they are attached. At present the sizes are not standardized therefore buy the cock and the fittings at the same time from the same maker.

Approximate guide:

Toilets
Small craft—Discharge, 38 mm/$1\frac{1}{2}$ in—Inlet, 20 mm/$\frac{3}{4}$ in.
Over 15 m/50 ft—Discharge, 50 mm/2 in—Inlet, 25 mm/1 in.

Basins and sinks
Small size—wastes, 20 mm/$\frac{3}{4}$ in.
Average size—wastes, 32–38 mm/$1\frac{1}{4}$–$1\frac{1}{2}$ in.

Steering—rudder, wheel etc.

Rudder
Rudder stops should normally be fitted at 33° each side, since beyond this angle the steering effect is lessened. Sometimes however, rudder stops are fitted beyond this angle to allow the rudder to swing to say 60° and act as a partial brake. If so the rudder, its stock and controls have to be made extra strong to withstand the pressure from full power going astern.

Normally rudder stall will occur at about 17° if the rudder is put over violently. Therefore where the helm is very light, e.g. where there is a tiller on a small craft, consideration should be given to introducing a light resisting pressure, or marking helm positions at 17°.

A balanced rudder normally has about $\frac{1}{6}$ of the area ahead of the centreline of the stock.

Wheel
A steering wheel should be as large as possible. About 75 mm (3 in) is needed outside a rim or spoke for knuckle clearance. The minimum practical diameter for continuous use is about 350 mm (14 in) and the larger the better. It is generally better to have a large diameter ungeared wheel than a small one with

gearing. In practice steering wheels are seldom fitted or available for small craft nowadays much over 1200 mm (4 ft) diameter though they used to be regularly made up to 2400 mm (8 ft) diameter.

Anchor cable and stowage space

Approximate stowage space for 20 metres (66 ft or 11 fathoms).

Notes:
Ample reserve space should always be allowed.
The compartment for chain cable should taper towards the bottom.
No overhang or other structure should protrude into the space.
The clench plate should always be above the stowed chain.

CABLE DIAMETER		APPROX STOWAGE SPACE	
MM.	INCHES	CUBIC METRES	CUBIC FEET
5	3/16	0·005	0·16
6·5	1/4	0·008	0·27
8	5/16	0·010	0·35
10	3/8	0·015	0·56
11	7/16	0·021	0·76
13	1/2	0·030	1·0
14	9/16	0·037	1·3
16	5/8	0·048	1·7
19	3/4	0·070	2·5

Ventilation

Ventilator diameter	Cross sectional Area		Notes
50mm/2 in	1900 mm²	3 in²	Too small. Promotes little ventilation especially in calm weather
75 mm/3 in	4400 mm²	7 in²	Suitable for craft below about 9 m (29 ft) overall
100 mm/4 in	7800 mm²	12·5 in²	Smallest reliable size for all-round effectiveness*
150 mm/6 in	17700 mm²	28 in²	Recommended for craft over about 13 m (43 ft) overall

*This is the 'Standard vent' size included in the table below

As a guide each person needs 0·4 cubic metres of air per minute (14 cu. ft).

An engine requires about 0·07 cubic metres per horse power per minute for combustion (2·5 cu. ft).

In temperate climates air intake should approximately equal exhaust but if the trunking is long or tortuous extra should be allowed for. Inflow will not travel as fast as exhaust gases and so extra area must be allowed for also.

Engine room ventilation is needed for the crew and the engine plus additional area of 650 sq. mm (1 sq. in) per horse power if the inlet is of the low speed type without fan assistance.

For personnel an air speed of about 900 mm/sec (3 ft/sec) is comfortable.

For hot weather an air speed of 1500 mm/sec (5 ft/sec) is pleasant.

Changes per hour and suggested ventilation

Compartment	Temperate climate	Hot climate	Very hot climate	Notes
Saloon cabins, etc.	8 ch/hr 1 'Standard vent' per 2 people	16 ch/hr 2 'Standard vents' per 2 people	24 ch/hr 3 'Standard vents' per 2 people	In hot climates vents will need wind scoops plus hatches and bigger than standard vents
Toilets of size 2 m × 2 m × 2 m (6·5 ft cube)	15 ch/hr	25 ch/hr	30 ch/hr	Extractor fan recommended when the compartment is occupied. Flow required 4·5 m/sec (15 ft/sec) with 'Standard vent'
Galley	30 ch/hr	36 ch/hr	40 ch/hr	Extractor fan required over cooker to draw off steam and smells and to ensure the required number of changes
Engine room	Depends on horse-power and crew (see above). Inlet area should be 1·5 times exhaust plus 950 sq mm (1½ sq in) per horse power of all engines			Minimum two cowls. One to be trunked to the bilge. Ventilation is often found to be inadequate.

Camber and sheer—how to calculate

Camber To work out the camber curve. The half beam is taken as 'B'. The maximum camber of a deckhead, 'C', is a height chosen by the designer depending on such factors as headroom, appearance, strength, the need to shed water quickly in rough conditions, the advantage of levelling up the weather side deck when the vessel is heeled if she is a sailing yacht, etc.

The camber 'a' at a distance 'd' off the centreline is:

$$a = C \times \frac{d^2}{B^2}$$

N.B. 'a' is the *downward* measurement from the level of maximum camber, as shown in the top sketch.

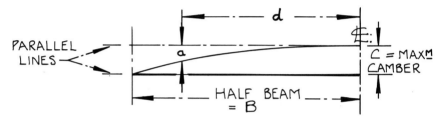

EXAMPLE: To find the drop in the camber curve at quarter beam width (1·1 m off centre-line) when the maximum camber height is 0·15 metres and the half beam is 2·2 metres:

$$a = 0·15 \times \frac{1·1^2}{2·2^2} \text{ metres}$$

$$= 0·0375 \text{ metres, measured downwards.}$$

Camber normally extends evenly from the centreline to the sheer though occasionally there is a flat horizontal section either side of the centreline. In such a case the half-beam (B) in the formula will extend from the side of the flat centre section to the deck edge.

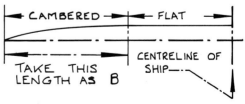

Sheer The same formula is used for measuring sheer, but the measurement is upwards from a horizontal line through the lowest point of the sheer. This point may be at $\frac{3}{4}$ of the length from the bow on a typical yacht and amidship on a traditional merchant vessel.

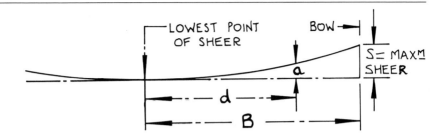

If 'S' is the maximum height of the sheer above the lowest point ('S' will naturally be at the bow) and 'B' is the distance from the lowest point to the highest point measured horizontally, then to find the height of the sheer ('a') at a distance 'd' from the lowest point:

$$a = S \times \frac{d^2}{B^2}$$

The formula can be used similarly for the part of the curve aft of the lowest point.

Diagrammatic method

1 Draw out the full maximum beam AC.
2 Erect the maximum camber height on the centreline BD.
3 Erect a perpendicular from A.
4 Draw a straight line from C to D and continue it to meet the perpendicular from A at X.
5 Divide AB into a number of equal parts.
6 Divide AX into the same number of equal parts.
7 Erect perpendiculars dividing the parts along AB, that is at p, q, r and s.
8 Join C to the dividing points on AX, that is at k, l, m and n.
9 The intersections of the perpendiculars from p, q, r and s with the respective diagonals from C give the points on the camber curve.

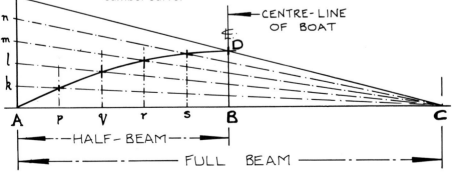

Open boats—average dimensions

Boats intended for rowing, for small outboards or for sailing should not be too extreme if they are to be safe. The graph opposite shows typical dimensions based on the load waterline. The bottom and left hand side of the graph are calibrated in metres while the top and right hand side are in feet. These dimensions are shown in the plan and elevation below, and for each dimension there is a graph.

In general the freeboard at the bow should be at least 115% of the freeboard at half L.W.L. The freeboard at the stern should be at least 85% of the freeboard at half L.W.L.

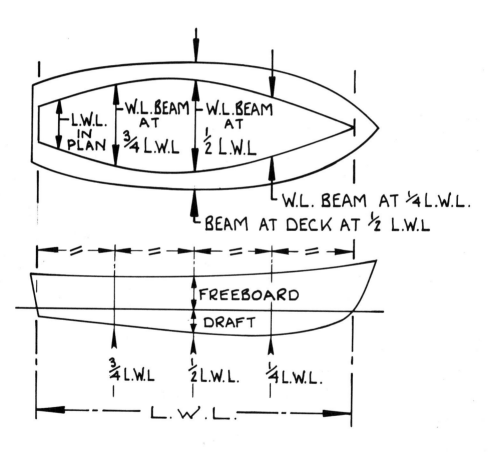

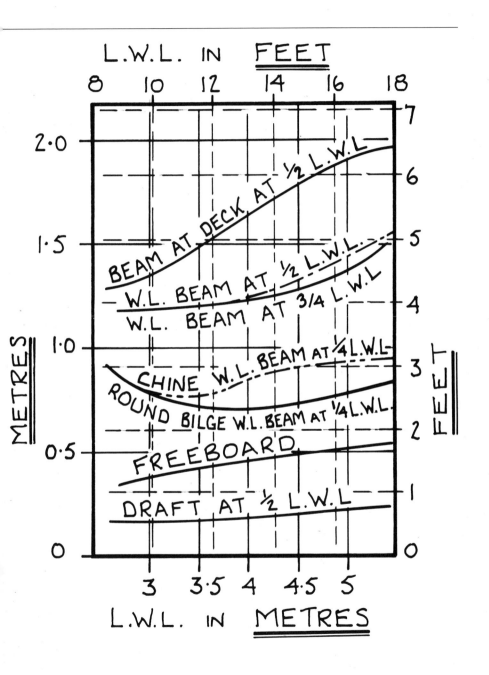

Open boats—typical sail areas

The graph shows safe sail areas for general use on boats between 3 and 5·5 metres and is calibrated in metres at the bottom and on the left hand side, in feet at the top and right hand side. Beginners may require less sail area than those shown but racing boats are likely to have somewhat greater sail areas.

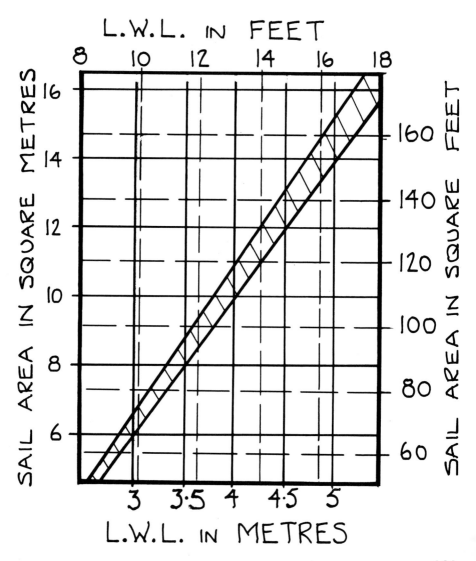

Common welding symbols

TYPE OF WELD	SECTION THROUGH	SYMBOL
FILLET		
SQUARE BUTT		
SINGLE V BUTT		
DOUBLE V BUTT		
SINGLE U BUTT		
DOUBLE U BUTT		
SINGLE BEVEL BUTT		
DOUBLE BEVEL BUTT		

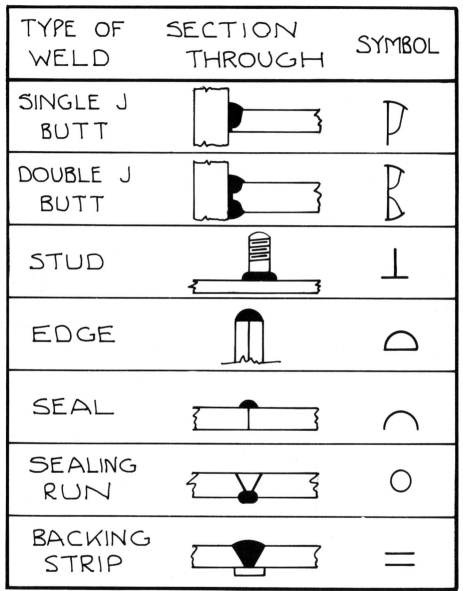

TYPE OF WELD	SECTION THROUGH	SYMBOL
SINGLE J BUTT		
DOUBLE J BUTT		
STUD		
EDGE		
SEAL		
SEALING RUN		
BACKING STRIP		

SECTION 7 — **Tables and formulae** *page*

Conversion factors

The reciprocal is used to convert the quantity in the second column into that in the first —

e.g. Inches × 25·4 = Millimetres
Millimetres × 0·0394 = Inches

To convert	into	Multiplier	Reciprocal
Inches	*Millimetres*	*25·4*	*0·0394*
Length			
$\frac{1}{8}$ths of inches	Millimetres	3·175	0·315
$\frac{1}{16}$ths of inches	Millimetres	1·587	0·630
Inches	Metres	0·025	39·37
Feet	Metres	0·305	3·281
Yards	Metres	0·914	1·094
Miles	Kilometres	1·609	0·621
Sea Miles	Metres	1853·1	0·000539
Miles	Metres	1609·3	0·000621
Area			
Square inches	Square centimetres	6·4516	0·155
Square feet	Square metres	0·0929	10·764
Volume			
Cubic inches	Cubic centimetres	16·387	0·061
Cubic inches	Litres	0·016	62·5
Cubic feet	Cubic metres	0·028	35·315
Cubic yards	Cubic metres	0·765	1·308
Imperial gallons	Litres	4·546	0·220
U.S.A. gallons	Litres	3·785	0·264
Imperial gallons	U.S.A. gallons	1·205	0·830

To convert	into	Multiplier	Reciprocal
Inches	Millimetres	25·4	0·0394

Weight

Grammes	Ounces	0·035	28·35
Pounds (lbs)	Kilogrammes	0·454	2·205
Hundredweights (cwt)	Kilogrammes	50·802	0·020
Tons	French tonnes	1·016	0·984

Density

Pounds per cubic foot	Kilograms per cubic metre	16·019	0·0624

Speed

Kilometres per hour	Metres per second	0·278	3·6
Metres per second	Knots	1·943	
Feet per second	Metres per second	0·305	3·281
Feet per second	Miles per hour	0·682	1·467
Feet per minute	Kilometres per hour	0·018	54·68
Miles per hour	Metres per second	0·447	2·237
Miles per hour	Kilometres per hour	1·609	0·621
Knots	Miles per hour	1·151	

Stress, Work, Energy

Kilograms per sq metre	Pounds per sq foot	0·205	4·88
Kilogram-metres	Foot-pounds	7·23	0·138
Horsepower (metric) Force de Cheval Cheval vapeur	Horsepower (British)	0·986	1·014
Kilowatts (kW)	Horsepower British	1·340	0·746
Watts	B. Th. U per second	0·00095	1055·36

Standard wire gauge—metric and imperial equivalents

MM.	IMPERIAL STANDARD W.G.	DECIMAL EQUIVALENTS INCHES	FRACTIONS INCHES
0·314	30	·0124	
0·345	29	·0136	
0·375	28	·0148	
0·396		·0156	1/64
0·416	27	·0164	
0·457	26	·018	
0·508	25	·020	
0·558	24	·022	
0·609	23	·024	
0·711	22	·028	
0·790		·0312	1/32
0·812	21	·032	
0·914	20	·036	
1		·039	
1·016	19	·040	
1·190		·0469	3/64
1·219	18	·048	
1·422	17	·056	
1·59		·0625	1/16
1·625	16	·064	
1·828	15	·072	
2		·0781	5/64
2·032	14	·080	
2·336	13	·092	
2·38		·0937	3/32
2·640	12	·104	
2·778		·1093	7/64
2·946	11	·116	
3		·118	

MM.	IMPERIAL STANDARD W.G.	DECIMAL EQUIVALENTS INCHES	FRACTIONS INCHES
3·17		·125	1/8
3·251	10	·128	
3·571	9	·1406	9/64
3·657		·144	
3·97		·1562	5/32
4		·1575	
4·064	8	·160	
4·365		·1718	11/64
4·470	7	·176	
4·76		·1875	3/16
4·876	6	·192	
5		·1968	
5·159		·2031	13/64
5·384	5	·212	
5·56		·2187	7/32
5·892	4	·232	
5·952		·2343	15/64
6		·2362	
6·35		·250	1/4
6·400	3	·252	
7		·2756	
7·010	2	·276	
7·14		·2812	9/32
7·620	1	·300	
7·94		·3125	5/16
8		·3150	
8·229	0	·324	
8·73		·3437	11/32
8·839	2/0	·348	

MM.	IMPERIAL STANDARD W.G.	DECIMAL EQUIVALENTS INCHES	FRACTIONS INCHES
9		·3543	
9·448	3/0	·372	
9·52		·375	3/8
10		·3937	
10·16	4/0	·400	
10·32		·4062	13/32
10·97	5/0	·432	
11		·4331	
11·11		·4375	7/16
11·8	6/0	·464	
11·91		·468	15/32
12		·472	
12·70	7/0	·500	1/2
13		·5118	
14		·5512	
14·29		·5625	9/16
15		·5905	
15·87		·625	5/8
16		·6299	
17		·6693	
17·46		·6875	11/16
18		·7087	
19		·7480	
19·05		·750	3/4
20		·7874	
20·64		·8125	13/16
22·22		·875	7/8
23·81		·9375	15/16
25·40		1·000	1

Metal gauges—metric and imperial equivalents

Gauge No.	Thickness	
	mm	*inches*
1	7·61	0·300
2	7·00	0·276
3	6·39	0·252
4	5·88	0·232
5	5·38	0·212
6	4·87	0·192
7	4·46	0·176
8	4·06	0·160
9	3·66	0·144
10	3·25	0·128
11	2·94	0·116
12	2·64	0·104
13	2·34	0·092
14	2·00	0·080
15	1·83	0·072
16	1·62	0·064
17	1·42	0·056
18	1·22	0·048
19	1·01	0·040
20	0·91	0·036
21	0·81	0·032
22	0·71	0·028
23	0·61	0·024
24	0·56	0·022
25	0·51	0·020
26	0·46	0·018
27	0·41	0·016
28	0·36	0·014
29	0·33	0·013
30	0·30	0·012

Millimetres in decimals of an inch

MM.	INCHES	MM.	INCHES	MM.	INCHES	MM.	INCHES	MM.	INCHES	MM.	INCHES	MM.	INCHES	MM.	INCHES	MM.	INCHES	MM.	INCHES
·01	·00039	·21	·00827	·41	·01614	·61	·02402	·81	·03189	2	·0787	22	·8661	42	1·6535	62	2·4409	82	3·2283
·02	·00079	·22	·00866	·42	·01654	·62	·02441	·82	·03228	3	·1181	23	·9055	43	1·6929	63	2·4803	83	3·2677
·03	·00118	·23	·00906	·43	·01693	·63	·02480	·83	·03268	4	·1575	24	·9449	44	1·7323	64	2·5197	84	3·3071
·04	·00157	·24	·00945	·44	·01732	·64	·02520	·84	·03307	5	·1968	25	·9842	45	1·7716	65	2·5590	85	3·3464
·05	·00197	·25	·00984	·45	·01772	·65	·02559	·85	·03346	6	·2362	26	1·0236	46	1·8110	66	2·5984	86	3·3858
·06	·00236	·26	·01024	·46	·01811	·66	·02598	·86	·03386	7	·2756	27	1·0630	47	1·8504	67	2·6378	87	3·4252
·07	·00276	·27	·01063	·47	·01850	·67	·02638	·87	·03425	8	·3150	28	1·1024	48	1·8898	68	2·6772	88	3·4646
·08	·00315	·28	·01102	·48	·01890	·68	·02677	·88	·03465	9	·3543	29	1·1417	49	1·9291	69	2·7165	89	3·5039
·09	·00354	·29	·01142	·49	·01929	·69	·02717	·89	·03504	10	·3937	30	1·1811	50	1·9685	70	2·7559	90	3·5433
·10	·00394	·30	·01181	·50	·01969	·70	·02756	·90	·03543	11	·4331	31	1·2205	51	2·0079	71	2·7953	91	3·5827
·11	·00433	·31	·01220	·51	·02008	·71	·02795	·91	·03583	12	·4724	32	1·2598	52	2·0472	72	2·8346	92	3·6220
·12	·00472	·32	·01260	·52	·02047	·72	·02835	·92	·03622	13	·5118	33	1·2992	53	2·0866	73	2·8740	93	3·6614
·13	·00512	·33	·01299	·53	·02087	·73	·02874	·93	·03661	14	·5512	34	1·3386	54	2·1260	74	2·9134	94	3·7008
·14	·00551	·34	·01339	·54	·02126	·74	·02913	·94	·03701	15	·5905	35	1·3779	55	2·1653	75	2·9527	95	3·7401
·15	·00591	·35	·01378	·55	·02165	·75	·02953	·95	·03740	16	·6299	36	1·4173	56	2·2047	76	2·9921	96	3·7795
·16	·00630	·36	·01417	·56	·02205	·76	·02992	·96	·03780	17	·6693	37	1·4567	57	2·2441	77	3·0315	97	3·8189
·17	·00669	·37	·01457	·57	·02244	·77	·03032	·97	·03819	18	·7087	38	1·4961	58	2·2835	78	3·0709	98	3·8583
·18	·00709	·38	·01496	·58	·02283	·78	·03071	·98	·03858	19	·7480	39	1·5354	59	2·3228	79	3·1102	99	3·8976
·19	·00748	·39	·01535	·59	·02323	·79	·03110	·99	·03898	20	·7874	40	1·5748	60	2·3622	80	3·1496	100	3·9370
·20	·00787	·40	·01575	·60	·02362	·80	·03150	1	·0394	21	·8268	41	1·6142	61	2·4016	81	3·1890		

Millimetres to inches

MILLIMETERS VERSUS INCHES

1 millimeter = 0.039370 inches

millimeters

	0	1	2	3	4	5	6	7	8	9
0	0	0.039370	0.078740	0.118110	0.157481	0.196851	0.236221	0.275591	0.314961	0.354331
10	0.393701	0.433072	0.472442	0.511812	0.551182	0.590552	0.629922	0.669292	0.708663	0.748033
20	0.787403	0.826773	0.866143	0.905513	0.944884	0.984254	1.02362	1.06299	1.10236	1.14173
30	1.18110	1.22047	1.25984	1.29291	1.33858	1.37796	1.41733	1.45670	1.49607	1.53544
40	1.57481	1.61418	1.65355	1.69292	1.73229	1.77166	1.81103	1.85040	1.88977	1.92914
50	1.96851	2.00788	2.04725	2.08662	2.12599	2.16536	2.20473	2.24410	2.28347	2.32284
60	2.36221	2.40158	2.44095	2.48032	2.51969	2.55906	2.59843	2.63780	2.67717	2.71654
70	2.75591	2.79528	2.83465	2.87402	2.91339	2.95276	2.99213	3.03150	3.07087	3.11024
80	3.14961	3.18898	3.22835	3.26772	3.30709	3.34646	3.38583	3.42520	3.46457	3.50394
90	3.54331	3.58268	3.62205	3.66142	3.70079	3.74016	3.77953	3.81890	3.85827	3.89764
100	3.93701	3.97638	4.01575	4.05513	4.09450	4.13387	4.17324	4.21261	4.25198	4.29135

1.0 inches

Inches to millimetres

INCHES VERSUS MILLIMETERS

1 inch = 25.4 millimeters

inches	0	1	2	3	4	5	6	7	8	9
						millimeters				
0	0	25.4	50.8	76.2	101.6	127.0	152.4	177.8	203.2	228.6
10	254.0	279.4	304.8	330.2	355.6	381.0	406.4	431.8	457.2	482.6
20	508.0	533.4	558.8	584.2	609.6	635.0	660.4	685.8	711.2	736.6
30	762.0	787.4	812.8	838.2	863.6	889.0	914.4	939.8	965.2	990.6
40	1016.0	1041.4	1066.8	1092.2	1117.6	1143.0	1168.4	1193.8	1219.2	1244.6
50	1270.0	1295.4	1320.8	1346.2	1371.6	1397.0	1422.4	1447.8	1473.2	1498.6
60	1524.0	1549.4	1574.8	1600.2	1625.6	1651.0	1676.4	1701.8	1727.2	1752.6
70	1778.0	1803.4	1828.8	1854.2	1879.6	1905.0	1930.4	1955.8	1981.2	2006.6
80	2032.0	2057.4	2082.8	2108.2	2133.6	2159.0	2184.4	2209.8	2235.2	2260.6
90	2286.0	2311.4	2336.8	2362.2	2387.6	2413.0	2438.4	2463.8	2489.2	2514.6
100	2540.0	2565.4	2590.8	2616.2	2641.6	2667.0	2692.4	2717.8	2743.2	2768.6

Inches to decimal parts of a foot

Inches	Foot	Inches	Foot
$\frac{1}{8}$	0·01	1	0·083
$\frac{1}{4}$	0·021	2	0·167
$\frac{3}{8}$	0·031	3	0·250
$\frac{1}{2}$	0·042	4	0·333
$\frac{5}{8}$	0·052	5	0·417
$\frac{3}{4}$	0·062	6	0·500
$\frac{7}{8}$	0·073	7	0·583
		8	0·667
		9	0·750
		10	0·833
		11	0·917

Modulus of elasticity and density

Material	Modulus of Elasticity		Density	
	kN/mm^2	lb/in^2	kg/m^3	lbs/ft^3
Aluminium – Sheet	69	10,000,000	2,770	196
– Cast	76	11,000,000	2,250	160
Brass – Common	63	9,170,000	7,500	533
– Wire Annealed	97	14,000,000	8,425	600
Steel	207	30,000,000	7,850	558
Concrete	13	1,900,000	2,400	170
Wood – Oak (White)	14·5	2,090,000	700	50
– Pine (Yellow)	11·0	1,600,000	540	38
Reinforced plastic	10·5	1,500,000	1,300	92
Nylon	2·0	300,000	1,000	70

Inches and eighths of an inch to millimetres

in	ft in	mm	in	ft in	mm	in	ft in	mm	in	ft in	mm
⅛		3·2	9⅛		231·8	18⅛	1 6⅛	460·4	27⅛	2 3⅛	689·0
¼		6·4	9¼		235·0	18¼	1 6¼	463·6	27¼	2 3¼	692·2
⅜		9·5	9⅜		238·1	18⅜	1 6⅜	466·7	27⅜	2 3⅜	695·3
½		12·7	9½		241·3	18½	1 6½	469·9	27½	2 3½	698·5
⅝		15·9	9⅝		244·5	18⅝	1 6⅝	473·1	27⅝	2 3⅝	701·7
¾		19·1	9¾		247·7	18¾	1 6¾	476·3	27¾	2 3¾	704·9
⅞		22·2	9⅞		250·8	18⅞	1 6⅞	479·4	27⅞	2 3⅞	708·0
1		25·4	10		254·0	19	1 7	482·6	28	2 4	711·2
1⅛		28·6	10⅛		257·2	19⅛	1 7⅛	485·8	28⅛	2 4⅛	714·4
1¼		31·8	10¼		260·4	19¼	1 7¼	489·0	28¼	2 4¼	717·6
1⅜		34·9	10⅜		263·5	19⅜	1 7⅜	492·1	28⅜	2 4⅜	720·7
1½		38·1	10½		266·7	19½	1 7½	495·3	28½	2 4½	723·9
1⅝		41·3	10⅝		269·9	19⅝	1 7⅝	498·5	28⅝	2 4⅝	727·1
1¾		44·5	10¾		273·1	19¾	1 7¾	501·7	28¾	2 4¾	730·3
1⅞		47·6	10⅞		276·2	19⅞	1 7⅞	504·8	28⅞	2 4⅞	733·4
2		50·8	11		279·4	20	1 8	508·0	29	2 5	736·6
2⅛		54·0	11⅛		282·6	20⅛	1 8⅛	511·2	29⅛	2 5⅛	739·8
2¼		57·2	11¼		285·8	20¼	1 8¼	514·4	29¼	2 5¼	743·0
2⅜		60·3	11⅜		288·9	20⅜	1 8⅜	517·5	29⅜	2 5⅜	746·1
2½		63·5	11½		292·1	20½	1 8½	520·7	29½	2 5½	749·3
2⅝		66·7	11⅝		295·3	20⅝	1 8⅝	523·9	29⅝	2 5⅝	752·5
2¾		69·9	11¾		298·5	20¾	1 8¾	527·1	29¾	2 5¾	755·7
2⅞		73·0	11⅞		301·6	20⅞	1 8⅞	530·2	29⅞	2 5⅞	758·8
3		76·2	12	1 0	304·8	21	1 9	533·4	30	2 6	762·0
3⅛		79·4	12⅛	1 0⅛	308·0	21⅛	1 9⅛	536·6	30⅛	2 6⅛	765·2
3¼		82·6	12¼	1 0¼	311·2	21¼	1 9¼	539·8	30¼	2 6¼	768·4
3⅜		85·7	12⅜	1 0⅜	314·3	21⅜	1 9⅜	542·9	30⅜	2 6⅜	771·5
3½		88·9	12½	1 0½	317·5	21½	1 9½	546·1	30½	2 6½	774·7
3⅝		92·1	12⅝	1 0⅝	320·7	21⅝	1 9⅝	549·3	30⅝	2 6⅝	777·9
3¾		95·3	12¾	1 0¾	323·9	21¾	1 9¾	552·5	30¾	2 6¾	781·1
3⅞		98·4	12⅞	1 0⅞	327·0	21⅞	1 9⅞	555·6	30⅞	2 6⅞	784·2
4		101·6	13	1 1	330·2	22	1 10	558·8	31	2 7	787·4
4⅛		104·8	13⅛	1 1⅛	333·4	22⅛	1 10⅛	562·0	31⅛	2 7⅛	790·6
4¼		108·0	13¼	1 1¼	336·6	22¼	1 10¼	565·2	31¼	2 7¼	793·8
4⅜		111·1	13⅜	1 1⅜	339·7	22⅜	1 10⅜	568·3	31⅜	2 7⅜	796·9
4½		114·3	13½	1 1½	342·9	22½	1 10½	571·5	31½	2 7½	800·1
4⅝		117·5	13⅝	1 1⅝	346·1	22⅝	1 10⅝	574·7	31⅝	2 7⅝	803·3
4¾		120·7	13¾	1 1¾	349·3	22¾	1 10¾	577·9	31¾	2 7¾	806·5
4⅞		123·8	13⅞	1 1⅞	352·4	22⅞	1 10⅞	581·0	31⅞	2 7⅞	809·6
5		127·0	14	1 2	355·6	23	1 11	584·2	32	2 8	812·8
5⅛		130·2	14⅛	1 2⅛	358·8	23⅛	1 11⅛	587·4	32⅛	2 8⅛	816·0
5¼		133·4	14¼	1 2¼	362·0	23¼	1 11¼	590·6	32¼	2 8¼	819·2
5⅜		136·5	14⅜	1 2⅜	365·1	23⅜	1 11⅜	593·7	32⅜	2 8⅜	822·3
5½		139·7	14½	1 2½	368·3	23½	1 11½	596·9	32½	2 8½	825·5
5⅝		142·9	14⅝	1 2⅝	371·5	23⅝	1 11⅝	600·1	32⅝	2 8⅝	828·7
5¾		146·1	14¾	1 2¾	374·7	23¾	1 11¾	603·3	32¾	2 8¾	831·9
5⅞		149·2	14⅞	1 2⅞	377·8	23⅞	1 11⅞	606·4	32⅞	2 8⅞	835·0
6		152·4	15	1 3	381·0	24	2 0	609·6	33	2 9	838·2
6⅛		155·6	15⅛	1 3⅛	384·2	24⅛	2 0⅛	612·8	33⅛	2 9⅛	841·4
6¼		158·8	15¼	1 3¼	387·4	24¼	2 0¼	616·0	33¼	2 9¼	844·6
6⅜		161·9	15⅜	1 3⅜	390·5	24⅜	2 0⅜	619·1	33⅜	2 9⅜	847·7
6½		165·1	15½	1 3½	393·7	24½	2 0½	622·3	33½	2 9½	850·9
6⅝		168·3	15⅝	1 3⅝	396·9	24⅝	2 0⅝	625·5	33⅝	2 9⅝	854·1
6¾		171·5	15¾	1 3¾	400·1	24¾	2 0¾	628·7	33¾	2 9¾	857·3
6⅞		174·6	15⅞	1 3⅞	403·2	24⅞	2 0⅞	631·8	33⅞	2 9⅞	860·4
7		177·8	16	1 4	406·4	25	2 1	635·0	34	2 10	863·6
7⅛		181·0	16⅛	1 4⅛	409·6	25⅛	2 1⅛	638·2	34⅛	2 10⅛	866·8
7¼		184·2	16¼	1 4¼	412·8	25¼	2 1¼	641·4	34¼	2 10¼	870·0
7⅜		187·3	16⅜	1 4⅜	415·9	25⅜	2 1⅜	644·5	34⅜	2 10⅜	873·1
7½		190·5	16½	1 4½	419·1	25½	2 1½	647·7	34½	2 10½	876·3
7⅝		193·7	16⅝	1 4⅝	422·3	25⅝	2 1⅝	650·9	34⅝	2 10⅝	879·5
7¾		196·9	16¾	1 4¾	425·5	25¾	2 1¾	654·1	34¾	2 10¾	882·7
7⅞		200·0	16⅞	1 4⅞	428·6	25⅞	2 1⅞	657·2	34⅞	2 10⅞	885·8
8		203·2	17	1 5	431·8	26	2 2	660·4	35	2 11	889·0
8⅛		206·4	17⅛	1 5⅛	435·0	26⅛	2 2⅛	663·6	35⅛	2 11⅛	892·2
8¼		209·6	17¼	1 5¼	438·2	26¼	2 2¼	666·8	35¼	2 11¼	895·4
8⅜		212·7	17⅜	1 5⅜	441·3	26⅜	2 2⅜	669·9	35⅜	2 11⅜	898·5
8½		215·9	17½	1 5½	444·5	26½	2 2½	673·1	35½	2 11½	901·7
8⅝		219·1	17⅝	1 5⅝	447·7	26⅝	2 2⅝	676·3	35⅝	2 11⅝	904·9
8¾		222·3	17¾	1 5¾	450·9	26¾	2 2¾	679·5	35¾	2 11¾	908·1
8⅞		225·4	17⅞	1 5⅞	454·0	26⅞	2 2⅞	682·6	35⅞	2 11⅞	911·2
9		228·6	18	1 6	457·2	27	2 3	685·8	36	3 0	914·4

in	ft in	mm	in	ft in	mm	in	ft in	mm	in	ft in	mm
36⅛	3 0⅛	917·6	45⅛	3 9⅛	1146·2	54⅛	4 6⅛	1374·8	63⅛	5 3⅛	1603·4
36¼	3 0¼	920·8	45¼	3 9¼	1149·4	54¼	4 6¼	1378·0	63¼	5 3¼	1606·6
36⅜	3 0⅜	923·9	45⅜	3 9⅜	1152·5	54⅜	4 6⅜	1381·1	63⅜	5 3⅜	1609·7
36½	3 0½	927·1	45½	3 9½	1155·7	54½	4 6½	1384·3	63½	5 3½	1612·9
36⅝	3 0⅝	930·3	45⅝	3 9⅝	1158·9	54⅝	4 6⅝	1387·5	63⅝	5 3⅝	1616·1
36¾	3 0¾	933·5	45¾	3 9¾	1162·1	54¾	4 6¾	1390·7	63¾	5 3¾	1619·3
36⅞	3 0⅞	936·6	45⅞	3 9⅞	1165·2	54⅞	4 6⅞	1393·8	63⅞	5 3⅞	1622·4
37	3 1	939·8	46	3 10	1168·4	55	4 7	1397·0	64	5 4	1625·6
37⅛	3 1⅛	943·0	46⅛	3 10⅛	1171·6	55⅛	4 7⅛	1400·2	64⅛	5 4⅛	1628·8
37¼	3 1¼	946·2	46¼	3 10¼	1174·8	55¼	4 7¼	1403·4	64¼	5 4¼	1632·0
37⅜	3 1⅜	949·3	46⅜	3 10⅜	1177·9	55⅜	4 7⅜	1406·5	64⅜	5 4⅜	1635·1
37½	3 1½	952·5	46½	3 10½	1181·1	55½	4 7½	1409·7	64½	5 4½	1638·3
37⅝	3 1⅝	955·7	46⅝	3 10⅝	1184·3	55⅝	4 7⅝	1412·9	64⅝	5 4⅝	1641·5
37¾	3 1¾	958·9	46¾	3 10¾	1187·5	55¾	4 7¾	1416·1	64¾	5 4¾	1644·7
37⅞	3 1⅞	962·0	46⅞	3 10⅞	1190·6	55⅞	4 7⅞	1419·2	64⅞	5 4⅞	1647·8
38	3 2	965·2	47	3 11	1193·8	56	4 8	1422·4	65	5 5	1651·0
38⅛	3 2⅛	968·4	47⅛	3 11⅛	1197·0	56⅛	4 8⅛	1425·6	65⅛	5 5⅛	1654·2
38¼	3 2¼	971·6	47¼	3 11¼	1200·2	56¼	4 8¼	1428·8	65¼	5 5¼	1657·4
38⅜	3 2⅜	974·7	47⅜	3 11⅜	1203·3	56⅜	4 8⅜	1431·9	65⅜	5 5⅜	1660·5
38½	3 2½	977·9	47½	3 11½	1206·5	56½	4 8½	1435·1	65½	5 5½	1663·7
38⅝	3 2⅝	981·1	47⅝	3 11⅝	1209·7	56⅝	4 8⅝	1438·3	65⅝	5 5⅝	1666·9
38¾	3 2¾	984·3	47¾	3 11¾	1212·9	56¾	4 8¾	1441·5	65¾	5 5¾	1670·1
38⅞	3 2⅞	987·4	47⅞	3 11⅞	1216·0	56⅞	4 8⅞	1444·6	65⅞	5 5⅞	1673·2
39	3 3	990·6	48	4 0	1219·2	57	4 9	1447·8	66	5 6	1676·4
39⅛	3 3⅛	993·8	48⅛	4 0⅛	1222·4	57⅛	4 9⅛	1451·0	66⅛	5 6⅛	1679·6
39¼	3 3¼	997·0	48¼	4 0¼	1225·6	57¼	4 9¼	1454·2	66¼	5 6¼	1682·8
39⅜	3 3⅜	1000·1	48⅜	4 0⅜	1228·7	57⅜	4 9⅜	1457·3	66⅜	5 6⅜	1685·9
39½	3 3½	1003·3	48½	4 0½	1231·9	57½	4 9½	1460·5	66½	5 6½	1689·1
39⅝	3 3⅝	1006·5	48⅝	4 0⅝	1235·1	57⅝	4 9⅝	1463·7	66⅝	5 6⅝	1692·3
39¾	3 3¾	1009·7	48¾	4 0¾	1238·3	57¾	4 9¾	1466·9	66¾	5 6¾	1695·5
39⅞	3 3⅞	1012·8	48⅞	4 0⅞	1241·4	57⅞	4 9⅞	1470·0	66⅞	5 6⅞	1698·6
40	3 4	1016·0	49	4 1	1244·6	58	4 10	1473·2	67	5 7	1701·8
40⅛	3 4⅛	1019·2	49⅛	4 1⅛	1247·8	58⅛	4 10⅛	1476·4	67⅛	5 7⅛	1705·0
40¼	3 4¼	1022·4	49¼	4 1¼	1251·0	58¼	4 10¼	1479·6	67¼	5 7¼	1708·2
40⅜	3 4⅜	1025·5	49⅜	4 1⅜	1254·1	58⅜	4 10⅜	1482·7	67⅜	5 7⅜	1711·3
40½	3 4½	1028·7	49½	4 1½	1257·3	58½	4 10½	1485·9	67½	5 7½	1714·5
40⅝	3 4⅝	1031·9	49⅝	4 1⅝	1260·5	58⅝	4 10⅝	1489·1	67⅝	5 7⅝	1717·7
40¾	3 4¾	1035·1	49¾	4 1¾	1263·7	58¾	4 10¾	1492·3	67¾	5 7¾	1720·9
40⅞	3 4⅞	1038·2	49⅞	4 1⅞	1266·8	58⅞	4 10⅞	1495·4	67⅞	5 7⅞	1724·0
41	3 5	1041·4	50	4 2	1270·0	59	4 11	1498·6	68	5 8	1727·2
41⅛	3 5⅛	1044·6	50⅛	4 2⅛	1273·2	59⅛	4 11⅛	1501·8	68⅛	5 8⅛	1730·4
41¼	3 5¼	1047·8	50¼	4 2¼	1276·4	59¼	4 11¼	1505·0	68¼	5 8¼	1733·6
41⅜	3 5⅜	1050·9	50⅜	4 2⅜	1279·5	59⅜	4 11⅜	1508·1	68⅜	5 8⅜	1736·7
41½	3 5½	1054·1	50½	4 2½	1282·7	59½	4 11½	1511·3	68½	5 8½	1739·9
41⅝	3 5⅝	1057·3	50⅝	4 2⅝	1285·9	59⅝	4 11⅝	1514·5	68⅝	5 8⅝	1743·1
41¾	3 5¾	1060·5	50¾	4 2¾	1289·1	59¾	4 11¾	1517·7	68¾	5 8¾	1746·3
41⅞	3 5⅞	1063·6	50⅞	4 2⅞	1292·2	59⅞	4 11⅞	1520·8	68⅞	5 8⅞	1749·4
42	3 6	1066·8	51	4 3	1295·4	60	5 0	1524·0	69	5 9	1752·6
42⅛	3 6⅛	1070·0	51⅛	4 3⅛	1298·6	60⅛	5 0⅛	1527·2	69⅛	5 9⅛	1755·8
42¼	3 6¼	1073·2	51¼	4 3¼	1301·8	60¼	5 0¼	1530·4	69¼	5 9¼	1759·0
42⅜	3 6⅜	1076·3	51⅜	4 3⅜	1304·9	60⅜	5 0⅜	1533·5	69⅜	5 9⅜	1762·1
42½	3 6½	1079·5	51½	4 3½	1308·1	60½	5 0½	1536·7	69½	5 9½	1765·3
42⅝	3 6⅝	1082·7	51⅝	4 3⅝	1311·3	60⅝	5 0⅝	1539·9	69⅝	5 9⅝	1768·5
42¾	3 6¾	1085·9	51¾	4 3¾	1314·5	60¾	5 0¾	1543·1	69¾	5 9¾	1771·7
42⅞	3 6⅞	1089·0	51⅞	4 3⅞	1317·6	60⅞	5 0⅞	1546·2	69⅞	5 9⅞	1774·8
43	3 7	1092·2	52	4 4	1320·8	61	5 1	1549·4	70	5 10	1778·0
43⅛	3 7⅛	1095·4	52⅛	4 4⅛	1324·0	61⅛	5 1⅛	1552·6	70⅛	5 10⅛	1781·2
43¼	3 7¼	1098·6	52¼	4 4¼	1327·2	61¼	5 1¼	1555·8	70¼	5 10¼	1784·4
43⅜	3 7⅜	1101·7	52⅜	4 4⅜	1330·3	61⅜	5 1⅜	1558·9	70⅜	5 10⅜	1787·5
43½	3 7½	1104·9	52½	4 4½	1333·5	61½	5 1½	1562·1	70½	5 10½	1790·7
43⅝	3 7⅝	1108·1	52⅝	4 4⅝	1336·7	61⅝	5 1⅝	1565·3	70⅝	5 10⅝	1793·9
43¾	3 7¾	1111·3	52¾	4 4¾	1339·9	61¾	5 1¾	1568·5	70¾	5 10¾	1797·1
43⅞	3 7⅞	1114·4	52⅞	4 4⅞	1343·0	61⅞	5 1⅞	1571·6	70⅞	5 10⅞	1800·2
44	3 8	1117·6	53	4 5	1346·2	62	5 2	1574·8	71	5 11	1803·4
44⅛	3 8⅛	1120·8	53⅛	4 5⅛	1349·4	62⅛	5 2⅛	1578·0	71⅛	5 11⅛	1806·6
44¼	3 8¼	1124·0	53¼	4 5¼	1352·6	62¼	5 2¼	1581·2	71¼	5 11¼	1809·8
44⅜	3 8⅜	1127·1	53⅜	4 5⅜	1355·7	62⅜	5 2⅜	1584·3	71⅜	5 11⅜	1812·9
44½	3 8½	1130·3	53½	4 5½	1358·9	62½	5 2½	1587·5	71½	5 11½	1816·1
44⅝	3 8⅝	1133·5	53⅝	4 5⅝	1362·1	62⅝	5 2⅝	1590·7	71⅝	5 11⅝	1819·3
44¾	3 8¾	1136·7	53¾	4 5¾	1365·3	62¾	5 2¾	1593·9	71¾	5 11¾	1822·5
44⅞	3 8⅞	1139·8	53⅞	4 5⅞	1368·4	62⅞	5 2⅞	1597·0	71⅞	5 11⅞	1825·6
45	3 9	1143·0	54	4 6	1371·6	63	5 3	1600·2	72	6 0	1828·8

Feet and inches to metres and millimetres

Feet	Inches											
	0	1	2	3	4	5	6	7	8	9	10	11
	Metres and millimetres											
0	—	25	51	76	102	127	152	178	203	229	254	279
1	305	330	356	381	406	432	457	483	508	533	559	584
2	610	635	660	686	711	737	762	787	813	838	864	889
3	914	940	965	991	1·016	1·041	1·067	1·092	1·118	1·143	1·168	1·194
4	1·219	1·245	1·270	1·295	1·321	1·346	1·372	1·397	1·422	1·448	1·473	1·499
5	1·524	1·549	1·575	1·600	1·626	1·651	1·676	1·702	1·727	1·753	1·778	1·803
6	1·829	1·854	1·880	1·905	1·930	1·956	1·981	2·007	2·032	2·057	2·083	2·108
7	2·134	2·159	2·184	2·210	2·235	2·261	2·286	2·311	2·337	2·362	2·388	2·413
8	2·438	2·464	2·489	2·515	2·540	2·565	2·591	2·616	2·642	2·667	2·692	2·718
9	2·743	2·769	2·794	2·819	2·845	2·870	2·896	2·921	2·946	2·972	2·997	3·023
10	3·048	3·073	3·099	3·124	3·150	3·175	3·200	3·226	3·251	3·277	3·302	3·327
11	3·353	3·378	3·404	3·429	3·454	3·480	3·505	3·531	3·556	3·581	3·607	3·632
12	3·658	3·683	3·708	3·734	3·759	3·785	3·810	3·835	3·861	3·886	3·912	3·937
13	3·962	3·988	4·013	4·039	4·064	4·089	4·115	4·140	4·166	4·191	4·216	4·242
14	4·267	4·293	4·318	4·343	4·369	4·394	4·420	4·445	4·470	4·496	4·521	4·547
15	4·572	4·597	4·623	4·648	4·674	4·699	4·724	4·750	4·775	4·801	4·826	4·851
16	4·877	4·902	4·928	4·953	4·978	5·004	5·029	5·055	5·080	5·105	5·131	5·156
17	5·182	5·207	5·232	5·258	5·283	5·309	5·334	5·359	5·385	5·410	5·436	5·461
18	5·486	5·512	5·537	5·563	5·588	5·613	5·639	5·664	5·690	5·715	5·740	5·766
19	5·791	5·817	5·842	5·867	5·893	5·918	5·944	5·969	5·994	6·020	6·045	6·071
20	6·096	6·121	6·147	6·172	6·198	6·223	6·248	6·274	6·299	6·325	6·350	6·375
21	6·401	6·426	6·452	6·477	6·502	6·528	6·553	6·579	6·604	6·629	6·655	6·680
22	6·706	6·731	6·756	6·782	6·807	6·833	6·858	6·883	6·909	6·934	6·960	6·985
23	7·010	7·036	7·061	7·087	7·112	7·137	7·163	7·188	7·214	7·239	7·264	7·290
24	7·315	7·341	7·366	7·391	7·417	7·442	7·468	7·493	7·518	7·544	7·569	7·595
25	7·620	7·645	7·671	7·696	7·722	7·747	7·772	7·798	7·823	7·849	7·874	7·899
26	7·925	7·950	7·976	8·001	8·026	8·052	8·077	8·103	8·128	8·153	8·179	8·204
27	8·230	8·255	8·280	8·306	8·331	8·357	8·382	8·407	8·433	8·458	8·484	8·509
28	8·534	8·560	8·585	8·611	8·636	8·661	8·687	8·712	8·738	8·763	8·788	8·814
29	8·839	8·865	8·890	8·915	8·941	8·966	8·992	9·017	9·042	9·068	9·093	9·119
30	9·144	9·169	9·195	9·220	9·246	9·271	9·296	9·322	9·347	9·373	9·398	9·423
31	9·449	9·474	9·500	9·525	9·550	9·576	9·601	9·627	9·652	9·677	9·703	9·728
32	9·754	9·779	9·804	9·830	9·855	9·881	9·906	9·931	9·957	9·982	10·008	10·033
33	10·058	10·084	10·109	10·135	10·160	10·185	10·211	10·236	10·262	10·287	10·312	10·338
34	10·363	10·389	10·414	10·439	10·465	10·490	10·516	10·541	10·566	10·592	10·617	10·643
35	10·668	10·693	10·719	10·744	10·770	10·795	10·820	10·846	10·871	10·897	10·922	10·947
36	10·973	10·998	11·024	11·049	11·074	11·100	11·125	11·151	11·176	11·201	11·227	11·252
37	11·278	11·303	11·328	11·354	11·379	11·405	11·430	11·455	11·481	11·506	11·532	11·557
38	11·582	11·608	11·633	11·659	11·684	11·709	11·735	11·760	11·786	11·811	11·836	11·862
39	11·887	11·913	11·938	11·963	11·989	12·014	12·040	12·065	12·090	12·116	12·141	12·167
40	12·192	12·217	12·243	12·268	12·294	12·319	12·344	12·370	12·395	12·421	12·446	12·471
41	12·497	12·522	12·548	12·573	12·598	12·624	12·649	12·675	12·700	12·725	12·751	12·776
42	12·802	12·827	12·852	12·878	12·903	12·929	12·954	12·979	13·005	13·030	13·056	13·081
43	13·106	13·132	13·157	13·183	13·208	13·233	13·259	13·284	13·310	13·335	13·360	13·386
44	13·411	13·437	13·462	13·487	13·513	13·538	13·564	13·589	13·614	13·640	13·665	13·691
45	13·716	13·741	13·767	13·792	13·818	13·843	13·868	13·894	13·919	13·945	13·970	13·995
46	14·021	14·046	14·072	14·097	14·122	14·148	14·173	14·199	14·224	14·249	14·275	14·300
47	14·326	14·351	14·376	14·402	14·427	14·453	14·478	14·503	14·529	14·554	14·580	14·605
48	14·630	14·656	14·681	14·707	14·732	14·757	14·783	14·808	14·834	14·859	14·884	14·910
49	14·935	14·961	14·986	15·011	15·037	15·062	15·088	15·113	15·138	15·164	15·189	15·215
50	15·240	15·265	15·291	15·316	15·342	15·367	15·392	15·418	18·443	15·469	15·494	15·519
51	15·545	15·570	15·596	15·621	15·646	15·672	15·697	15·723	15·748	15·773	15·799	15·824
52	15·850	15·875	15·900	15·926	15·951	15·977	16·002	16·027	16·053	16·078	16·104	16·129
53	16·154	16·180	16·205	16·231	16·256	16·281	16·307	16·332	16·358	16·383	16·408	16·434
54	16·459	16·485	16·510	16·535	16·561	16·586	16·612	16·637	16·662	16·688	16·713	16·739
55	16·764	16·789	16·815	16·840	16·866	16·891	16·916	16·942	16·967	16·993	17·018	17·043
56	17·069	17·094	17·120	17·145	17·170	17·196	17·221	17·247	17·272	17·297	17·323	17·348
57	17·374	17·399	17·424	17·450	17·475	17·501	17·526	17·551	17·577	17·602	17·628	17·653
58	17·678	17·704	17·729	17·755	17·780	17·805	17·830	17·856	17·882	17·907	17·932	17·958
59	17·983	18·009	18·034	18·059	18·085	18·110	18·136	18·161	18·186	18·212	18·237	18·263
60	18·288	18·313	18·339	18·364	18·390	18·415	18·440	18·466	18·491	18·517	18·542	18·567
61	18·593	18·618	18·644	18·669	18·694	18·720	18·745	18·771	18·796	18·821	18·847	18·872
62	18·898	18·923	18·948	18·974	18·999	19·025	19·050	19·075	19·101	19·126	19·152	19·177
63	19·202	19·228	19·253	19·279	19·304	19·329	19·355	19·380	19·406	19·431	19·456	19·482
64	19·507	19·533	19·558	19·583	19·609	19·634	19·660	19·685	19·710	19·736	19·761	19·787
65	19·812	19·837	19·863	19·888	19·914	19·939	19·964	19·990	20·015	20·041	20·066	20·091
66	20·117	20·142	20·168	20·193	20·218	20·244	20·269	20·295	20·320	20·345	20·371	20·396
67	20·422	20·447	20·472	20·498	20·523	20·549	20·574	20·599	20·625	20·650	20·676	20·701
68	20·726	20·752	20·777	20·803	20·828	20·853	20·879	20·904	20·930	20·955	20·980	21·006
69	21·031	21·057	21·082	21·107	21·133	21·158	21·184	21·209	21·234	21·260	21·285	21·311

4/4/4 (1

6 longths x 4 m.

Base.

Feet	Inches											
	0	1	2	3	4	5	6	7	8	9	10	11
	Metres and millimetres											
70	21·336	21·361	21·387	21·412	21·438	21·463	21·488	21·514	21·539	21·565	21·590	21·615
71	21·641	21·666	21·692	21·717	21·742	21·768	21·793	21·819	21·844	21·869	21·895	21·920
72	21·946	21·971	21·996	22·022	22·047	22·073	22·098	22·123	22·149	22·174	22·200	22·225
73	22·250	22·276	22·301	22·327	22·352	22·377	22·403	22·428	22·454	22·479	22·504	22·530
74	22·555	22·581	22·606	22·631	22·657	22·682	22·708	22·733	22·758	22·784	22·809	22·835
75	22·860	22·885	22·911	22·936	22·962	22·987	23·012	23·038	23·063	23·089	23·114	23·139
76	23·165	23·190	23·216	23·241	23·266	23·292	23·317	23·343	23·368	23·393	23·419	23·444
77	23·470	23·495	23·520	23·546	23·571	23·597	23·622	23·647	23·673	23·698	23·724	23·749
78	23·774	23·800	23·825	23·851	23·876	23·901	23·927	23·952	23·978	24·003	24·028	24·054
79	24·079	24·105	24·130	24·155	24·181	24·206	24·232	24·257	24·282	24·308	24·333	24·359
80	24·384	24·409	24·435	24·460	24·486	24·511	24·536	24·562	24·587	24·613	24·638	24·663
81	24·689	24·714	24·740	24·765	24·790	24·816	24·841	24·867	24·892	24·917	24·943	24·968
82	24·994	25·019	25·044	25·070	25·095	25·121	25·146	25·171	25·197	25·222	25·248	25·273
83	25·298	25·324	25·349	25·375	25·400	25·425	25·451	25·476	25·502	25·527	25·552	25·578
84	25·603	25·629	25·654	25·679	25·705	25·730	25·756	25·781	25·806	25·832	25·857	25·883
85	25·908	25·933	25·959	25·984	26·010	26·035	26·060	26·086	26·111	26·137	26·162	26·187
86	26·213	26·238	26·264	26·289	26·314	26·340	26·365	26·391	26·416	26·441	26·467	26·492
87	26·518	26·543	26·568	26·594	26·619	26·645	26·670	26·695	26·721	26·746	26·772	26·797
88	26·822	26·848	26·873	26·899	26·924	26·949	26·975	27·000	27·026	27·051	27·076	27·102
89	27·127	27·153	27·178	27·203	27·229	27·254	27·280	27·305	27·330	27·356	27·381	27·407
90	27·432	27·457	27·483	27·508	27·534	27·559	27·584	27·610	27·635	27·661	27·686	27·711
91	27·737	27·762	27·788	27·813	27·838	27·864	27·889	27·915	27·940	27·965	27·991	28·016
92	28·042	28·067	28·092	28·118	28·143	28·169	28·194	28·219	28·245	28·270	28·296	28·321
93	28·346	28·372	28·397	28·423	28·448	28·473	28·499	28·524	28·550	28·575	28·600	28·626
94	28·651	28·677	28·702	28·727	28·753	28·778	28·804	28·829	28·854	28·880	28·905	28·931
95	28·956	28·981	29·007	29·032	29·058	29·083	29·108	29·134	29·159	29·185	29·210	29·235
96	29·261	29·286	29·312	29·337	29·362	29·388	29·413	29·439	29·464	29·489	29·515	29·540
97	29·566	29·591	29·616	29·642	29·667	29·693	29·718	29·743	29·769	29·794	29·820	29·845
98	29·870	29·896	29·921	29·947	29·972	29·997	30·023	30·048	30·074	30·099	30·124	30·150
99	30·175	30·201	30·226	30·251	30·277	30·302	30·328	30·353	30·378	30·404	30·429	30·455
100	30·480	—	—	—	—	—	—	—	—	—	—	—

Feet and inches to metres

Feet	Inches											
	0	1	2	3	4	5	6	7	8	9	10	11
	Metres											
0	—	0·0254	0·0508	0·0762	0·1016	0·1270	0·1524	0·1778	0·2032	0·2286	0·2540	0·2794
1	0·3048	0·3302	0·3556	0·3810	0·4064	0·4318	0·4572	0·4826	0·5080	0·5334	0·5588	0·5842
2	0·6096	0·6350	0·6604	0·6858	0·7112	0·7366	0·7620	0·7874	0·8128	0·8382	0·8636	0·8890
3	0·9144	0·9398	0·9652	0·9906	1·0160	1·0414	1·0668	1·0922	1·1176	1·1430	1·1684	1·1938
4	1·2192	1·2446	1·2700	1·2954	1·3208	1·3462	1·3716	1·3970	1·4224	1·4478	1·4732	1·4986
5	1·5240	1·5494	1·5748	1·6002	1·6256	1·6510	1·6764	1·7018	1·7272	1·7526	1·7780	1·8034
6	1·8288	1·8542	1·8796	1·9050	1·9304	1·9558	1·9812	2·0066	2·0320	2·0574	2·0828	2·1082
7	2·1336	2·1590	2·1844	2·2098	2·2352	2·2606	2·2860	2·3114	2·3368	2·3622	2·3876	2·4130
8	2·4384	2·4638	2·4892	2·5146	2·5400	2·5654	2·5908	2·6162	2·6416	2·6670	2·6924	2·7178
9	2·7432	2·7686	2·7940	2·8194	2·8448	2·8702	2·8956	2·9210	2·9464	2·9718	2·9972	3·0226
10	3·0480	3·0734	3·0988	3·1242	3·1496	3·1750	3·2004	3·2258	3·2512	3·2766	3·3020	3·3274
11	3·3528	3·3782	3·4036	3·4290	3·4544	3·4798	3·5052	3·5306	3·5560	3·5814	3·6068	3·6322
12	3·6576	3·6830	3·7084	3·7338	3·7592	3·7846	3·8100	3·8354	3·8608	3·8862	3·9116	3·9370
13	3·9624	3·9878	4·0132	4·0386	4·0640	4·0894	4·1148	4·1402	4·1656	4·1910	4·2164	4·2418
14	4·2672	4·2926	4·3180	4·3434	4·3688	4·3942	4·4196	4·4450	4·4704	4·4958	4·5212	4·5466
15	4·5720	4·5974	4·6228	4·6482	4·6736	4·6990	4·7244	4·7498	4·7752	4·8006	4·8260	4·8514
16	4·8768	4·9022	4·9276	4·9530	4·9784	5·0038	5·0292	5·0546	5·0800	5·1054	5·1308	5·1562
17	5·1816	5·2070	5·2324	5·2578	5·2832	5·3086	5·3340	5·3594	5·3848	5·4102	5·4356	5·4610
18	5·4864	5·5118	5·5372	5·5626	5·5880	5·6134	5·6388	5·6642	5·6896	5·7150	5·7404	5·7658
19	5·7912	5·8166	5·8420	5·8674	5·8928	5·9182	5·9436	5·9690	5·9944	6·0198	6·0452	6·0706
20	6·0960	—	—	—	—	—	—	—	—	—	—	—

Inches and thirty-seconds of an inch to millimetres

Inches	0	1	2	3	4	5	6	7	8	9	10	11
	Millimetres											
—	—	25·4	50·8	76·2	101·6	127·0	152·4	177·8	203·2	228·6	254·0	279·4
1/32	0·8	26·2	51·6	77·0	102·4	127·8	153·2	178·6	204·0	229·4	254·8	280·2
1/16	1·6	27·0	52·4	77·8	103·2	128·6	154·0	179·4	204·8	230·2	255·6	281·0
3/32	2·4	27·8	53·2	78·6	104·0	129·4	154·8	180·2	205·6	231·0	256·4	281·8
1/8	3·2	28·6	54·0	79·4	104·8	130·2	155·6	181·0	206·4	231·8	257·2	282·6
5/32	4·0	29·4	54·8	80·2	105·6	131·0	156·4	181·8	207·2	232·6	258·0	283·4
3/16	4·8	30·2	55·6	81·0	106·4	131·8	157·2	182·6	208·0	233·4	258·8	284·2
7/32	5·6	31·0	56·4	81·8	107·2	132·6	158·0	183·4	208·8	234·2	259·6	285·0
1/4	6·4	31·8	57·2	82·6	108·0	133·4	158·8	184·2	209·6	235·0	260·4	285·8
9/32	7·1	32·5	57·9	83·3	108·7	134·1	159·5	184·9	210·3	235·7	261·1	286·5
5/16	7·9	33·3	58·7	84·1	109·5	134·9	160·3	185·7	211·1	236·5	261·9	287·3
11/32	8·7	34·1	59·5	84·9	110·3	135·7	161·1	186·5	211·9	237·3	262·7	288·1
3/8	9·5	34·9	60·3	85·7	111·1	136·5	161·9	187·3	212·7	238·1	263·5	288·9
13/32	10·3	35·7	61·1	86·5	111·9	137·3	162·7	188·1	213·5	238·9	264·3	289·7
7/16	11·1	36·5	61·9	87·3	112·7	138·1	163·5	188·9	214·3	239·7	265·1	290·5
15/32	11·9	37·3	62·7	88·1	113·5	138·9	164·3	189·7	215·1	240·5	265·9	291·3
1/2	12·7	38·1	63·5	88·9	114·3	139·7	165·1	190·5	215·9	241·3	266·7	292·1
17/32	13·5	38·9	64·3	89·7	115·1	140·5	165·9	191·3	216·7	242·1	267·5	292·9
9/16	14·3	39·7	65·1	90·5	115·9	141·3	166·7	192·1	217·5	242·9	268·3	293·7
19/32	15·1	40·5	65·9	91·3	116·7	142·1	167·5	192·9	218·3	243·7	269·1	294·5
5/8	15·9	41·3	66·7	92·1	117·5	142·9	168·3	193·7	219·1	244·5	269·9	295·3
21/32	16·7	42·1	67·5	92·9	118·3	143·7	169·1	194·5	219·9	245·3	270·7	296·1
11/16	17·5	42·9	68·3	93·7	119·1	144·5	169·9	195·3	220·7	246·1	271·5	296·9
23/32	18·3	43·7	69·1	94·5	119·9	145·3	170·7	196·1	221·5	246·9	272·3	297·7
3/4	19·1	44·5	69·9	95·3	120·7	146·1	171·5	196·9	222·3	247·7	273·1	298·5
25/32	19·8	45·2	70·6	96·0	121·4	146·8	172·2	197·6	223·0	248·4	273·8	299·2
13/16	20·6	46·0	71·4	96·8	122·2	147·6	173·0	198·4	223·8	249·2	274·6	300·0
27/32	21·4	46·8	72·2	97·6	123·0	148·4	173·8	199·2	224·6	250·0	275·4	300·8
7/8	22·2	47·6	73·0	98·4	123·8	149·2	174·6	200·0	225·4	250·8	276·2	301·6
29/32	23·0	48·4	73·8	99·2	124·6	150·0	175·4	200·8	226·2	251·6	277·0	302·4
15/16	23·8	49·2	74·6	100·0	125·4	150·8	176·2	201·6	227·0	252·4	277·8	303·2
31/32	24·6	50·0	75·4	100·8	126·2	151·6	177·0	202·4	227·8	253·2	278·6	304·0

Cubic feet to cubic metres

Cubic feet	0	1	2	3	4	5	6	7	8	9
	Cubic metres (m³)									
0	—	0·03	0·06	0·08	0·11	0·14	0·17	0·20	0·23	0·25
10	0·28	0·31	0·34	0·37	0·40	0·42	0·45	0·48	0·51	0·54
20	0·57	0·59	0·62	0·65	0·68	0·71	0·73	0·76	0·79	0·82
30	0·85	0·88	0·91	0·93	0·96	0·99	1·02	1·05	1·08	1·10
40	1·13	1·16	1·19	1·22	1·25	1·27	1·30	1·33	1·36	1·39
50	1·42	1·44	1·47	1·50	1·53	1·56	1·59	1·61	1·64	1·67
60	1·70	1·73	1·76	1·78	1·81	1·84	1·87	1·90	1·93	1·95
70	1·98	2·01	2·04	2·07	2·10	2·12	2·15	2·18	2·21	2·24
80	2·27	2·29	2·32	2·35	2·38	2·41	2·44	2·46	2·49	2·52
90	2·55	2·58	2·61	2·63	2·66	2·69	2·72	2·75	2·78	2·80
100	2·83	—	—	—	—	—	—	—	—	—

Square feet to square metres

Square feet	0	1	2	3	4	5	6	7	8	9
	Square metres (m²)									
0	—	0·09	0·19	0·28	0·37	0·46	0·56	0·65	0·74	0·84
10	0·93	1·02	1·11	1·21	1·30	1·39	1·49	1·58	1·67	1·77
20	1·86	1·95	2·04	2·14	2·23	2·32	2·42	2·51	2·60	2·69
30	2·79	2·88	2·97	3·07	3·16	3·25	3·34	3·44	3·53	3·62
40	3·72	3·81	3·90	3·99	4·09	4·18	4·27	4·37	4·46	4·55
50	4·65	4·74	4·83	4·92	5·02	5·11	5·20	5·30	5·39	5·48
60	5·57	5·67	5·76	5·85	5·95	6·04	6·13	6·22	6·32	6·41
70	6·50	6·60	6·69	6·78	6·87	6·97	7·06	7·15	7·25	7·34
80	7·43	7·53	7·62	7·71	7·80	7·90	7·99	8·08	8·18	8·27
90	8·36	8·45	8·55	8·64	8·73	8·83	8·92	9·01	9·10	9·20
100	9·29	9·38	9·48	9·57	9·66	9·75	9·85	9·94	10·03	10·13
110	10·22	10·31	10·41	10·50	10·59	10·68	10·78	10·87	10·96	11·06
120	11·15	11·24	11·33	11·43	11·52	11·61	11·71	11·80	11·89	11·98
130	12·08	12·17	12·26	12·36	12·45	12·54	12·63	12·73	12·82	12·91
140	13·01	13·10	13·19	13·29	13·38	13·47	13·56	13·66	13·75	13·84
150	13·94	14·03	14·12	14·21	14·31	14·40	14·49	14·59	14·68	14·77
160	14·86	14·96	15·05	15·14	15·24	15·33	15·42	15·51	15·61	15·70
170	15·79	15·89	15·98	16·07	16·17	16·26	16·35	16·44	16·54	16·63
180	16·72	16·82	16·91	17·00	17·09	17·19	17·28	17·37	17·47	17·56
190	17·65	17·74	17·84	17·93	18·02	18·12	18·21	18·30	18·39	18·49
200	18·58	18·67	18·77	18·86	18·95	19·05	19·14	19·23	19·32	19·42
210	19·51	19·60	19·70	19·79	19·88	19·97	20·07	20·16	20·25	20·35
220	20·44	20·53	20·62	20·72	20·81	20·90	21·00	21·09	21·18	21·27
230	21·37	21·46	21·55	21·65	21·74	21·83	21·93	22·02	22·11	22·20
240	22·30	22·39	22·48	22·58	22·67	22·76	22·85	22·95	23·04	23·13
250	23·23	23·32	23·41	23·50	23·60	23·69	23·78	23·88	23·97	24·06
260	24·15	24·25	24·34	24·43	24·53	24·62	24·71	24·81	24·90	24·99
270	25·08	25·18	25·27	25·36	25·46	25·55	25·64	25·73	25·83	25·92
280	26·01	26·11	26·20	26·29	26·38	26·48	26·57	26·66	26·76	26·85
290	26·94	27·03	27·13	27·22	27·31	27·41	27·50	27·59	27·69	27·78
300	27·87	27·96	28·06	28·15	28·24	28·34	28·43	28·52	28·61	28·71
310	28·80	28·89	28·99	29·08	29·17	29·26	29·36	29·45	29·54	29·64
320	29·73	29·82	29·91	30·01	30·10	30·19	30·29	30·38	30·47	30·57
330	30·66	30·75	30·84	30·94	31·03	31·12	31·22	31·31	31·40	31·49
340	31·59	31·68	31·77	31·87	31·96	32·05	32·14	32·24	32·33	32·42
350	32·52	32·61	32·70	32·79	32·89	32·98	33·07	33·17	33·26	33·35
360	33·45	33·54	33·63	33·72	33·82	33·91	34·00	34·10	34·19	34·28
370	34·37	34·47	34·56	34·65	34·75	34·84	34·93	35·02	35·12	35·21
380	35·30	35·40	35·49	35·58	35·67	35·77	35·86	35·95	36·05	36·14
390	36·23	36·33	36·42	36·51	36·60	36·70	36·79	36·88	36·98	37·07
400	37·16	37·25	37·35	37·44	37·53	37·63	37·72	37·81	37·90	38·00
410	38·09	38·18	38·28	38·37	38·46	38·55	38·65	38·74	38·83	38·93
420	39·02	39·11	39·21	39·30	39·39	39·48	39·58	39·67	39·76	39·86
430	39·95	40·04	40·13	40·23	40·32	40·41	40·51	40·60	40·69	40·78
440	40·88	40·97	41·06	41·16	41·25	41·34	41·43	41·53	41·62	41·71
450	41·81	41·90	41·99	42·09	42·18	42·27	42·36	42·46	42·55	42·64
460	42·74	42·83	42·92	43·01	43·11	43·20	43·29	43·39	43·48	43·57
470	43·66	43·76	43·85	43·94	44·04	44·13	44·22	44·31	44·41	44·50
480	44·59	44·69	44·78	44·87	44·97	45·06	45·15	45·24	45·34	45·43
490	45·52	45·62	45·71	45·80	45·89	45·99	46·08	46·17	46·27	46·36
500	46·45									

Pounds to kilogrammes

Pounds	0	1	2	3	4	5	6	7	8	9
	Kilogrammes (kg)									
0	—	0·45	0·91	1·36	1·81	2·27	2·72	3·18	3·63	4·08
10	4·54	4·99	5·44	5·90	6·35	6·80	7·26	7·71	8·16	8·62
20	9·07	9·53	9·98	10·43	10·89	11·34	11·79	12·25	12·70	13·15
30	13·61	14·06	14·52	14·97	15·42	15·88	16·33	16·78	17·24	17·69
40	18·14	18·60	19·05	19·50	19·96	20·41	20·87	21·32	21·77	22·23
50	22·68	23·13	23·59	24·04	24·49	24·95	25·40	25·85	26·31	26·76
60	27·22	27·67	28·12	28·58	29·03	29·48	29·94	30·39	30·84	31·30
70	31·75	32·21	32·66	33·11	33·57	34·02	34·47	34·93	35·38	35·83
80	36·29	36·74	37·19	37·65	38·10	38·56	39·01	39·46	39·92	40·37
90	40·82	41·28	41·73	42·18	42·64	43·09	43·54	44·00	44·45	44·91
100	45·36	45·81	46·27	46·72	47·17	47·63	48·08	48·53	48·99	49·44
110	49·90	50·35	50·80	51·26	51·71	52·16	52·62	53·07	53·52	53·98
120	54·43	54·88	55·34	55·79	56·25	56·70	57·15	57·61	58·06	58·51
130	58·97	59·42	59·87	60·33	60·78	61·24	61·69	62·14	62·60	63·05
140	63·50	63·96	64·41	64·86	65·32	65·77	66·22	66·68	67·13	67·59
150	68·04	68·49	68·95	69·40	69·85	70·31	70·76	71·21	71·67	72·12
160	72·57	73·03	73·48	73·94	74·39	74·84	75·30	75·75	76·20	76·66
170	77·11	77·56	78·02	78·47	78·93	79·38	79·83	80·29	80·74	81·19
180	81·65	82·10	82·55	83·01	83·46	83·91	84·37	84·82	85·28	85·73
190	86·18	86·64	87·09	87·54	88·00	88·45	88·90	89·36	89·81	90·26
200	90·72	91·17	91·63	92·08	92·53	92·99	93·44	93·89	94·35	94·80
210	95·25	95·71	96·16	96·62	97·07	97·52	97·98	98·43	98·88	99·34
220	99·79	100·24	100·70	101·15	101·61	102·06	102·51	102·97	103·42	103·87
230	104·33	104·78	105·23	105·69	106·14	106·59	107·05	107·50	107·96	108·41
240	108·86	109·32	109·77	110·22	110·68	111·13	111·58	112·04	112·49	112·95
250	113·40	113·85	114·31	114·76	115·21	115·67	116·12	116·57	117·03	117·48
260	117·93	118·39	118·84	119·30	119·75	120·20	120·66	121·11	121·56	122·02
270	122·47	122·92	123·38	123·83	124·28	124·74	125·19	125·65	126·10	126·55
280	127·01	127·46	127·91	128·37	128·82	129·27	129·73	130·18	130·64	131·09
290	131·54	132·00	132·45	132·90	133·36	133·81	134·26	134·72	135·17	135·62
300	136·08	136·53	136·99	137·44	137·89	138·35	138·80	139·25	139·71	140·16
310	140·61	141·07	141·52	141·97	142·43	142·88	143·34	143·79	144·24	144·70
320	145·15	145·60	146·06	146·51	146·96	147·42	147·87	148·33	148·78	149·23
330	149·69	150·14	150·59	151·05	151·50	151·95	152·41	152·86	153·31	153·77
340	154·22	154·68	155·13	155·58	156·04	156·49	156·94	157·40	157·85	158·30
350	158·76	159·21	159·67	160·12	160·57	161·03	161·48	161·93	162·39	162·84
360	163·29	163·75	164·20	164·65	165·11	165·56	166·02	166·47	166·92	167·38
370	167·83	168·28	168·74	169·19	169·64	170·10	170·55	171·00	171·46	171·91
380	172·37	172·82	173·27	173·73	174·18	174·63	175·09	175·54	175·99	176·45
390	176·90	177·36	177·81	178·26	178·72	179·17	179·62	180·08	180·53	180·98
400	181·44	181·89	182·34	182·80	183·25	183·71	184·16	184·61	185·07	185·52
410	185·97	186·43	186·88	187·33	187·79	188·24	188·69	189·15	189·60	190·06
420	190·51	190·96	191·42	191·87	192·32	192·78	193·23	193·68	194·14	194·59
430	195·05	195·50	195·95	196·41	196·86	197·31	197·77	198·22	198·67	199·13
440	199·58	200·03	200·49	200·94	201·40	201·85	202·30	202·76	203·21	203·66
450	204·12	204·57	205·02	205·48	205·93	206·39	206·84	207·29	207·75	208·20
460	208·65	209·11	209·56	210·01	210·47	210·92	211·37	211·83	212·28	212·74
470	213·19	213·64	214·10	214·55	215·00	215·46	215·91	216·36	216·82	217·27
480	217·72	218·18	218·63	219·09	219·54	219·99	220·45	220·90	221·35	221·81
490	222·26	222·71	223·17	223·62	224·08	224·53	224·98	225·44	225·89	226·34
500	226·80	—	—	—	—	—	—	—	—	—

Kilogrammes to pounds

KILOGRAMS	0	1	2	3	4	5	6	7	8	9
0		2·205	4·409	6·614	8·818	11·023	13·228	15·432	17·637	19·842
10	22·046	24·251	26·455	28·660	30·865	33·069	35·274	37·479	39·683	41·888
20	44·092	46·297	48·502	50·706	52·911	55·116	57·320	59·525	61·729	63·934
30	66·139	68·343	70·548	72·752	74·957	77·162	79·366	81·571	83·776	85·980
40	88·185	90·389	92·594	94·799	97·003	99·208	101·41	103·62	105·82	108·03
50	110·23	112·44	114·64	116·84	119·05	121·25	123·46	125·66	127·87	130·07
60	132·28	134·48	136·69	138·89	141·10	143·30	145·51	147·71	149·91	152·12
70	154·32	156·53	158·73	160·94	163·14	165·35	167·55	169·76	171·96	174·17
80	176·37	178·57	180·78	182·98	185·19	187·39	189·60	191·80	194·01	196·21
90	198·42	200·62	202·83	205·03	207·23	209·44	211·64	213·85	216·05	218·26
100	220·46	222·67	224·87	227·08	229·28	231·49	233·69	235·89	238·10	240·30

Pounds force per sq. ft to kilonewtons per sq. m

lbf/ft:	0	10	20	30	40	50	60	70	80	90
	Kilonewtons per square metre									
0	—	0·479	0·958	1·436	1·915	2·394	2·873	3·352	3·830	4·309
100	4·788	5·267	5·746	6·224	6·703	7·182	7·661	8·140	8·618	9·097
200	9·576	10·055	10·534	11·013	11·491	11·970	12·449	12·928	13·407	13·885
300	14·364	14·843	15·322	15·801	16·279	16·758	17·237	17·716	18·195	18·673
400	19·152	19·631	20·110	20·589	21·067	21·546	22·025	22·504	22·983	23·461
500	23·940	24·419	24·898	25·377	25·855	26·334	26·813	27·292	27·771	28·249
600	28·728	29·207	29·686	30·165	30·643	31·122	31·601	32·080	32·559	33·037
700	33·516	33·995	34·474	34·953	35·431	35·910	36·389	36·868	37·347	37·825
800	38·304	38·783	39·262	39·741	40·219	40·698	41·177	41·656	42·135	42·613
900	43·092	43·571	44·050	44·529	45·007	45·486	45·965	46·444	46·923	47·402
1000	47·880									

Speed conversions—knots, mph, kph

Knots	Miles per hour	Kilometres per hour
1	1·152	1·85
2	2·303	3·70
3	3·455	5·55
4	4·606	7·41
5	5·758	9·26
6	6·909	11·13
7	8·061	12·98
8	9·212	14·83
9	10·364	16·68
10	11·515	18·55
11	12·667	20·40
12	13·818	22·25
13	14·970	24·10
14	16·121	25·95
15	17·273	27·80
16	18·424	29·65
17	19·576	31·50
18	20·727	33·35
19	21·879	35·21
20	23·031	36·70
21	24·182	38·91
22	25·333	40·80
23	26·485	42·62
24	27·636	44·50
25	28·788	46·33
26	29·939	48·20
27	31·091	49·03
28	32·242	51·90
29	33·394	53·74
30	34·545	55·60
31	35·697	57·34
32	36·848	59·30
33	38·000	61·15
34	39·152	63·00
35	40·303	64·86
36	41·455	66·70
37	42·606	68·56
38	43·758	70·42
39	44·909	72·27
40	46·061	73·40

Volume conversions—Imp galls, litres, US galls

Imperial gallons	Litres	U.S. Gallons
0·125	0·57	0·15
0·22	1·00	0·26
0·83	3·78	1·0
1·0	4·55	1·2
2	9·09	2·4
3	13·6	3·6
4	18·2	4·8
5	22·7	6·0
6	27·3	7·2
7	31·8	8·4
8	36·4	9·6
9	40·9	10·8
10	45·5	12·0
11	50·0	13·2
12	54·6	14·4
13	59·1	15·6
14	63·6	16·8
15	68·2	18·0
16	72·7	19·2
17	77·3	20·4
18	81·8	21·6
19	86·4	22·8
20	90·9	24·0
50	227	60
100	445	120

Tons per sq. in to kg per sq. mm—and vice versa

UK Tons per Sq. Inch		Kg. per Sq. mm.	UK Tons per Sq. Inch		Kg per Sq. mm.
0.635	1	1.575	32.38	51	80.32
1.27	2	3.15	33.02	52	81.89
1.90	3	4.72	33.65	53	83.47
2.54	4	6.30	34.29	54	85.04
3.17	5	7.87	34.92	55	86.62
3.81	6	9.45	35.56	56	88.19
4.44	7	11.02	36.19	57	89.77
5.08	8	12.60	36.83	58	91.34
5.71	9	14.17	37.46	59	92.92
6.35	10	15.75	38.10	60	94.49
6.98	11	17.32	38.73	61	96.07
7.62	12	18.90	39.37	62	97.64
8.25	13	20.47	40.00	63	99.22
8.89	14	22.05	40.64	64	100.79
9.52	15	23.62	41.27	65	102.37
10.16	16	25.20	41.91	66	103.94
10.79	17	26.77	42.54	67	105.52
11.43	18	28.35	43.18	68	107.09
12.06	19	29.92	43.81	69	108.67
12.70	20	31.50	44.45	70	110.24
13.33	21	33.07	45.08	71	111.82
13.97	22	34.65	45.72	72	113.39
14.60	23	36.22	46.35	73	114.97
15.24	24	37.80	46.99	74	116.54
15.87	25	39.37	47.62	75	118.12
16.51	26	40.95	48.26	76	119.69
17.14	27	42.52	48.89	77	121.27
17.78	28	44.10	49.53	78	122.84
18.41	29	45.67	50.16	79	124.42
19.05	30	47.25	50.80	80	125.99
19.68	31	48.82	51.43	81	127.57
20.32	32	50.40	52.07	82	129.14
20.95	33	51.97	52.70	83	130.72
21.59	34	53.55	53.34	84	132.29
22.22	35	55.12	53.97	85	133.86
22.86	36	56.70	54.61	86	135.44
23.49	37	58.27	55.24	87	137.01
24.13	38	59.85	55.88	88	138.59
24.76	39	61.42	56.51	89	140.16
25.40	40	63.00	57.15	90	141.74
26.03	41	64.57	57.78	91	143.31
26.67	42	66.14	58.42	92	144.89
27.30	43	67.72	59.05	93	146.46
27.94	44	69.29	59.69	94	148.04
28.57	45	70.87	60.32	95	149.61
29.21	46	72.44	60.96	96	151.19
29.84	47	74.02	61.59	97	152.76
30.48	48	75.59	62.23	98	154.34
31.11	49	77.17	62.86	99	155.91
31.75	50	78.74	63.50	100	157.49

Read known figure in bold face type. Corresponding figure in Kilogrammes per Square Millimetre will be found in column to the right. Corresponding figure in U.K. Tons per Square Inch will be found in column to the left.

Temperatures—Fahrenheit/Centigrade

0 to 100						0 to 1000						1000 to 2000					
C.		F.	C.		F.	C.		F.	C.		F.	C.		F.	C.		F.
-17.8	**0**	32	10.0	**50**	122.0	-17.8	**0**	32	260	**500**	932	538	**1000**	1832	816	**1500**	2732
-17.2	**1**	33.8	10.6	**51**	123.8	-12.2	**10**	50.0	266	**510**	950	543	**1010**	1850	821	**1510**	2750
-16.7	**2**	35.6	11.1	**52**	125.6	-6.67	**20**	68.0	271	**520**	968	549	**1020**	1868	827	**1520**	2768
-16.1	**3**	37.4	11.7	**53**	127.4	-1.11	**30**	86.0	277	**530**	986	554	**1030**	1886	832	**1530**	2786
-15.6	**4**	39.2	12.2	**54**	129.2	4.44	**40**	104.0	282	**540**	1004	560	**1040**	1904	838	**1540**	2804
-15.0	**5**	41.0	12.8	**55**	131.0	10.0	**50**	122.0	288	**550**	1022	566	**1050**	1922	843	**1550**	2822
-14.4	**6**	42.8	13.3	**56**	132.8	15.6	**60**	140.0	293	**560**	1040	571	**1060**	1940	849	**1560**	2840
-13.9	**7**	44.6	13.9	**57**	134.6	21.1	**70**	158.0	299	**570**	1058	577	**1070**	1958	854	**1570**	2858
-13.3	**8**	46.4	14.4	**58**	136.4	26.7	**80**	176.0	304	**580**	1076	582	**1080**	1976	860	**1580**	2876
-12.8	**9**	48.2	15.0	**59**	138.2	32.2	**90**	194.0	310	**590**	1094	588	**1090**	1994	866	**1590**	2894
-12.2	**10**	50.0	15.6	**60**	140.0	38	**100**	212	316	**600**	1112	593	**1100**	2012	871	**1600**	2912
-11.7	**11**	51.8	16.1	**61**	141.8	43	**110**	230	321	**610**	1130	599	**1110**	2030	877	**1610**	2930
-11.1	**12**	53.6	16.7	**62**	143.6	49	**120**	248	327	**620**	1148	604	**1120**	2048	882	**1620**	2948
-10.6	**13**	55.4	17.2	**63**	145.4	54	**130**	266	332	**630**	1166	610	**1130**	2066	888	**1630**	2966
-10.0	**14**	57.2	17.8	**64**	147.2	60	**140**	284	338	**640**	1184	616	**1140**	2084	893	**1640**	2984
-9.44	**15**	59.0	18.3	**65**	149.0	66	**150**	302	343	**650**	1202	621	**1150**	2102	899	**1650**	3002
-8.89	**16**	60.8	18.9	**66**	150.8	71	**160**	320	349	**660**	1220	627	**1160**	2120	904	**1660**	3020
-8.33	**17**	62.6	19.4	**67**	152.6	77	**170**	338	354	**670**	1238	632	**1170**	2138	910	**1670**	3038
-7.78	**18**	64.4	20.0	**68**	154.4	82	**180**	356	360	**680**	1256	638	**1180**	2156	916	**1680**	3056
-7.22	**19**	66.2	20.6	**69**	156.2	88	**190**	374	366	**690**	1274	643	**1190**	2174	921	**1690**	3074
-6.67	**20**	68.0	21.1	**70**	158.0	93	**200**	392	371	**700**	1292	649	**1200**	2192	927	**1700**	3092
-6.11	**21**	69.8	21.7	**71**	159.8	99	**210**	410	377	**710**	1310	654	**1210**	2210	932	**1710**	3110
-5.56	**22**	71.6	22.2	**72**	161.6	104	**220**	428	382	**720**	1328	660	**1220**	2228	938	**1720**	3128
-5.00	**23**	73.4	22.8	**73**	163.4	110	**230**	446	388	**730**	1346	666	**1230**	2246	943	**1730**	3146
-4.44	**24**	75.2	23.3	**74**	165.2	116	**240**	464	393	**740**	1364	671	**1240**	2264	949	**1740**	3164
-3.89	**25**	77.0	23.9	**75**	167.0	121	**250**	482	399	**750**	1382	677	**1250**	2282	954	**1750**	3182
-3.33	**26**	78.8	24.4	**76**	168.8	127	**260**	500	404	**760**	1400	682	**1260**	2300	960	**1760**	3200
-2.78	**27**	80.6	25.0	**77**	170.6	132	**270**	518	410	**770**	1418	688	**1270**	2318	966	**1770**	3218
-2.22	**28**	82.4	25.6	**78**	172.4	138	**280**	536	416	**780**	1436	693	**1280**	2336	971	**1780**	3236
-1.67	**29**	84.2	26.1	**79**	174.2	143	**290**	554	421	**790**	1454	699	**1290**	2354	977	**1790**	3254
-1.11	**30**	86.0	26.7	**80**	176.0	149	**300**	572	427	**800**	1472	704	**1300**	2372	982	**1800**	3272
-0.56	**31**	87.8	27.2	**81**	177.8	154	**310**	590	432	**810**	1490	710	**1310**	2390	988	**1810**	3290
0	**32**	89.6	27.8	**82**	179.6	160	**320**	608	438	**820**	1508	716	**1320**	2408	993	**1820**	3308
0.56	**33**	91.4	28.3	**83**	181.4	166	**330**	626	443	**830**	1526	721	**1330**	2426	999	**1830**	3326
1.11	**34**	93.2	28.9	**84**	183.2	171	**340**	644	449	**840**	1544	727	**1340**	2444	1004	**1840**	3344
1.67	**35**	95.0	29.4	**85**	185.0	177	**350**	662	454	**850**	1562	732	**1350**	2462	1010	**1850**	3362
2.22	**36**	96.8	30.0	**86**	186.8	182	**360**	680	460	**860**	1580	738	**1360**	2480	1016	**1860**	3380
2.78	**37**	98.6	30.6	**87**	188.6	188	**370**	698	466	**870**	1598	743	**1370**	2498	1021	**1870**	3398
3.33	**38**	100.4	31.1	**88**	190.4	193	**380**	716	471	**880**	1616	749	**1380**	2516	1027	**1880**	3416
3.89	**39**	102.2	31.7	**89**	192.2	199	**390**	734	477	**890**	1634	754	**1390**	2534	1032	**1890**	3434
4.44	**40**	104.0	32.2	**90**	194.0	204	**400**	752	482	**900**	1652	760	**1400**	2552	1038	**1900**	3452
5.00	**41**	105.8	32.8	**91**	195.8	210	**410**	770	488	**910**	1670	766	**1410**	2570	1043	**1910**	3470
5.56	**42**	107.6	33.3	**92**	197.6	216	**420**	788	493	**920**	1688	771	**1420**	2588	1049	**1920**	3488
6.11	**43**	109.4	33.9	**93**	199.4	221	**430**	806	499	**930**	1706	777	**1430**	2606	1054	**1930**	3506
6.67	**44**	111.2	34.4	**94**	201.2	227	**440**	824	504	**940**	1724	782	**1440**	2624	1060	**1940**	3524
7.22	**45**	113.0	35.0	**95**	203.0	232	**450**	842	510	**950**	1742	788	**1450**	2642	1066	**1950**	3542
7.78	**46**	114.8	35.6	**96**	204.8	238	**460**	860	516	**960**	1760	793	**1460**	2660	1071	**1960**	3560
8.33	**47**	116.6	36.1	**97**	206.6	243	**470**	878	521	**970**	1778	799	**1470**	2678	1077	**1970**	3578
8.89	**48**	118.4	36.7	**98**	208.4	249	**480**	896	527	**980**	1796	804	**1480**	2696	1082	**1980**	3596
9.44	**49**	120.2	37.2	**99**	210.2	254	**490**	914	532	**990**	1814	810	**1490**	2714	1088	**1990**	3614
10.0	**50**	122.0	37.8	**100**	212.0	260	**500**	932	538	**1000**	1832	816	**1500**	2732	1093	**2000**	3632

Read known temperature in bold face type. Corresponding temperature in degrees Fahrenheit will be found in column to the right. Corresponding temperature in degrees Centigrade will be found in column to the left.

FOR INTERMEDIATE VALUES ADD THE FOLLOWING:—

C.		F.	C.		F.
0.56	1	1.8	3.33	6	10.8
1.11	2	3.6	3.89	7	12.6
1.67	3	5.4	4.44	8	14.4
2.22	4	7.2	5.00	9	16.2
2.78	5	9.0	5.56	10	18.0

Temperature Conversion Formulae :—°C. = °F. — 32 × 5/9.
°F. = °C. × 9/5 + 32.

183

ISO and metric thread equivalents

NOMINAL THREAD SIZE	I.S.O. PITCH		NEAREST ENGLISH EQUIVALENT	NEAREST UNIFIED SIZE	INCH EQUIVALENT	GERMAN D.I.N. PITCH	FRENCH C.N.M. PITCH
	COARSE	FINE					
M2	0·40	—	9BA	—	—	—	—
M2·5	0·45	—	7BA (·098)	4UN (·112)	—	—	0·45
M3	0·50	—	6BA (·110)	5UN (·125)	0·1181	0·50	0·60
M3·5	0·60	—	4BA (·142)	6UN (·138)	0·1378	0·60	0·60
M4	0·70	—	3BA (·161)	8UN (·164)	0·1575	0·70	0·75
M4·5	0·75	—	—	—	0·1772	0·75	0·75
M5	0·80	—	2BA (·185)	10UN (·190)	0·1968	0·80	0·90
M6	1·00	—	0BA (·236)	—	0·2362	1·00	1·00
M7·0	1·00	—	¼ (·250)	¼UN (·250)	0·2756	1·00	1·00
M8·0	1·25	1·00	$\frac{5}{16}$ (·312)	$\frac{5}{16}$UN (·312)	0·3150	1·25	1·25
M10·0	1·50	1·25	$\frac{3}{8}$ (·375)	$\frac{3}{8}$UN (·375)	0·3937	1·50	1·50
M12·0	1·75	1·25	—	½UN (·500)	0·4724	1·75	1·75

Wind speeds and pressures

Velocity in kilometres per hour	Pressure in kilos per sq metre	Beaufort Scale	Description	Velocity in knots	Pressure in lbs per sq foot
0	0	0	Calm	0	0
2– 6	0·049	1	Light Air	1– 3	0·01
7– 12	0·390	2	Light Breeze	4– 6	0·08
13– 19	1·366	3	Gentle Breeze	7–10	0·28
20– 28	3·270	4	Moderate Breeze	11–15	0·67
29– 37	6·393	5	Fresh Breeze	16–20	1·31
38– 48	11·224	6	Strong Breeze	21–26	2·30
49– 61	17·575	7	Moderate Gale	27–33	3·60
62– 74	26·363	8	Fresh Gale	34–40	5·40
75– 87	37·591	9	Strong Gale	41–47	7·70
88–102	51·261	10	Whole Gale	48–55	10·50
103–120	68·348	11	Storm	56–65	14·00
above 120	above 82·994	12	Hurricane	above 65	above 17·00

TRIGONOMETRY

SINE $A = \frac{a}{c}$ COSINE $A = \frac{b}{c}$

SECANT $A = \frac{c}{b}$ COSECANT $A = \frac{c}{a}$

TANGENT $A = \frac{a}{b}$ COTANGENT $A = \frac{b}{a}$

$$b = \frac{a \sin B}{\sin A} = \frac{a}{\cos C + \sin C \cot B}$$

$$b = \frac{c}{\cos A + \sin A \cot B} = \frac{c \sin B}{\sin C}$$

$$b = a \cos C + a \sin C . \cot A$$

$$b = c \cos A + c \sin A . \cot C$$

$$= \sqrt{a^2 + c^2 - 2a \times c \cos B}$$

$$A + B + C = 180° \qquad \sin A = \frac{a \sin C}{c} = \frac{a \sin B}{b}$$

$$\cos A = \frac{b^2 + c^2 - a^2}{2bc} \qquad \tan A = \frac{a \sin C}{b - a \cos C} = \frac{a \sin B}{c - a \cos B}$$

$$\tan A = \frac{\tan B + \tan C}{\tan B . \tan C - 1}$$

$$\text{AREA} = \frac{b.c. \sin A}{2} = \frac{a.b. \sin C}{2} = \frac{c.a. \sin B}{2}$$

186

Buckling loads on pillars

E = MODULUS OF ELASTICITY   L = UNSUPPORTED LENGTH
I = LEAST MOMENT OF INERTIA   OF CROSS–SECTION

	END CONDITION	BUCKLING LOAD	NOTES
	PIN JOINED BOTH ENDS	$\dfrac{\pi^2 E I}{L^2}$	
	BUILT IN AT BOTH ENDS	$\dfrac{4\pi^2 E I}{L^2}$	STRONGEST CONDITION
	BUILT IN AT ONE END, FREE AT OTHER END.	$\dfrac{\pi^2 E I}{4 L^2}$	WEAKEST CONDITION
	BUILT IN AT ONE END OTHER END PIN JOINED	$\dfrac{2\pi^2 E I}{L^2}$	

EXAMPLE

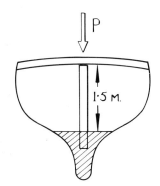

PILLAR OF 76·2 × 50·8 MM [3 × 2 INCH]
R.H.S. STEEL FIXED RIGIDLY AT KEEL
AND SUPPORTING A CROSS–BEAM AT THE
OTHER END BUT NOT FIXED TO THE BEAM.

$$P_{BUCKLING} = \frac{\pi^2 E I}{4 L^2}$$

$$= \frac{\pi^2\ 207\ \frac{KN}{MM^2} \times 38\cdot5 \times 10^4\,MM}{4 \times 1\cdot5 \times 10^6\ MM}$$

$$= 87\cdot5\ KN\ =\ 8\cdot9\ TONNES$$

IN PRACTICE THE LOAD SHOULD NEVER BE
ALLOWED TO EXCEED HALF THIS FIGURE.
I.E. THE FACTOR OF SAFETY
SHOULD BE 2 OR MORE.

187

Simple bending theory for a uniform beam

$$\frac{M}{I}=\frac{E}{R}=\frac{a}{y} \quad - \quad \textbf{Equation 1}$$

M is the applied bending moment.
I is the second moment of area of the cross-section about its neutral axis Z–Z.
a is the longitudinal stress in the beam.
y is the distance from the neutral axis.
E is Young's Modulus of Elasticity for the material. Some values are given on page 171.
R is the radius of curvature the beam takes up when the bending moment is applied.

Method of Finding the Required Section to Support a Load
First one must find the maximum stress that the material can withstand. Then using part of the equation above, i.e.

$$M_{max}=a_{max}\frac{I}{y} \quad - \quad \textbf{Equation 2}$$

the section of the material may be determined. The maximum value of the bending moment depends upon the way the beam is loaded.

Note: $\frac{I}{y}$ is known as the section modulus. Values for a variety of sections are given on pages 190/1.

Loading	Maximum bending moment
1 Beam supported at both ends with a point load W at the mid-length point.	$\dfrac{WL}{4}$
2 Beam supported at both ends with a uniformly distributed loading of w/unit length.	$\dfrac{wL^2}{8}$
3 Beam supported at both ends and having a concentrated load W at a distance A from the left end.	$\dfrac{W \times A \times (L-A)}{L}$

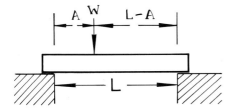

4 Beam built in at one end and having a concentrated load W at free end.	WL
5 Beam, built in at one end, with a uniformly distributed load W over the whole length.	$\dfrac{WL}{2}$

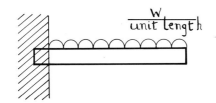

Substitute into Equation 2 values for M_{max} and a_{max} to give a suitable value of section modulus for the beam.

This calculation has produced a section of sufficient strength to support the applied loads. It is now necessary to determine the possible deflection of the beam when loads are applied. For example flexing of decks when walked on may not be harmful from a strength consideration but can be most disconcerting to the crew.

From Equation I above:

$$\frac{I}{R} = \frac{M}{E} \quad \text{or} \quad R = \frac{EI}{M}$$

Sectional areas, y_{max}, I and I/y_{max}

SECTION	AREA [A]	y_{max}	I	$\dfrac{I}{y_{max}}$ = SECTION MODULUS
(rectangle, width d, height b)	bd	$\dfrac{d}{2}$	$\dfrac{bd^3}{12}$	$\dfrac{bd^2}{6}$
(hollow rectangle, d, b, d_1, b_1)	$bd - b_1 d_1$	$\dfrac{d}{2}$	$\dfrac{bd^3 - b_1 d_1^3}{12}$	$\dfrac{bd^2 - b_1 d_1^2}{6}$
(circle, diameter d)	$\dfrac{\pi d^2}{4}$	$\dfrac{d}{2}$	$\dfrac{\pi d^4}{64}$	$\dfrac{\pi d^3}{32}$
(hollow circle, d, d_1)	$\dfrac{\pi \left(d^2 - d_1^2 \right)}{4}$	$\dfrac{d}{2}$	$\dfrac{\pi \left(d^4 - d_1^4 \right)}{64}$	$\dfrac{\pi}{32} \dfrac{\left(d^4 - d_1^4 \right)}{d}$
(ellipse, d, b)	$\dfrac{\pi b d}{4}$	$\dfrac{d}{2}$	$\dfrac{\pi b d^3}{64}$	$\dfrac{\pi b d^2}{32}$

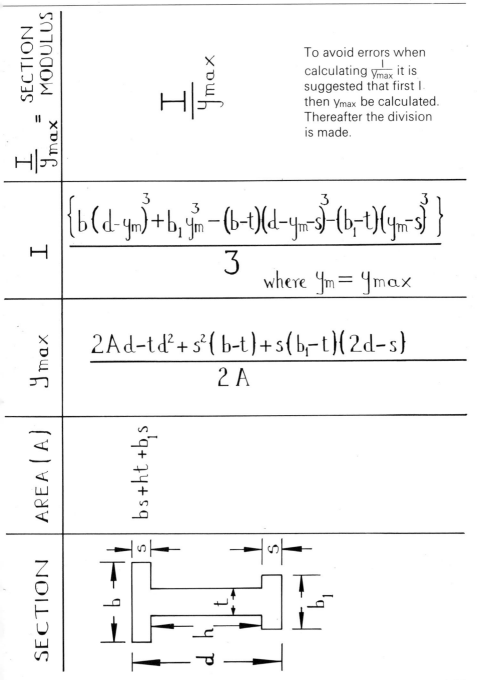

$\dfrac{I}{y_{max}} =$ SECTION MODULUS

To avoid errors when calculating $\frac{I}{y_{max}}$ it is suggested that first I then y_{max} be calculated. Thereafter the division is made.

I

$$\frac{\left\{ b\left(d-y_m\right)^3 + b_1 y_m^3 - (b-t)(d-y_m-s)^3 - (b_1-t)(y_m-s)^3 \right\}}{3}$$

where $y_m = y_{max}$

y_{max}

$$\frac{2Ad - td^2 + s^2(b-t) + s(b_1-t)(2d-s)}{2A}$$

AREA (A)

$bs + ht + b_1 s$

SECTION